Working-class organisations and popular tourism, 1840–1970

STUDIES IN
POPULAR
CULTURE

General editor: Professor Jeffrey Richards

Working-class organisations and popular tourism, 1840–1970

SUSAN BARTON

Manchester University Press

Manchester and New York

distributed exclusively in the USA by Palgrave

Published by Manchester University Press
Oxford Road, Manchester M13 9NR, UK
and Room 400, 175 Fifth Avenue, New York, NY 10010, USA
www.manchesteruniversitypress.co.uk

Distributed in the United States exclusively by
Palgrave Macmillan, 175 Fifth Avenue,
New York, NY 10010, USA

Distributed in Canada exclusively by
UBC Press, University of British Columbia, 2029 West Mall,
Vancouver, BC, Canada V6T 1Z2

British Library Cataloguing-in-Publication Data is available

Library of Congress Cataloging-in-Publication Data is available

ISBN 978 0 7190 6591 0 paperback

First published by Manchester University Press in hardback 2005

This paperback edition first published 2011

The publisher has no responsibility for the persistence or accuracy of URLs for any external
or third-party internet websites referred to in this book, and does not guarantee that any content
on such websites is, or will remain, accurate or appropriate.

Printed by Lightning Source

STUDIES IN
POPULAR
CULTURE

There has in recent years been an explosion of interest in culture and cultural studies. The impetus has come from two directions and out of two different traditions. On the one hand, cultural history has grown out of social history to become a distinct and identifiable school of historical investigation. On the other hand, cultural studies has grown out of English literature and has concerned itself to a large extent with contemporary issues. Nevertheless, there is a shared project, its aim, to elucidate the meanings and values implicit and explicit in the art, literature, learning, institutions and everyday behaviour within a given society. Both the cultural historian and the cultural studies scholar seek to explore the ways in which a culture is imagined, represented and received, how it interacts with social processes, how it contributes to individual and collective identities and world views, to stability and change, to social, political and economic activities and programmes. This series aims to provide an arena for the cross-fertilisation of the discipline, so that the work of the cultural historian can take advantage of the most useful and illuminating of the theoretical developments and the cultural studies scholars can extend the purely historical underpinnings of their investigations. The ultimate objective of the series is to provide a range of books which will explain in a readable and accessible way where we are now socially and culturally and how we got to where we are. This should enable people to be better informed, promote an interdisciplinary approach to cultural issues and encourage deeper thought about the issues, attitudes and institutions of popular culture.

Jeffrey Richards

Contents

List of illustrations

General editor's introduction

Holidays are today taken for granted by almost everyone – a right and not a privilege. Many people now have several holidays a year. But it was not until Parliament passed the 1938 Holidays with Pay Act that the majority of the population could even contemplate a week away from home. Even then the outbreak of the Second World War the following year delayed the full implementation of the Act until the late 1940s.

Susan Barton's fascinating book traces the century-long process by which the working classes fought for, argued for and saved for their right to take an annual holiday. She identifies the 1851 Great Exhibition as the key event which established the viability of the working-class package holiday. The fears of a horde of working-class revolutionists descending on the capital and causing mayhem were unrealised and within a few years Engels was observing sadly, 'The English proletariat is becoming more and more bourgeois.' That may have been so, but the working-class holiday was to become a distinctive part of a purely working-class culture.

Susan Barton explores in detail the ways in which the time available for holidays was extended by, for instance, the passing of the 1870 Bank Holidays Act and the collective bargaining which secured unpaid holidays within individual industries before the goal of paid holidays for all was finally achieved. She examines the activities of a range of working-class organisations in providing holidays, the role of savings clubs and organised excursions and the expansion of holiday accommodation to cater for the growing working-class market.

Where the middle-class holiday tended to be individualistic, the working-class holiday was from the first and remained a communal experience – in travel (steamboats, trains, charabancs), in accommodation (from seaside boarding houses where you rubbed shoulders with neighbours from home to holiday camps where collective activities were organised for the happy campers) and in pleasures often taken in groups rather than singly. Even when from the 1960s the working classes took to the skies and sought the sun in overseas package holidays, collectivity ruled. Drawing on vivid contemporary accounts, Susan Barton provides a meticulously researched, readable and persuasive analysis of a much-valued working-class institution.

Jeffrey Richards

I

Introduction

Honest travelling have been so rascally abused since I was a boy in pinners, by tribes of nobodies tearing from one end of the country to t'other, to see the sun go down in salt water, or the moon play jack-lantern behind some rotten tower or other, that, upon my song, when life and death's in the wind there's no telling the difference.[1]

This quotation from Thomas Hardy's novel *The hand of Ethelberta*, set in the third quarter of the nineteenth century, conveys a sense of the changes that had been taking place in the experience of travel during that time. An elderly countryman living near a seaside town has been asked if he has noticed whether anything unusual is happening in the town because of the number of people travelling towards it. In his reply he tells the enquirer that he would not be able to notice if there was. He emphasises the increase in the numbers of visitors, who are just 'nobodies', to the seaside witnessed during his lifetime. The next generation of residents would have seen an even bigger expansion of the number of visitors to the town on the Dorset coast and it would become pointless to ask if there were strangers about. Over just one lifetime or two or three generations the mobility of the British population for leisure purposes grew explosively, and formerly quiet coastal towns and villages became the venues for all manner of fun and entertainment. During the summer months the peaceful days before the railway arrived would be just a memory, like that of Hardy's old man, 'of a boy in pinners'.

Although each shows a unique experience, the photographs in this book are all instantly recognisable as being of holidays. In the creation of memory photography is a vitally important factor. Holiday photos are more common than pictures taken at home or at work although a holiday is only a short period in life compared with other activities. At the seaside towns, professional photographers created visual records of the holiday experience for those who did not own a camera. Holidays and photographs of them create a memory of family life to look back on, a means of social and familial bonding. Although modern holidays are part of a consumerist, hedonistic culture they have a value beyond the immediate and the present. Nothing else in British culture, apart from Christmas, has quite the same effect at the psychological level. As well as providing a focal point in the past for the mind – memories of holidays provide something pleasant and shared to look back on and to talk about and relive at family gatherings, creating a collective experience for bonding and integration purposes – holidays also create future reference points. They provide something to look forward to in the not-too-distant future, in effect a punctuation point in the routine of work and the annual cycle. Just as religious 'holy days', holidays are a time set aside, neither work nor domestic, apart from normal routine, liminal periods spent in what Rob Shields describes as liminal places, usually between sea and land.[2]

Looking at the holiday snap of a girl, wrapped in a home-made cape as sun protection attending to a younger boy (plate 1) we get a glimpse of a typical holiday scene. But who is on holiday? The photo shows us what a 1920s holiday ought to have been like but the girl is not on holiday; she is in service,

Plate 1 Winnie Feltwell and young charge on the beach at Littlehampton, 1930

working to supervise the younger child. The little boy is being looked after while his middle-class parents have a holiday. They are outside the picture; perhaps one of them is holding the camera. The picture shows an empty beach, the middle-class ideal, although other people may have been out of range of the camera.

Another photograph is an image contemporary with that of the girl and little boy on the beach. Both of these show working-class holidays. Reproduced on the cover of this book, it shows two little girls on a beach, wearing rubber knickers over their clothes to keep them clean and dry while they play on the sand and paddle in the sea. This time, though, the beach is crowded and it is the older girl from the first photograph, their big sister on leave from her job in service, who points the camera, creating her own holiday images to pass on to future generations.[3] The crowded beach indicates that this is a resort frequented by the working class and is not one of the quieter, more select places favoured by the middle-class family. These are also the only photographs, apart from formal studio family portraits, of these girls as children. Many were taken of the middle-class children, creating memories for them of all aspects and stages of family life. For the working-class children and their family these are their only physically visible memories, the only remaining images of their childhood together. The few short days spent at the seaside and wake have therefore taken on a significance far greater than its length in relation to the other more mundane aspects of life. Social class determined where their 'tourist gaze' would fall and just how far away that gaze could focus.[4]

This shows that, although there were outward similarities, the holiday was a different experience for working and middle-class participants. The middle-class family includes not just the nuclear family but a servant as well. This would ensure that the parents actually had an opportunity to enjoy being together and have a break, free, if they chose, from the responsibilities of child care. Having a nanny, especially once the children were away at boarding school, could have meant that, for them and similar parents, actually taking part in the care of the children could have become a leisure activity, in the sense of a break from routine, in itself.

It is the intention of this work to examine what the working class and its organisations did to achieve holidays independently of middle-class patronage to enable holidays to become less of an extraordinary experience. Works relating specifically to tourism and holidaymaking, when discussing working-class leisure travel, are more concerned with its effects on the growth and development of resorts than with workers actually shaping these developments through their own demands and cultural expression. This study covers a relatively long period, looking at the pre-industrial roots of holidaymaking before moving on to investigate the period from around 1830 to 1970, examining a process of change rather than an event static in time. The text is arranged thematically rather than chronologically and each chapter covers a different aspect affecting workers' ability to go on holiday. This is also a study of the English labour movement and how it was able to secure self-directed time away from employers as well as travel for personal fulfilment. Recognising that many workers were unorganised, the cultural preferences and collective experience of people who may not necessarily have been trade union members is examined to see how this influenced the kind of tourist experience offered. It begins by looking at excursions of just a day, usually by rail. It discusses the proto-package tours to the Great Exhibition and investigates the ways and means used by workers to get a holiday before payment for the 'lost time' was received. Trade unions' efforts to secure holidays with pay for their members are examined, looking at their campaigning and, in 1938, their contribution to the Amulree Committee, or Select Committee on Holidays with Pay. All these new holidaymakers had to be catered for and so a section of the book is dedicated to the provision of accommodation such as boarding houses, holiday camps, chalets and caravans, taking alternative employment like hop picking to get a change of air and a few weeks of country life, and – an important but often forgotten sector – staying with friends and relatives. After the Holidays with Pay legislation, governments were concerned that there would be too many people all trying to go away to the same places at the same time. These concerns led to a number of official investigations and quasi-government bodies being established to try to regulate these potentially massive population movements, to stagger the times holidays were taken and to spread the distribution across a wider range of destinations. From the 1950s, with rising working-class standards of living, growing confidence about travel and lowering of the price of air travel to cheaper locations abroad, package holidays began to cater for working-class tastes in the sunny climes of the Mediterranean, particularly Spain, from the late 1950s.

The point of the work is not to investigate the activities of working-class people on holiday. Discussion will focus on how workers have managed to claim the right to blocks of time away from work, a period of leave during which the worker has autonomy and control over what is done in his or her own time. This area of study seems neglected even though free time is fundamental to any kind of leisure or tourism. Looking at the eighteenth century roots of working-class travel, although taking place within a different cultural context and therefore not to be labelled tourism in the modern sense of the word, tramping by craft workers enabled men in skilled occupations to travel from place to place on foot, receiving sustenance during their journeys from trade society funds while ostensibly looking for employment when trade was slack in their home town. That some men travelled for reasons other than economic necessity has been highlighted by R. A. Leeson, and by Eric Hobsbawm, who called it a kind of 'artisan's grand tour'.[5] In small workshops and among craft workers and, as we shall see in Chapters 4 and 5, by coal miners, Monday was a day of rest or used for socialising. The work of Douglas Reid on St Monday shows how this group of workers was able to control its own hours of work and the length of the working week until their control was weakened by industrialisation and factory discipline.[6]

The summer of 1851 saw around 6 million, including many working people, heading for London and the Great Exhibition. Chapter 3 demonstrates how workers were able to work collectively to enable visits to London to take place. Arrangements for transport, accommodation and finance had to be made. Clubs were formed to collect regular savings to cover the cost of the train or steamer fare, accommodation and spending money. In many cases these clubs undertook all the practical arrangements themselves for the benefit of their members, providing what in effect was a prototype for the later inclusive tour or package holiday. While other authors, such as Jeffrey Auerbach, Michael Leapman and Louise Purbrick, have written about the Great Exhibition, work has tended to focus on consumption, design or behaviour rather than how ordinary men and women came to be there at all.[7] The trips to the exhibition of workers from Leeds were the subject of a local case study by R. J. Morris.[8] Excursions there organised as works outings for employees by the organisations they worked for and the accommodation and travel arrangements available were described by Alan Degado in his book entitled *The annual outing and other excursions.*[9] The chapter in this book is based on new research using minute books and correspondence of working men's committees for the Great Exhibition as primary sources.

Looking at the mid to late nineteenth century, John Walton has proposed some explanation of how taking holidays had become common among the Lancashire working class by the beginning of the twentieth century and not so elsewhere. Craftsmen and labourers in other regions and occupational groups could have secured periods of free time and perhaps have used it to take holidays but spent their money on localised leisure activities and festivals instead, rather than developing a habit of saving up for extended periods of time off work and to go to the seaside.[10] For Lancashire in particular, Robert Poole has described how the previously Church-centred wakes holidays became secularised and extended from a day or two to a collectively enforced whole week's duration for cotton industry workers.[11] For this free time to be translated into leisure or holidays, provision had to be made to ensure that no financial hardship occurred as a result of not earning a wage. The evolution of this can be traced from community-based holidays without official sanction from the employers, through holidays taken with the agreement of the employer but for which workers themselves had made financial provision, to breaks from work of a week or two during which the employee received the normal remuneration. Holiday savings clubs were popular in the North-western cotton-producing towns from the middle of the nineteenth century when they were used to accumulate enough money to enable people to enjoy the wakes holiday with as little hardship as possible. Savings covered the loss of income during the holiday, new clothes to wear and the cost of going to the fair, a seaside excursion and later a few days' stay on the Lancashire coast.[12] For other groups of workers, saving was less ingrained as a habit even when it could be afforded. In mining, steel, hosiery and some workshop industries where the worker maintained some control over the production process, extra effort and longer hours were put in during the week or two preceding a holiday to earn enough to cover the additional expenses of a break from work. Regular disciplined habits of labour eluded these groups of workers, who enjoyed leisure based around their own communities rather than saving and going away for holidays.[13]

The type of accommodation available was important: not only had it to be appropriate to working-class tastes and lifestyles but ways had to be devised to make it affordable yet still provide a livelihood for the host or hostess and their employees. Different aspects of the accommodation sector have been the subjects of previous historical investigation. The pivotal role of Blackpool landladies in providing culturally appropriate lodgings at an affordable price for a large proportion of Lancashire cotton textile workers has been emphasised by John Walton.[14] His findings and conclusions are relevant to apartments (where guests provided their own food for the landlady to prepare) and boarding-house accommodation in other resorts where the scale of provision was not so great. The regimentation and restrictions of apartment and boarding houses were not always the preference of guests, especially those who could afford to make a real choice of the kind of holiday they had. That sector providing a more free-and-easy atmosphere, entertainment and activities at an inclusive price, the holiday camp, which emerged in the 1920s, has been the subject of a study by Colin Ward and Dennis Hardy.[15] They are also the authors of an engaging study of alternative accommodation for those who, even though they could afford a catered holiday, wanted more freedom than holiday camps allowed or who could not afford anything other than improvised huts they themselves built and 'chalets' by the shore.[16] The impact of working-class visitors and those of other backgrounds on resort development and 'social tone' has been discussed by Harold Perkin, who emphasises that social tone was affected by ownership and leasehold patterns in the resorts themselves, which influenced the kind of market developers aimed for.[17] In the present work the findings contained within this literature are placed within a working-class cultural and social context and are supplemented by additional primary source materials, including oral history recordings and interviews.

Work and leisure are not exclusive areas; both are an integral part of modern existence. The quality of leisure for working people, its amount and content are directly related to working conditions and hence to workplace organisation. Better or more secure incomes, as well as improved conditions and shorter hours of work, meant that by the mid-twentieth century many workers were less physically tired than in the previous century, which in turn helped to facilitate leisure travel. In the early twentieth century some groups of workers, such as miners, boot and shoe and cotton textile workers, managed to secure agreements with their employers for sanctioned leave although it was unpaid, firms organised savings clubs and in some cases made a contribution to the workers' funds, although the Lancashire cotton workers retained their own independent schemes.[18] According to the TUC, the increased regimentation, decreased autonomy, intensified production and, in some cases, deskilling and loss of productive control all led to a greater need for workers to have periods away from the work environment and routine in order to recuperate and benefit from 'recreation', literally the re-creation of physical and mental productive capacities. Using trade union histories and new material from the TUC archive, a chapter in this book is devoted to showing how the organised working class was able to ensure that workers in many industries were able to enjoy paid leave of a week or two through the collective bargaining process and how the TUC was able to influence the government through its membership of the Select Committee on Holidays with Pay which led to the Act of 1938.

Following the introduction of legislation aiming to give most workers a paid holiday there were fears that the existing accommodation sector would not be able to cope with the extra demand. Unfortunately war postponed the full implementation of the Holidays with Pay Act until 1945 and beyond in many cases, by which time most workers had secured paid leave by negotiated or informal agreement.[19] The predicted surge in demand would be exacerbated because there was even less suitable accommodation than in 1938, as many boarding houses and holiday camps had been requisitioned for military use and sections of the coast had been damaged. The inaccessibility of a seaside holiday with all the family present in most areas of the country during the war years and the return home of servicemen would mean a rush to the coast as soon as people were able. Chapter 7 therefore will look at research and planning by government bodies and quangos to try to find solutions to the projected problems of a massive rush to the resorts in July and August 1945 and in subsequent summers. This chapter reassesses some of the material produced by these organisations and also brings into use information from government records of the time relating to planning for future holiday expansion.

The final chapter looks at the rise of the relatively cheap package holiday overseas. The example of holidays in Spain, as the archetypal package holiday resort is looked at in detail, using oral reminiscence from working people who first took vacations on the Costas or in Majorca in the 1950s and 1960s. The Workers' Travel Association archive also produced some interesting information on this developmental period for inclusive tours and workers travelling abroad. Government policy and legislation regulating this emergent industry are discussed with reference to previously unused sources from the National Archive. Regulation of charter air traffic and restrictions to protect the flag-carrying airlines BEA and BOAC from competition helped create the stereotypical 'Brit abroad' when holiday prices were artificially increased because of Board of Trade requirements and tour operators compensated their clients by offering free excursions, barbecues and limitless wine at no extra charge. These sources have not been analysed elsewhere, although there are publications on the theme of tourism and of the British in Spain. There has been some investigation of the package holidaymakers of the 1960s, looking at some of the individual experiences and motivations of this group, by Sue Wright, published in a chapter in *The making of modern tourism* edited by Berghoff *et al.*[20] Karen O'Reilly investigates the *British on the Costa del Sol*, but this work is a study of people who have moved to Spain permanently and how they are creating a community of English residents, many of whom are retired.[21] A volume of essays, *Tourism in Spain*, edited by Barke *et al.*, presents quantitative information about the relatively sudden rise of mass tourism in Spain and the subsequent effects.[22] Another book of essays, edited by Allan M. Williams and Gareth Shaw, *Tourism and economic development: European experiences*, also contains chapters discussing the rise and consequences of mass tourism in Spain, but neither this nor the other works in this area, apart from that of Wright, deal with qualitative aspects using the experiences of holidaymakers who decided to take the adventure of a holiday abroad in the 1950s or 1960s.[23] Although they look at the Spanish government's tourism strategies, they ignore the critical effect that the British government's policies had on the development of the package holiday industry in Spain and elsewhere. The research undertaken to produce this chapter was facilitated with the help of a British Academy small research grant.

The modern distinction between the ideas of work and leisure and their separateness as concepts and experiences is a product of industrial capitalism. Prior to this there were festivals together with informal and irregular breaks from work; leisure was integrated into the routine of work. Industrial societies have leisure, weekends and vacations. The emergence of distinct periods of leisure is therefore part of the process of industrialisation. In his 1994 paper 'The invention of leisure in early modern Europe' Peter Burke uses this concept to show that the history of leisure is discontinuous.[24] If this theory is correct there is what Michel Foucault called a conceptual break or 'rupture' between the two periods and so the very idea of the history of leisure before the industrial revolution is anachronistic.[25] Foucault's thesis, according to Burke, cuts history in two slices, but the supposed dichotomy is misleading, as it reduces the great variety of medieval and early modern European ideas, assumptions and practices into a single 'festival culture'. This argument demonstrates the danger of projecting modern concepts of leisure on to the past without looking at the meanings given by contemporaries to their activities. While not concerned with the ideas of the early modern period, this work takes this argument on board by setting leisure in context, clearly relating it to the quest for free time as an element of labour history in industrial society. Leisure is now integral to working life and cannot be separated from conditions of employment, although the concepts of work and leisure are discrete in time and place. Unemployment and retirement are composed of large amounts of free time but in themselves are not leisure, as this involves voluntary control of that free time and what activities take place within it.

For working people, holidays have become a part of the routine of working life, periodic breaks from employment while still receiving a wage or salary for that employment. While not projecting modern concepts of leisure and holidays backwards in time, some pre-industrial celebratory or 'festival' activities can be seen to have had an influence on modern leisure activities, but the cultural meanings attached to them by participants have changed. Although ways of enjoying modern leisure and vacations are not continuous with the pre-industrial past, obviously different and holding different meanings for industrial workers than their ancestors would have recognised, in England at least Foucault's dichotomy is not always so clear as to be described as a rupture. There was no sudden change from pre-industrial to industrialised leisure forms. Cultural changes are influenced by existing and previous cultural preferences and cannot be divorced entirely from the past although their origins are forgotten, with no apparent relevance to industrial life. For example, wakes holidays ostensibly focused around the Church certainly influenced the early advance of industrial holidays in Lancashire, but the modern wakes holidays of the late nineteenth and early twentieth centuries, or the savings clubs to finance them, carried no association with religious ritual in the minds of those participating.

As living standards rose after 1850, working-class culture itself began to change. Greater security raised people's expectations and a higher emphasis was placed on the importance of family life. James Walvin has identified Sunday dinner, clothing and, later, holidays as becoming part of the working-class lifestyle.[26] By the mid-1870s, the ability to save up money had become, for an increasing number, a feature of working-class life; the virtues of thrift which in the harsher times of the 1830s and 1840s had been vital for survival were now, in changed economic circumstances, turned to more profitable and pleasurable ends. It is from this period that the wakes savings clubs in the North-west of England originate. It is important to emphasise here the contrast between skilled workers, the unskilled and 'the poor'. Obviously this lifestyle was not available equally to all the working class. Only those skilled workers able to command a relatively high price for their labour and who could obtain some job security were able to afford it. In the middle years of the nineteenth century, reformers, radicals and socialists had thought that the responsible use of free time by workers might hasten political emancipation. Many of them were also opposed to the ensuing commercialisation of leisure, which they believed bred 'false consciousness' and apathy. Religious reformers, like Lord Shaftesbury and the Lord's Day Observance Society, also demanded more leisure time for workers, particularly the Saturday half-holiday, which by giving additional time for amusements might have encouraged people to keep the Sabbath for worship rather than pleasure. Christians would also be able to mix with non-churchgoers in Saturday afternoon activities and so give them the benefit of their moral example. Unlike evangelical reformers, socialists saw the enemy as the capitalist system of exploitation rather than any particular kinds of amusements happening on Sundays. The desire for profit in commercialised leisure resulted in a double exploitation; that of the entertainment providers or workers in the leisure industry as well as the entertained, who were rarely offered edifying activities, while at the same time entertainment was becoming more standardised. Standardisation and the development of a national market in the drive to maximise profit seemed by the late nineteenth century to be threatening to overwhelm the pre-existing regional diversity in culture and recreational life. Golby and Purdue, however, claim that 'popular culture and the changes in it were largely made by the people, their appetites, demands and aspirations', to which commercial forces merely acceded.[27] Some, from Christian Socialists and the Chartist Thomas Cooper to the Independent Labour Party and the Clarion Fellowship at the turn of the century, saw entrepreneurs' manipulation of workers' leisure activities for profit as a threat to developing an independent class-consciousness. This aspect of leisure and labour history has been analysed by Chris Waters who points out that the late nineteenth century condemnation of amusements that offered fun and frivolity at the expense of rest and recreation also involved the condemnation of an industry that grew rich by manipulating the desire for such amusements.[28] The new 'fun morality' offered by seaside entertainments threatened an older, more radical culture and the appeal of commercial entertainment reduced the ability of men and women to develop any alternatives. It was these concerns that motivated elements of the socialist movement to become involved in alternative holiday provision which will be discussed later in this volume, in particular the work of the Workers' Travel Association, the Co-operative Holiday Association and the founders of early holiday camps.

Holidaymaking, though still a luxury affordable only to a minority, had become part of the expectations of mainstream English working-class culture by 1914. During the period immediately following the First World War many organised groups of workers secured paid holidays through the collective bargaining process for the first time. With the onset of recession and the defeat of the General Strike in 1926 the majority of workers had to wait until the late 1930s to secure the same right. However, expectations had been raised to such an extent that 'the inability to afford such pleasures did not prevent the poor from believing they had a right to enjoy them; leisure as a natural aspiration of life became a major feature of English society, contemporary social investigators were surprised to discover'.[29] In order to enjoy an annual trip to the seaside, the poorest of families were prepared to resort to petty social crime in order to attain their goal. In his study of working-class childhood, Stephen Humphries discovered that in the 1930s, lacking the rail fare, mothers would go with their children to the station and wait until there was a big crowd on the platform. They would sneak behind them past the ticket inspector both on the way there and on the way back.[30] Despite the ways and means employed to achieve a holiday, seaside vacations were often an unattainable luxury, especially for families with young children. By the 1930s the rise of the seaside holiday may have caused feelings of deprivation to be sharpened for those unable to afford one. Andrew Davies concluded that while some working-class families were enjoying new levels of affluence and acquired status symbols such as gramophones, wireless and holidays, those trapped in the poverty cycle or unemployment were made to feel acutely aware that they were missing out.[31]

With the acceptance that ordinary working people had the right to anticipate periods of leisure without financial hardship, the proposition first put to the TUC in 1911 began to look less outrageous. Over the next twenty years the demand for paid holidays was raised in more and more unions at a national level until it became an aspiration of the entire labour movement.[32] During the 1930s the Labour Party developed its reformist policies in preparation and anticipation of when it became elected. The Trades Union Congress, in response to industrial defeat after the General Strike and disappointment in the second Labour government of 1929–31, developed a corporate bias and a conciliatory and consultative role with employers and the government.[33] Both the unions and the Labour Party were more interested in class collaboration than conflict.[34] In the depths of depression neither the government nor employers had much motivation to consult the weakened unions. Walter Citrine of the TUC emphasised the research function of its General Council and the need for patient lobbying of the government which resulted in TUC representation on a number of parliamentary committees. Importantly to this study, one was that on Holidays with Pay, which probably would not have been established without trade union pressure.[35] According to James Hinton, the narrowly electoral policies of the Labour Party grew at the expense of extraparliamentary action.

The Communist Party of Great Britain (CPGB) had been small but, although excluded from official influence, during the 1920s it had been able to exert a greater influence than its size would suggest because of its effective organisation, acting through the Minority Movement, the National Unemployed Workers' Committees and the Left Wing Movement. This influence declined with the onset of the party's sectarian policy in 1929, which lasted until the mid-1930s. By the time that the demand for holidays with pay was on the mainstream political agenda in the 1930s there were within the working-class movement two main political outlooks in the campaign, the reformist Labour Party followers and the revolutionary CPGB. In addition these were countered by the attempts of the establishment to manipulate working-class leisure as a means of social control or exploit collectivist tradition for commercial gain. It is essential to understand the relationship between working-class culture, reformist and revolutionary socialist theories and political and actual practice when looking at leisure and holidays. By the 1930s the campaign for paid holidays united the two strands of the labour movement. Both the reformists of the Labour Party and the revolutionary left, mainly in the Communist Party, agreed with the principle of holidays with pay for all workers. The timing of the main thrust of the official campaign coincided with the Communist Party's abandonment of the extreme sectarianism of Stalinism's so-called 'third period'.[36] Then there was a switch to a Popular Front policy with the slogan 'Peace, Freedom, Democracy' emphasising what all workers had in common. On the massive May Day march, organised by the co-operative movement, in London in 1938 during the time the parliamentary committee on Holidays with Pay was working, there was a float decorated to publicise the campaign, a symbol of how far the idea of holidays had become part of mainstream working-class culture.[37]

In the Labour Party in the 1930s and 1940s the debate could be portrayed as an attempt to create efficiency that would allow people to take greater charge of their lives.[38] A central feature of the party's thinking in this period was equality, justified by the desire to release the potential within people. Following the 1931 election, trade unionists predominated in the parliamentary party: the Miners' Federation alone sponsored half the MPs.[39] The subsequent Labour Party Conference demanded that any future Labour government must undertake 'definite socialist legislation'. From 1934 plans were formulated to nationalise major industries and for emergency powers to resist ruling-class opposition, although there was disagreement over priorities. Some felt that public ownership and planning were imperative; others believed that redistribution of material rewards through taxation was sufficient; others stressed a more qualitative vision of socialist fellowship.[40] The problem faced by the Labour Party was that, despite its intention to promote equality and social participation with its policies, to enable the vast majority of producers to share in a classless society offering individual moral improvement, material prosperity was a prerequisite. The Labour Party developed its own social strategy which included improved leisure facilities such as swimming pools, amenities in parks, recreation grounds and so on to be established during its next anticipated period of government. Unlike the Communists, Labour did not see leisure as part of a wider materialist world but, as Frank Betts put it, 'an ethical foundation for joy'.[41] The constitution called for the state to actively brighten 'the lives of those now condemned to almost ceaseless toil' by a 'great development of the means of recreation'.[42] Leisure was an outlet for individual choice away from the dictates of work, essential to body and mind. Little attempt was made to see leisure in relation to the dominant mode of production, ultimately determined by the capitalist order of society – the leisure question was never linked with a systematic overview of the capitalist way of life as a whole. According to Stephen G. Jones, Labour identified the role of workers' organisations as being to fight for a fair share of leisure and to extract benefits from the capitalist system. This was symptomatic of the labour movement's political shift to the left in terms of rhetoric, but mirrored in practical terms by its industrial weakness. Trade unions were the vehicles for the construction of social reform, first by campaigning for paid holidays, the forty-hour week and other leisure demands. Only when these were achieved would they be able to consider the creation of a society guaranteeing fair shares of leisure for all. As Jones put it:

> Although not precluding the need for socialism, the labour argument for the shorter working week was based on the reformist premise that, with capitalist prosperity, benefits would percolate through the system into the palms of the workers – a premise to some extent evidenced by the increase in real wages, reduction in hours and the expansion of capitalist forms for those in work. It was not the overt task of the Labour Socialist, so it seems, to overthrow the society that others on the left suggested restricted the quality and quantity of leisure, but rather to secure labour its just rewards out of capitalism.[43]

Leisure was seen as something to be demanded in its own right, clearly accepting the dominant institutions and order of society. In 1938 the TUC president and secretary of the National Union of Clerks and Administrative Workers, Herbert Elvin, felt a Ministry of Leisure would best serve working-class people. A new economic system, based on need, and not profit, was not a prerequisite for real gains in workers' leisure: capital could be reformed and concede benefits to the working class.

Although the Communist Party was fundamentally opposed to capitalism it was not above reformism as a political tactic. Leisure and holidays were seen as the right of all workers. The party demanded two weeks with pay even during its sectarian period. In its general election programme of 1929, entitled *Class against class*, two of the demands it put forward to solve the unemployment problem were for a seven-hour day and a fortnight's holiday a year with pay.[44] The importance placed on these demands is emphasised in their positioning within the manifesto as the top two points out of the twelve in the programme, above housing, social legislation, education, taxation and the fight against a probable future war. This prominence was because greater workers' control in the workplace was seen as a key part of the defensive strategy against the capitalist offensive. Revolutionary socialists realised that the dominant mode of production depressed the cultural level of the masses. Capitalism had made everything a commodity, a potential source of profit. People had become consumers of culture rather than partners in its production. A socialist system of production would produce more free time together with better leisure and cultural facilities. 'It is the capitalist ownership of the land, industries and banks which is preventing the development of wealth-producing power in order to provide the wealth and leisure for all workers . . . Decaying and parasitic capitalism had to be wiped out and replaced by a planned socialist economy.'[45]

From this analysis it is clear that there was no contradiction between the struggle for reforms, including paid holidays, and the long term goal of socialist revolution, providing reforms were not substituted for class struggle but became a means of raising the level of workers' class consciousness during campaigns for their achievement. When addressing the British Youth Peace Assembly in 1937, Vincent Duncan Jones, secretary of the Youth Charter Group, called for a forty hour maximum working week, a minimum wage scale for young workers and two weeks annual holiday with pay. In his speech to 250 enthusiastic delegates and observers at the assembly, Jones invoked class to support his argument: 'Young men, told that industry would collapse if they were given two weeks' annual paid holiday, see every day plans and pictures of "southern cruises" undertaken by sons of the rich.'[46] By working with non-Communists towards a common goal, be it holidays with pay or higher wages, Communists could influence them and hopefully win them over to revolutionary politics through their example as the best activists. For this reason revolutionaries became involved in the struggle for paid holidays and other reforms not solely for the primary objective of securing a vacation but also to influence and to gain a position to lead the working-class movement.

As the demand for paid holidays became a viable and serious proposition, it was widely believed that free time, not the endless increase in consumption, would be a consequence of economic growth. The application of Fordism and Taylorism to industrial production as well as technological advances meant that production could be rationalised by the effective use of labour.[47] More could be produced in less time, meaning that industry could reduce working hours and grant more holidays to workers without loss of productivity. Everyone working for fewer hours, sharing the benefits of cheap, mass-produced consumer goods, could eradicate unemployment and the problems of overproduction. It would also create a mass leisure society and undermine the work ethic. It was assumed that people only had limited consumer needs and once these were satisfied they would be content to spend more time on their own interests. In her study of working-class women in Lancashire, Elizabeth Roberts found from early twentieth-century working wives that it was clear they had an ideal income that would clothe, feed and house the family and leave a surplus for savings. Once that ideal was reached it was more important to have less work than more money.[48] The demand for the eight-hour day and paid holidays after the First World War seemed to prove this point. The campaign for holidays with pay became a symbol of a social solidarity to be realised in leisure beyond the control of the market and the state.[49] During the inter-war years it became accepted that working people had the right to expect a break from the routine of work. It was at this time, culminating in the Amulree report of the Select Committee on Holidays with Pay and the ensuing legislation, that paid holidays were campaigned for seriously within the working-class movement.

This vision of contentment through increased free time with all other needs fulfilled never became a reality. From the 1930s, and especially after the Second World War, Gary Cross argues, in the United States increased output came to be seen as the means to prosperity for all, and more time for leisure was of only secondary importance. High wages gained a priority over reduced working hours as a way to encourage economic growth. Shorter hours and more holidays suggested economic constraint and limited growth. The paradox of workers who claim to want more free time and yet clamour for more and more overtime with higher rates of pay is raised by the American Sebastian de Grazia.[50] These changes in outlook also affected the British working class, and by the 1960s trade unions were campaigning not to share in economic prosperity through more and longer paid holidays but through higher wage rates, bonus pay and overtime agreements. Having achieved a two-week summer holiday with pay and perhaps a third elsewhere in the year, in addition to bank holidays, workers seemed content and focused on money rather than more time off as the central employment issue, before industrial decline and the right to employment and union organisation themselves became paramount.

The text that follows will attempt to demonstrate working-class agency in the development of popular tourism and offers a perspective distinct from other histories of tourism and holidaymaking, such as *The Englishman's holiday* by J. A. R. Pimlott, one of the first authors to produce a serious history of the subject, dating from 1945 but still interesting and relevant, especially in the chapters on holidays with pay.[51] Other general texts covering leisure and tourism history from a wide perspective were written by James Walvin and John Walton in the late 1970s and early 1980s.[52] These have had an important influence on the present work, which now attempts to reinterpret and fill in the narrow gaps in these studies regarding how lower-income groups came to have holidays at all, let alone spend them at the seaside. The historical study of British holidaymaking is brought into the more recent past, again by John Walton, in *The British seaside: holidays and resorts in the twentieth century*.[53] Here still, apart from a chapter on the 'holidaymakers' and on 'travelling to the coast' this work is about the seaside rather than how people managed to be able to go there in financial and social terms. The role of local government in seaside development and marketing is analysed by Nigel J. Morgan and Annette Pritchard in their study of Devon resorts, *Power and politics at the seaside*.[54] The theme of this work is municipal involvement in tourism influenced by local politics and it opens a new perspective on the evolution of seaside facilities and social tone. Also looking at the political implications of advertising and marketing of resorts is a chapter by John Beckerson again in Berghoff et al.'s *The making of modern tourism*.[55] Purporting to be a general history of tourism, Fred Inglis's *The delicious history of the holiday*, despite some useful and novel ideas, is neither delicious nor an accurate history.[56] The cultural studies approach he adopts often says more about his own sensitivities and preoccupations, although a strength of the work is that it does deal with the darker side of holidays, specifically sex tourism in the Far East. John Urry, in *The tourist gaze* and *Consuming places*, takes a different approach.[57] Although influential, Urry's work offers little in historical terms that is not available in the works already discussed apart from a useful catch phrase. What he does do, however, is bridge the gap between the academic study of tourism history and that of marketing the tourism product. Urry presents ideas regarding the directing of the tourism consumer's interest and also the nature of that product, which unlike other commodities is consumed at the same time as it is produced and cannot be stored to be sold later, making for an immediacy and urgency in its sale and consumption. Similar ideas have influenced the business of tourism since the 1980s but were presented as useful information for those concerned professionally with marketing the tourism product.[58]

The present work has the acknowledged weakness of not dealing either with holidaymaking in the wider British Isles or with issues relating to gender in depth and detail. It is mainly about the English and to a certain extent the Welsh working class, although there are occasional examples from Scotland. It was felt that there are too many cultural differences regarding the labour movement, class and leisure to deal with adequately in the present volume. This needs a comprehensive study in its own right to avoid the tokenism that might inadvertently occur if this work were to pretend to cover the whole of Britain. Gender is not specifically discussed in relation to tourism, although undoubtedly there are differences in the way men and women perceive and use leisure. The role of women as the main carers for children means that even on holiday they might not be able to completely relax because of that continuing responsibility. However, this needs to be put into context. For working mothers, as well as men, time spent with children can be a leisure activity in its own right. In the 1930s Mass-Observation's study of Bolton people on holiday in Blackpool showed that many women enjoyed watching their children playing on the sand and felt proud that were able to give them the opportunity.[59] As it was particularly difficult for families with young children to go away on holiday they were right to feel proud. It would have been women's thrift and housekeeping skills that enabled the family to go away as much as men's provision of a wage. Most working women would have contributed financially to the household income in some way, even if it was not acknowledged in the historical record, by cleaning, taking in washing or lodgers. Many women in lower income groups had paid work outside the home, especially in the Northern cotton and woollen districts and in the East Midland hosiery and boot and shoe trades where they would take part in savings schemes, perhaps run them and have a say in how their money was spent. It is recognised that going away on holiday can involve women in more work than usual, buying new clothes for the family, extra washing, ironing and packing in the days leading up to departure. Even on holiday, unless in full-board accommodation, married women might still have to shop for food and prepare it. Even so this continuation of domestic responsibility, for many women part of their normal routine of unwaged work, may have been less onerous if undertaken in a different environment. This statement is not meant to belittle the hard work of women, without whom, like Christmas, holidays as we know them would not have happened. Compare it with the hop pickers, who worked extremely long and hard, living in poor conditions where they had to cook and wash after an exhausting day in the fields. Despite the hardships, they regarded the work in the Kent countryside as a holiday away from the urban sprawl of London. Where specific evidence regarding women exists, it has been utilised. Unfortunately because of past omissions it is difficult to write of the different experiences of men and women in the facilitation of holidays. Working-class women's cultural experiences shaped the way that holidays evolved as much as men's. Women were sometimes part of the organised working class in the trade union movement when they were employed in cotton and woollen textiles, shoe manufacture, hosiery, pottery, shops (especially the Co-op) and clerical work. Collective and trade union campaigns for paid leave, whilst usually excluding women from being negotiating officials for reasons discussed elsewhere, included women workers in the results of negotiations, even if they were not actually members of the union.[60] The subject of women's leisure has been discussed by Claire Langhamer. Although her work is not specifically about holidays it incorporates ideas about leisure in the context of female exclusion from the workplace and the contradiction of spare time for people who do not go out to work and whose main employment was unmeasurable, unpaid and in the home.[61]

Having outlined the intellectual background to the present study and where it will hopefully contribute new knowledge and expand on existing themes it remains now to begin to interpret the role of the working class and its organisations in the development of popular tourism in England.

Notes

1 Thomas Hardy, *The hand of Ethelberta*, 1876, New Wessex edn 1975, p. 367.

2 Rob Shields, *Places on the margin: alternative geographies of modernity*, London, 1991.

3 Family testimonies to the author, whose mother and aunt appear in the photograph.

4 John Urry, *The tourist gaze: leisure and travel in contemporary societies*, London, 1990.

5 R. A. Leeson, *Travelling brothers*, London, 1979; Eric Hobsbawm, 'The tramping artisan', in *Labouring men*, London, 1964.

6 D. Reid, 'The decline of St Monday, 1766–1876', *Past and Present* 71, 1976, pp. 76–101.

7 Jeffrey Auerbach, *The Great Exhibition of 1851: a nation on display*, New Haven CT, 1999; Michael Leapman, *The world for a shilling: how the Great Exhibition of 1851 shaped a nation*, London, 2002; Louise Purbrick (ed.), *The Great Exhibition of 1851*, Manchester, 2001.

8 R. J. Morris, 'Leeds and the Crystal Palace', *Victorian Studies* 13, 1970, pp. 283–300.

9 Alan Delgado, *The annual outing and other excursions*, London, 1977.

10 John K. Walton, 'The demand for working-class seaside holidays in Victorian England', *Economic History Review* 34, 1981, pp. 249–65.

11 Robert Poole, 'Oldham wakes', in J. K. Walton and J. Walvin (eds), *Leisure in Britain, 1780–1939*, London, 1983, pp. 71–98; also John K. Walton and Robert Poole, 'The Lancashire wakes in the nineteenth century', in Robert Storch (ed.), *Popular culture and custom in nineteenth-century England*, Beckenham, 1982, pp. 100–24.

12 Stephen G. Jones, 'The Lancashire wakes, holiday savings and holiday pay in the textile districts', *Eccles and District Local History Society*, 1983, pp. 27–39; Poole, 'Oldham wakes'.

13 Walton, 'The demand for working-class seaside holidays'; Reid, 'The decline of St Monday'; John Benson, *British coal miners in the nineteenth century*, Dublin, 1980, pp. 56–7; G. I. H. Lloyd, *The cutlery trade: an historical essay in the economics of small-scale production*, London, 1913, p. 181; Ronald E. Wilson, *Two hundred precious metal years: a history of the Sheffield Smelting Company, 1760–1960*, London, 1960, p. 75; W. Felkin, 'An account of the machine-wrought hosiery trade: its extent and the condition of the framework knitters', paper read at the second York meeting of the British Association, 1844; Felkin, *Evidence given under the Hosiery Commission enquiry*, London, 1845, pp. 19–20.

14 John K. Walton, *The Blackpool landlady*, Manchester, 1979; John K. Walton, 'The Blackpool landlady revisited', *Manchester Region History Review*, 1994, pp. 23–31.

15 Colin Ward and Dennis Hardy, *Goodnight, campers!*, London, 1986.

16 Colin Ward and Dennis Hardy, *Arcadia for all*, London, 1984.

17 Harold Perkin, *The structured crowd*, Sussex, 1981.

18 Edwin Hopwood, *A history of the Lancashire cotton industry and the Amalgamated Weavers' Association*, Manchester, 1969, p. 124; J. E. Williams, *The Derbyshire miners*, London, 1962, pp. 628–9; Alan Fox, *A history of the National Union of Boot and Shoe Operatives*, Oxford, 1958, p. 408.

19 John K. Walton, *The British seaside: holidays and resorts in the twentieth century*, Manchester, 2000, pp. 58–62.

20 Sue Wright, 'Sun, sea, sand and self-expression: mass tourism as an individual experience', in Hartmut Berghoff, Barbara Korte, Ralf Schneider and Christopher Harvie (eds), *The making of modern tourism: the cultural history of the British experience, 1600–2000*, Basingstoke, 2002, pp. 181–202.

21 Karen O'Reilly, *The British on the Costa del Sol: transnational identities and local community*, London, 2000.

22 M. Barke, J. Towner and M. Newton (eds), *Tourism in Spain: critical issues*, London, 1995.

23 Allan M. Williams and Gareth Shaw, *Tourism and economic development: European experiences*, 3rd edn, Chichester, 1998.

24 Peter Burke, 'Viewpoint: the invention of leisure in early modern Europe', *Past and Present* 146, February 1995, pp. 136–50.

25 Michel Foucault, *The order of things*, trans. A. Sheridan, London, 1970, p. xxii.

26 James Walvin, *Leisure and society, 1830–1950*, London, 1978, p. 61.

27 J. M. Golby and A.W. Purdue, *The civilisation of the crowd: popular culture in England, 1750–1900*, rev. edn, Stroud, 1999, p. 7.

28 Chris Waters, *British socialists and the politics of popular culture*, Manchester, 1990, and also 'Social reformers, socialists and the opposition to the commercialisation of leisure in late Victorian England', in Wray Vamplew (ed.), *The economic history of leisure: papers presented at the eighth International Economic History Conference*, Budapest, 1982, p. 109; Harvey Taylor, *A claim on the countryside: a history of the British outdoor movement*, Keele, 1997.

29 Walvin, *Leisure and society*, p. 63.

30 Stephen Humphries, *Hooligans or rebels? An oral history of working-class childhood and youth, 1889–1939*, Oxford, 2nd edn, 1995, p. 166.

31 Andrew Davies, *Leisure, gender and poverty: working-class culture in Salford and Manchester, 1900–1939*, Buckingham, 1992, p. 42.

32 Trades Union Congress archive, Modern Records Office, University of Warwick, MSS 292/114.

33 James Hinton, *Labour and socialism: a history of the British labour movement, 1867–1974*, Brighton, 1983, p. 128.

34 Stephen G. Jones, 'The British labour movement and working-class leisure, 1918–1939', Ph.D. thesis, University of Manchester, 1983, p. 86.

35 Hinton, *Labour and socialism*, p. 150.

36 Leon Trotsky, 'What next?' (1932), in *Fascism, Stalinism and the United Front, 1930–1934*, special issue of *International Socialism Journal*, London, 1969, p. 28.

37 *Advance democracy* (film) dir. Ralph Bond, Co-op Film Unit, 1938.

38 M. J. Daunton, 'Payment and participation: welfare and state formation in Britain, 1900–1951', *Past and Present* 150, February 1996, pp. 169–216, 212.

39 Hinton, *Labour and socialism*, p. 148.

40 Daunton, 'Payment and participation', p. 210.

41 Jones, 'The British labour movement and working-class leisure', p. 93.

42 Waters, *British socialists and the politics of popular culture*, pp. 154–5.

43 Jones, 'The British labour movement and working-class leisure', p. 94.

44 *Class against class*, the general election programme of the Communist Party of Great Britain, London, 1929, pp. 22–3.

45 *Daily Worker*, 31 March 1934, p. 2.

46 *Ibid.*, 21 May 1937, p. 4.

47 Eric Hobsbawm, *The Age of Empire, 1875–1914*, London, 1987, p. 45.

48 Elizabeth Roberts, *A woman's place: an oral history of working-class women, 1890–1940*, Oxford, 1984, p. 142.

49 Gary Cross, *Time and money: the making of consumer culture*, London and New York, 1993, pp. 7–8.

50 Sebastian de Grazzia, *Of work, time and leisure*, New York, 1962, pp. 139–40.

51 J. A. R. Pimlott, *The Englishman's holiday*, 1947, Hassocks, 1976 edn.

52 Walton and Walvin, *Leisure in Britain*; John K. Walton, *The English seaside resort: a social history, 1750–1914*, Leicester, 1983; James Walvin, *Beside the seaside*, London, 1978; Walvin, *Leisure and society*.

53 Walton, *The British seaside*.

54 Nigel J. Morgan and Annette Pritchard, *Power and politics at the seaside: the development of Devon's resorts in the twentieth century*, Exeter, 1999.

55 John Beckerson, 'Marketing British tourism: government approaches to the stimulation of a service sector', in Hartmut Berghoff *et al.* (eds), *The making of modern tourism*, pp. 133–57.

56 Fred Inglis, *The delicious history of tourism*, London, 2001.

57 Urry, *The tourist gaze*; *id.*, *Consuming places*, London, 1995.

58 J. C. Holloway and R. V. Plant, *Marketing for tourism*, London, 1988.

59 Gary Cross, *Worktowners at Blackpool: Mass-Observation and popular leisure in the 1930s*, London, 1990.

80 Hopwood, *Lancashire cotton industry*; Fox, *National Union of Boot and Shoe Operatives*; Gurnham, *200 years: the hosiery unions, 1776–1976*, Leicester, 1976; F. Birchall and R. Ross, *A history of the potters' union*, Stoke on Trent, 1977.

61 Claire Langhamer, *Women's leisure in England, 1920–1960*, Manchester, 2000.

2

No Grand Tours:
tourism before 1850

When discussing travel in the period before 1850 it should not be assumed that working people never travelled for pleasure, despite ostensibly economic reasons for their journeys. Although some of the activities described in this chapter have similarities to later practices and are relevant to this study and suggest continuity and development into later tourism-related ones, the cultural meanings attached to these activities would also have changed over time. For instance, artisans on the tramping circuit may well have found it an interesting or even enjoyable experience and carried with them a type of 'cheque book' with vouchers to exchange for lodgings and money *en route* but they would not have thought of themselves as tourists or on holiday.

While there have always been people who travelled, the significant feature of modern tourism, imbuing it with more meaning than simply travelling and staying away from home, is that it is undertaken for pleasure. Even as recently as the late nineteenth century, most poor people who travelled were doing so out of necessity. They moved about the country in search of work or left their own country altogether through emigration. In England, Scotland, Wales and Ireland economic change caused many dislocated people to move from the countryside into the growing towns and cities. From the middle of the nineteenth century, not just in Britain but all over Europe, the number of people leaving their own country and emigrating overseas increased. Before 1845 in only one year had more than 100,000 migrated to the United States. Between 1846 and 1859 an annual average of more than a quarter of a million left Europe, followed in the next five years by an annual average of almost 350,000 people. America gained 428,000 immigrants in 1854 alone. The bulk of these migrants were from Western Europe. Some artisans would migrate to earn money and return to their homeland after a few years. A considerable proportion, between

30 per cent and 40 per cent, returned home usually because they had failed to settle down in the United States. Many British craft union leaders worked for a spell in America or elsewhere overseas and then came back.[1] Irish migrant workers would have been familiar to British town dwellers. Witnessing migration and emigration meant that the idea of travel, even over long distances, was not an unfamiliar concept. The difference between this and tourist travel was motivation. Migration and emigration were usually because of compulsion or to better oneself whereas tourism is usually undertaken by choice and for pleasure.

Emigration was a feature of life for agricultural workers and urban craftsmen and their families. Many of those who left Britain returned, either because they didn't settle or because they had never intended to remain permanently overseas. Others migrated within the home country in search of work, to distant growing towns or to neighbouring communities. The craft organisations of skilled artisans paid out-of-work members an allowance as they travelled the country on foot in search of work. This aspect of working-class mobility has been researched and documented by both R. A. Leeson[2] and Eric Hobsbawm,[3] who investigated this feature of craft organisation. Eric Hobsbawm described tramping in his paper 'The tramping artisan':

> The man who wished to leave town to look for work elsewhere received a 'blank' or 'clearance' or 'document', showing him to be a member in good standing of the society. This he presented to the local secretary or relieving officer in the 'lodge house' or 'club house' or 'house of call' of the strange town – generally a pub – receiving in return supper, lodging, perhaps beer, and a tramp allowance. If there was work he took it; the call book (if there was one) was of course kept at the house of call, an unofficial labour exchange.[4]

This system, though outwardly a means of support for the unemployed and a way of regulating the supply of skilled labour, must also have encouraged in some men the desire to travel for its own sake. As a means of assisting the unemployed journeyman it would have been less efficient than paying a man relief to stay at home. It was not a system suited to the needs of a married man with a family who would be forced to abandon them to the rates if he used this form of relief. Yet the tramping system persisted, in the case of stonemasons until the First World War. During the time of the repressive Combination Acts tramping was also a means of developing links between workers in one town with those in another, passing on information relating to rates of pay, disputes and working conditions as well as dispersing a pool of potential scab labour in times of conflict. The circulation of tradesmen around the country forged an embryonic national trade union structure which proved vital in the transition from craft society to trade unions. By 1800 the system was highly developed, although its origins were much older, being in existence among Devon wool combers as early as 1700.[5]

The adaptation of tramping to the needs of single men and the emphasis on travel suggest that the earlier craft organisations fostered touring the country for other than purely economic reasons. Travel could have been encouraged because of its educational value for young men just out of their apprenticeship. It enabled them to experience working life in a variety of contexts in order to expand their skills as all-round craftsmen. In the clothing industry, at one time, a man was scarcely considered a good tailor unless he had done his turn on the road.[6] It was a sort of 'artisans' Grand Tour', as Eric Hobsbawm described it.[7] That some men travelled because they chose to rather than being compelled to by unemployment or industrial conflict is proposed in the book *Travelling brothers*, by R. A. Leeson, who found evidence that many tramps took to the road in times of full employment in their home town. The only reason for going on the tramp would have been personal choice, travelling for the pleasure of doing so or to broaden experience.[8] By the early nineteenth century tramping was widely practised in most trades. The Select Committee on Artisans and Machinery, looking into the Combination Acts, in 1824 found networks of houses of call and arrangements between Dublin-based and English crafts.[9] Hatters, smiths, carpenters, boot and shoe makers, metalworkers, bakers, tailors, plumbers, painters, glaziers, bookbinders and others had houses of call in London.[10] In April 1848 the Masons' corresponding secretary was sent to Stalybridge, where he believed a strike was in progress after a bill of £45 arrived from the Moulders' Arms. On his arrival he found that the scene of action for the previous fortnight was a wakes or fair instead of a strike, 'to the utter disgrace of officers of the lodge'. The pub landlord had been so simple as to allow customers money, meat and drink with the idea of keeping unprincipled rascals from working.[11] The expenses for these men's holiday had been charged to the unemployed artisans' fund. This story shows the link between collectively enforced wakes weeks in cotton textile towns and going on strike to obtain a holiday. It also demonstrates that the tramping artisan funds could be abused by those seeking pleasure rather than genuinely in search of work.

Because of its practice among a wide variety of trades, with tramping circuits of over a thousand miles in some cases,[12] the custom must have been widely accepted and familiar not just among all skilled workers but among the communities around them. For this reason the concept of tourism, though not the word itself, would have been familiar to most people, even given it was formed within a different cultural context.

The tramping system may have had another important influence on one aspect of the tourism industry's later development. This was through the use of a cheque system by those on the tramp. On setting out the traveller would be given a cheque book valid for a certain number of days[13] and would cash the relief cheques at each branch or house of call for hospitality and an allowance. This was to guard against abuses of the system by those not entitled to benefit. The fact that craft societies felt the system was being brought into disrepute by lazy people who were travelling to escape work, rather than to find it, also suggests that at least some of those on the road were doing so for their own satisfaction and pleasure.[14]

A similar scheme to the cheques of travelling artisans was introduced in the developing travel and tourism industry in the 1860s. An unsuccessful system of travellers' cheques was introduced by the early travel agent Henry Gaze. An earlier system of circular notes had been devised by the banker Herries almost a century previously in 1772, but Cook's was the firm that made a success of the innovation. In 1865 John Mason Cook, the son of Thomas Cook, copied Gaze's scheme and introduced the hotel coupon for use by tourists who had paid their accommodation costs in advance.[15] From 1868 Cook's sold coupons for 8s which entitled tourists to a bed, two meals, lights (candle or lamp fuel) and attendance (service by a member of staff) at participating hotels. Tourists benefited from the assurance that they would not be overcharged or have problems carrying and exchanging currency. By 1872 120,000 sets of coupons had been sold with a network of 150 Continental hotels joining the scheme. In 1871 the American Express Company introduced travellers' cheques, known then as 'circular notes', in the United States which were to replace letters of credit and the need for travellers to carry large amounts of currency. Soon, from 1872, travellers' cheques were issued in Britain, again by Thomas Cook & Son. As we have seen, those on the tramp were already using their own kind of hotel coupons and travellers' cheques; their blanks or cheques, which they cashed in at the houses of call in the network. As formal reference is made in the rules for Operative Stonemasons from 1871 and in 1873 in the Operative Bakers' rules,[16] it is unlikely that the firm of Thomas Cook or even Henry Gaze would not have been aware of their use before instituting their own system of coupons. Thomas Cook had himself been an artisan in the printing trade before entering the travel business full-time and Gaze's early initiatives had been among workers in the North-west industrial area. They were both well placed to have observed the practices of tramping first-hand. Because of the number of migrants to America from among the artisan community it is likely that the system would also have been known to members of the American Express Company. Although no direct evidence links these commercial schemes with the cheques of the tramping artisans, the similarities are remarkable and it seems unlikely that the two systems could have flourished contemporaneously without the older being the inspiration of the newer.

Turning now to consider trips undertaken simply for pleasure, Londoners had been able to travel to Gravesend and Margate by sailing hoy from the middle of the eighteenth century. In 1757 the fare was 2s. The number of passenger hoys plying this route rose from four in 1763 to eleven by 1801.[17] As steamboats came into use, conditions for passengers improved and the journey became much quicker. An anonymous diarist, apparently a young man, 'left London in the *Emerald* Steam Packet to Gravesend – twenty miles in two and a half hours' in September 1835.[18] He found Gravesend 'much enlarged since a former visit'. The town had grown and been 'improved' to cater for the new trade from trippers, thanks to the steamboats. 'The views from the Tivoli Gardens and particularly from Windmill Hill were extensive and picturesque, the Thames shipping adding much to the beauty and interest of the scene.' Margate too had 'also much increased' since a previous visit; there were

> many grand hotels and the new church was very striking. The promenade attached to the pier is a fine gravel walk which holds the ground firm and dry – length about 300 yards by six or seven yards wide and about six feet above the pier.

There was no charge to walk on the lower part of the pier where boat passengers landed. Paying attention to passenger comfort, some boats even employed stewardesses to look after female passengers. In Arthur Sketchley's comic story *Mrs Brown at the seaside*, written in Cockney dialect around the middle of the nineteenth century, the heroine is obliged to turn to the stewardess for help when a fall causes her dress to come undone at the back.

> I was shook by the fall, with my 'ooks and eyes bust out of my back, that I was obligated to go down to the stewardess to be set to rights . . . A werry nice lady that stewardess were, thro' bein' a widder and 'ad buried seven poor things, and all under five years old . . . I could 'ave set all day along with that stewardess as 'aad only rared three out of ten as fine babbies as ever was born.[19]

On the deck it was very pleasant, we are told,

with a breeze a-blowin' and the band a-playin' as makes the time pass that agree-
able, and werry different to the time when parties was days a-gettin to Margate
thro' goin' in a Hoy, as it were called, and the fust families in the land a-goin' by
it, the same as I 'ave 'eard say.[20]

Steam-powered boats were very much faster than the hoys but that did not
much impress Mrs Brown, who associated speed with danger. She remarked
that the hoys' trade

was run down thro' steamboats a-comin' in as is frightful dangerous, and
knocked my dear aunt over the side of a barge, as kept the ferry 'ouse near Erith
Church, and was pertikler fond of being a-board on the water, and went to
fill the kettle jest as the steamer come by, never thinkin' of no danger thro'
bein' 'ard of 'earin, and the fust steamer as ever run to Margate and come on 'er
that sudden as nobody wasn't aware on in them days, a-comin' so quick and must
'ave been drownded but for 'er gownd a-ketchin' in the rullock as 'eld 'er up by
the 'eel, till she was drawed out with a 'itcher as was kep' for the purpose.[21]

Not easy to please, Mrs Brown was not nostalgic for the hoys which themselves
had had many faults. 'As to them Hoys, they were as bad as a man-of-war for
seasickness I've 'eard say, and nobody went aboard 'em without preparin' their-
selves for the worst; and 'ave been know'd to be wrecked off Greenithe, as is
a wild spot on the Essex side.' Of her journey to Margate, Mrs Brown told the
reader, 'I can't say as I ever fancies the sea myself, and would 'ave gone by
train, only it's a savin'.' Her husband enjoyed the experience more than she
did. 'Brown enjoys 'is pipe with a glass of stout on deck,' and for her 'it was
a real pleasure to 'ear 'im talk to them sailors'.[22] The journey by steamer may
have been an attraction in itself to trippers. As well as music, sea air and drink,
passengers could enjoy a meal on board. Mrs Brown appreciated this too.

There was a werry nice dinner aboard that steamer, as I calls a biled leg of
mutton and a roast line of pork, with summer cabbage and peas, and green
gooseberry pies as was that acid thro' a-gettin nearly ripe; in all my life I never
tasted a better cheese, tho' the reddishes was as big as 'a'penny balls, and the
lettices run werry much up the middle, as makes 'em all stalk and bitter as sut.
    They certinly do 'ave lovely bottled stout aboard them boats, and altogether,
what with 'avin' a little somethin' 'ot along with Brown, I never did enjoy a meal
more.

The piers at Gravesend and Margate where the steamers landed attracted
crowds, not just of passengers but of people who just wanted to watch what
was going on and enjoy the views. Crowds themselves provided an attraction
for thieves and both the factual diary and the fictional Mrs Brown refer to this

problem. The diarist above reported that at Margate people were 'not allowed on the free pier when steamers were in to prevent London blacklegs from fingering luggage'.[23] Mrs Brown was wary of the porters who carried her luggage aboard the boat. When they grabbed her boxes she 'overpaid the cabman frightful, in fear as they'd been and collared the lot'.[24]

Although there had been excursions by steamboat, notably from London to Gravesend, described above, which was a popular trippers' resort before the railways opened up towns farther afield,[25] and even some trips by horse and cart before the coming of the railway, it was the railway excursion that launched the era of cheap holiday travel for the masses.[26] Probably the first steam-powered rail excursion took place, at normal fares, on the Liverpool & Manchester Railway on 16 September 1830, only one day after the line's opening. Earlier than that, there had been excursions by horse-drawn train on the Swansea to Mumbles line of the Oystermouth Railway. The first rail excursion at reduced fares was probably in 1839 on the Whitby & Pickering Railway, using horse-drawn trains for transport to the Grosmont church bazaar.[27]

Since the very beginning of the Railway Age in the 1830s, organisations catering for the needs of at least some sections of the working class had organised excursions primarily for leisure purposes. Examples of these were the Mechanics' Institutes and Friendly Societies. These early excursions usually had some aspect of self-improvement in them such as a visit to an exhibition or even some moral edification such as teetotalism. Despite the justifications for these excursions, putting them firmly in the field of rational recreation, the main motivation of trippers was the hope of enjoyment. The earliest excursions took place in a ceremonial atmosphere, accompanied by brass bands, jollity and feasting.[28] A welcoming party and passengers on the trip from Nottingham to an exhibition organised by the Mechanics' Institute in Leicester in 1840 formed a procession four abreast. This parade from the station to the exhibition venue was greeted by the Duke of Rutland's band playing 'God save the Queen' followed by further musical entertainment.[29] Even Thomas Cook's first temperance excursion was far from being a solemn occasion, the festive event in Loughborough being open to all, even drinkers of alcohol. Cook recalled, 'We carried music and music met us at the Loughborough station. The people crowded the streets, filled windows, covered the housetops and cheered all along the line.'[30]

The work of the Mechanics' Institutes, though, pioneered the way for the development of cheap, popular excursions utilising the power of steam-driven locomotives to convey large crowds of people, including many members of the working class. The first recorded of these excursions happened in 1839 when York Mechanics' Institute members went by train to visit the Leeds Public Exhibition of the Works of Art, Science, Natural History and Manufacturing Skill, a trip organised by the Leeds Mechanics' Institute in collaboration with the local Literary and Philosophical Society.[31] Another early Mechanics' excursion at reduced fares ran on 13 May 1840, involving the Newcastle & Carlisle Railway.[32] That year, 1840, saw the major launch of popular rail excursion travel. There were several exhibitions in the summer of that year. The Leicester and Nottingham Mechanics' Institutes followed the example of their more northern sister organisations when they arranged excursions between the two towns to visit each other's exhibitions. This particular reciprocal trip was acknowledged to have been his inspiration by Thomas Cook, whose more famous excursion from Leicester to Loughborough took place a year later.

> I believe that the Midland Railway from Derby to Rugby via Leicester was opened in 1840 ... the reports in the papers of the opening of the new line created astonishment in Leicestershire and I had read of an interchange of visits between the Leicester and Nottingham Mechanics' Institutes ... About midway between Harborough and Leicester ... a thought flashed through my brain – what a glorious thing it would be if the newly developed powers of railways and locomotives could be made subservient to the promotion of temperance![33]

This admission contradicts an early biographer of Cook, William Fraser Rae, who stated that Cook 'is none the less an originator, because he never heard of anyone doing what he had accomplished' and 'nothing more can be proved in opposition to his claim' to have been the originator of excursion travel 'than the probable fact of the idea which flashed upon him in his lonely walk, having passed through other minds beforehand or contemporaneously'.[34] Fraser Rae's enthusiastic claims can perhaps be explained as his book was published by Thomas Cook & Son to commemorate the fiftieth anniversary of the firm. Fraser Rae was also mistaken in his assertion that the Mechanics' excursions were not publicly advertised and were open only to their own organisation's members, crediting Cook with running the first advertised excursion open to the general public. The *Leicester Chronicle* in July 1840 carried an advertisement from the Leicester Mechanics' Institute addressed to the 'Ladies and Gentlemen' who were not members 'intending to join the party' for the excursion to Nottingham.[35] The number who travelled, approximately 400 people, with a further 2,400 on a second trip later that summer, far outnumbered the membership of the Institute which totalled between 600 and 700 at that time.[36]

For the first of these trips 'Not less than 420 took their places, 100 in the first class, 150 in the second and 150 in the third class [*sic*]'.[37] From these estimates, although they don't add up, it can be seen that the number of travellers spending 6*s* on first-class tickets, and 4*s* 6*d* on second-class seats, outnumbered those paying the third-class fare of 2*s* by a ratio of five to three. This is indicative of the experience of many Mechanics' Institutes that had problems attracting genuine mechanics or working men.[38] As the combined quantity of excursionists on both trips outnumbered the total membership of the institutes it is not possible to tell which category of passengers contained most actual members. A journalist travelling with the party described the exhilaration of the fastest movement he had ever yet experienced:

> We need scarcely say, how they bowled along; what a 'hith' was made on passing a bridge or another train of carriages, how objects on either side seem to flit from view; horses, cows, calves, colts, and sheep, scampered off in surprise; and cottagers, labourers and villagers gazed and wondered at the sight . . . The grove of Clifton, the bridge over the Trent, the Red-hill tunnel with its darkened shadows, all engaged attention and furnished topics of conversation.[39]

The second excursion from Nottingham to Leicester a month later was even more popular. The train of sixteen carriages and two engines was the longest ever seen up to that time on the Midland Counties line and it drew considerable attention, with villagers stopping to stare as it passed through the countryside. After adding more carriages and engines to accommodate the growing numbers of excursionists as the train progressed towards Leicester, the final total was seventy carriages drawn by four engines. The party was hours late in arriving and the crowds assembled at Leicester station grew extremely anxious. A search party was sent forth on an engine from Leicester to locate the awaited train. Eventually the party arrived safely. For the journey home it was wisely decided to despatch two separate trains to accommodate the massive number of excursionists.[40]

A motivation for both the Leicester and the Nottingham institutes was the desire to acquire premises that could house their resources and activities under one roof. With this objective in mind, both groups hoped to use the excursions and exhibitions as fund-raising initiatives towards their expensive ventures. Another unwritten objective was the desire to promote the cause of political reform. The Chartist movement was a growing force among working people, very few of whom, other than those who were freemen by birth or apprenticeship, had the right to vote at this time.[41] An article in the *Leicester Journal* that same summer[42] announced a plan to reform Chartist organisations as the

National Charter Association of Great Britain in order to reconstitute their scattered forces and to put pressure on the government to introduce democratic reforms. The vice-president of the Leicester Mechanics, John Biggs, was an advocate of political reform, by moral force rather than by violent struggle. Within this context, the exhibition and the excursions would have presented an excellent opportunity to demonstrate the intelligence, abilities and good behaviour of respectable working men and so dispel some of the arguments against their enfranchisement.[43] The Mechanics' exhibitions formed the ideal prototype for the Great Exhibition of the Works of Industry of all Nations a decade later, which inspired so many to travel and made it imperative to devise new ways of meeting the needs of very large numbers of working-class travellers.[44]

Railway transport was essential for the organisation of all these excursions, which would have been impossible to organise only a few weeks earlier. A large number of people had been enabled to travel a comparatively long distance, quickly and cheaply. The *Leicester Exhibition Gazette*, a magazine to accompany the town's Mechanics' exhibition in 1840, acknowledged the major contribution of the railway to transport and its potential as a liberator of humankind from the barriers imposed by distance, the triumph of science over matter, the annihilation of space and the economy of time.

> Had a visit like this been contemplated a year since, how could it have been carried into effect? At the most moderate computation, thirty coaches must have been engaged, two hundred horses employed, six hours consumed in the journey to and fro, far greater fatigue and risk, in the aggregate incurred, and the time afforded for the objects of the journey shortened by four hours. Almost any one of these obstacles is singly sufficient to have deterred anyone from the proposal of such a visit as we have the pleasure to record, while their amount would have rendered the bare contemplation preposterous.[45]

Other methods of transport could not match the railway trains for speed, capacity and eventually the range of destinations. Right from the start, working-class trippers took advantage of the railway excursion. After the pioneering trips of the Mechanics' Institutes, Friendly Societies soon followed suit. The Oddfellows and Foresters were both organising trips from Leeds to the North-east coast and Scarborough in 1840.[46] A survey by Douglas Reid of the excursions leaving Birmingham showed that six years later, in 1846, nearly half of them were organised by those characteristically working-class institutions, Friendly Societies.[47] The societies that promoted the Birmingham excursions originated among and attracted better-paid and more skilled working men. These trips were all organised by 'affiliated orders': the Manchester Unity, the

Wolverhampton Loyal Order, the London Independent, the Druids, the Foresters, the Free Gardeners, organisations whose membership comprised, as Reid says, precisely the social stratum we would envisage as most capable of going on excursions. Most of the trips advertised were relatively inexpensive, at prices for day trips ranging from 6d, for a trip to Gloucester for a rally addressed by Henry Vincent, up to 8s for a visit to Chester for the races and some sight-seeing, the average price of the excursions being 4s.

As well as trips for just a single day there were a number of more expensive ones lasting for several days, such as a week in London at a fare of 12s or a few days in Liverpool for 10s,[48] prices which were rather expensive if there were additional accommodation costs and loss of earnings to be taken into account. Although these trips were organised by Friendly Societies, Reid's figures do not show what proportion of travellers were working-class. Significantly, though, organisations with a substantial upper working-class membership were actually organising collective holidays to places of interest for several days as early as the mid-1840s. A trip to London organised by the Manchester Unity Society even included the services of a guide. Most of the trips seem to have included pleasurable pastimes such as boat trips rather than purely educational activities. Reid has been unable to determine whether or not accommodation arrangements were made for members travelling. The prices advertised may have been for non-members to fill empty seats or to raise funds. That was the arrangement in June 1857 when the Shropshire Provident Society hired a train to go to the Manchester Art Treasures Exhibition. Tickets included the fare for the return journey and entrance to the exhibition at a combined cost of 5s to non-members of the society but a cheaper rate of 4s for members and their families,[49] an early inclusive or package tour. In like manner, members of the Birmingham societies themselves may have been offered a cheaper fare or even a package including lodgings during the 1846 excursions. The register of accommodation in London suitable for working men and artisans, compiled in 1850, shows that lodging houses were in existence catering for that share of the market.[50] Thomas Cook had attempted to compile such a register for Leicester in the early 1840s.[51] Prospective travellers may also have been offered savings scheme facilities to spread the cost. Not all the excursions analysed by Reid were run by Friendly Societies; some of them were organised by private promoters, presumably to make a profit, although their prices were no higher than those of the societies.

What, though, is the significance of these initiatives that enabled working-class people to take part in tourist-related leisure activities? Why weren't workers simply imitating middle-class travellers and tourists? Railway travel was, after all, equally available to the middle class, even more available when the amount that could be spent on leisure from disposable income is taken into account. Train travel and especially the excursion organised by workers' own organisations were particularly suited to working-class taste and culture. Group travel in a shared railway carriage was never appealing to the middle class, whose more reserved, private culture meant that they shunned group or communal activities in favour of individual or family ones. Middle-class passengers, in general, shied away from the type of trip where working-class excursionists crammed into the cheaper seats. Middle-class trippers would have been very reluctant to subject themselves to literally rubbing shoulders with the mass of their fellow travellers. The collectivist culture of the workers with its strong sense of group identity was positively at home on an organised rail excursion. Overcrowded housing in working-class districts made this aspect of culture integral to daily existence.[52] The middle-class ideal was a separate family holiday rather than merely 'clubbing together' on a day or even longer trip.[53] While Reid recognises that there is no precise way of knowing the class composition of excursionists, non-working-class participants were very likely to have been from the ranks of master tradesmen or small-scale manufacturers who had not yet acquired either middle-class respectability or income and the social distancing that went with them. They would have felt no affront to their status by travelling on an excursion, albeit not always in the third-class carriages with their employees. Rail travel itself was socially segregated from the start, with separate waiting rooms and sections of the train for different classes of passenger. On any rail excursion the majority of accommodation, unless the train was reserved specifically for first-class passengers,[54] was in the third-class carriages, so obviously the greatest number of trippers was expected to be from lower or moderate-income groups.

The garrulousness of workers meant that sharing accommodation on the train was not beneath their dignity. In the dialect account of a Bolton weaver and his wife's visit to the Paris Exhibition of 1867 the couple engage in conversation with their fellow passengers, from their local region, on the initial stage of the journey to London. They talk about people's family business, make personal remarks, quarrel and exchange insults with strangers and encounter drunks in a way that would surely have been offensive to more genteel middle-class passengers. Having been startled by a small explosion caused by putting her foot on a box of matches on the floor, Sarah Shuttle, the weaver's wife, enters into banter with an unknown male passenger. 'Sink their apishness, aw wish thoose ut had done this trick mut ha th' toothwertch till they'd etten a box o' lucifers t' their supper,' she exclaims. The male passenger tells her the matches wouldn't have been put on the floor on purpose.

> 'Heaw does theaw know, Mester Pepperpod?' retorted Sayroh in her best snappish style. 'Well, in course,' wur th'onswer, 'aw know nowt abeawt it for a sartinty, but aw should think o my heart ut nobuddy would ever do a trick o that sort.' 'If theaw knows nowt abeawt it,' said Sayroh, 'say nowt abeawt it, un show thy wisdom.'[55]

An elderly widow joins them in the carriage and proceeds to complain about her daughter 'hoo'd no mooaar sense than wed a coaler ust fond uv his drink'.

> Eh, dear, aye; un he keeps pidjuns, un goes eawt uv a Sunday mornin' o whistlin um off th' heawse tops, un catchin straggs; un then he goes to an owd durty jerry-shop wheere they sell 'n thripenny ale; un hobbles whoam to his dinner drunk, un raises a regilur hallibash if oather me or Sally looks cruckt.[56]

The widow then hurls an insult at another man who speaks to her:

> Theaw looks clivver; theaw's made thy own clugs, aaw'll bet tuppence, un fashunt um after th' make o thy yed. Theaw'rt thick at booath eends.[57]

During the same journey a drunken man sits opposite Sarah and, pulling a flask from his side pocket, offers it to her:

> In this, fair Amazon there is liquor fit for the gods; it is terrestrial ambrosia; the elixir of life. Pray, take the flask from mine hand and moisten it with those chaste lips. In plain English, take a swig, old cockolorum. 'Tis brandy – brandy![58]

This man does not share the Bolton dialect of Sarah and her other fellow passengers, his words are given in standard English. Perhaps there is another discourse here of the socially fallen alcoholic, who has lost his former station in life and now travels third-class with the lower orders. Sarah is reluctant to accept the invitation but the man forces the flask to her lips and she takes a drink, pretending to like it. Then, at his request, she passes it round the compartment to another seven passengers, who all pronounce it liquor of the finest quality. These incidents do not take place on an excursion trip but in a third-class carriage of a timetabled train. No pretence of edification or self-improvement is demonstrated on this journey: the travellers have not yet adopted the aloof behaviour of public transport users. The railway carriage was a public space and its occupiers were subject to scrutiny although its liminality and the transience of encounters could have had the effect of allowing people freedom to behave in a more extrovert way because of the anonymity.

Middle-class travellers were able to segregate themselves to a certain extent by purchasing tickets for the more expensive second-class carriages. Railway carriages formed a physical space where travelling companions were not chosen and the close proximity of fellow passengers made interaction hard to avoid. Carriages were not segregated by gender, and so female travellers could find themselves alone with strange men, a social experience not approved of in normal middle-class etiquette. As a newly emerging public activity, travel offered a cultural space for interactions that reflected negotiations in power relations between gender and class. The enhanced social status of middle-class passengers would have offered some protection from unwelcome advances from the 'lower orders'. Writing about travel in nineteenth-century America, Patricia Cline Cohen suggests that the worrisome possibilities inherent in travel within the public space of railway carriages produced in response an etiquette of travel that emphasised rigid codes of conduct, rules of politeness and sex segregation where feasible.[59] This took place in a very public arena where normal codes of behaviour were tested. Using the behaviour of modern travellers as evidence, the development of an evolving set of manners also happened in Britain. Norbert Elias described this change in behaviour and attitudes as the civilising process in which the standard of what 'society demands and prohibits changes and the threshold of socially instilled displeasure moves'.[60] Although some passengers do engage in conversation with each other, unwritten rules about physical proximity are observed, for instance people do not sit next to strangers if empty seats are available elsewhere. It is quite normal for travellers to ignore each other, keeping themselves to themselves as if protected by an unseen bubble.

Returning to the theme of excursions, not all those patronised by members of the working class were edifying or educational by twenty-first-century Western standards but sometimes trips reflected the demand created by the cultural taste for the macabre. Before the abolition of public hanging in 1868 excursions were run to executions. In 1840 the murderer of Mr Norway of Wadebridge was hanged at Bodmin. Three special trains were put on by the Bodmin & Wadebridge Railway so that Wadebridge people could watch. Almost half the Wadebridge population, 11,000 people, joined the trip and were able to watch the spectacle from the comfort of the railway carriages, as the railway station was adjacent to the gaol. In 1849 J. Gleeson Wilson, convicted of the murder of a woman, her two sons and a servant, was hanged at Kirkdale Gaol. A massive crowd of between 80,000 and 90,000 went to Liverpool to view the execution, many of them arriving by excursion train.[61]

It should not be thought that railway companies were initially motivated by benevolence in providing cheap travel facilities for ordinary people. Their primary trade was moving industrial goods and raw materials rather than a large volume of passenger traffic. Developments in passenger traffic were mainly concentrated in the middle-class market. Despite the growth in the number of excursions from 1839 onwards and the huge numbers who travelled to London for the Great Exhibition, it was not until 1872 that British railway companies earned 50 per cent of their total passenger receipts from third-class traffic. In fact, they made little effort to develop the working-class market despite government compulsion to provide a minimum amount of cheaper third-class accommodation.[62]

A newspaper advertisement of 1855 demonstrates the popularity of excursions and their effect on the imagination. The heading CHEAP EXCURSION is used as an eye-catcher over text that reads: 'J. Levy begs to inform the inhabitants of Leicester and the surrounding neighbourhood, that the Cheapest Trip they can make is to his large and spacious premises . . . where a splendid assortment of Ready Made Clothing is now awaiting their inspection.'[63] Exhibitions were a popular excursion destination for workers, as they were not just entertaining but could be patriotic and edifying, and at the same time educational and improving. From those of the Mechanics' Institutes, the Great Exhibition, visited by millions in 1851, the follow-up exhibition at the Crystal Palace in 1862, and even overseas trips to the Paris exhibitions in 1855 and 1867, and into the twentieth century for the British Empire Exhibition at Wembley in 1924, exhibitions have been a major attraction for excursionists. Continuity of theme at these World's Fairs celebrating industrial and colonial achievement was coupled with continual evolution in transport and visitor expectations. The entertainment aspect of ostensibly educational events cannot be overestimated. Sensationalist publicity was used to advertise the early Mechanics' exhibitions and this conflict between education and entertainment continues to the present.[64] The 1851 exhibition was the motivation for a vast influx of excursionists to London from all over Britain, Europe and the rest of the world.[65] This event truly popularised not just the excursion but, for those living too far away to make the return journey the same day, a stay away from home was also experienced.

Thomas Cook is often credited with the invention of both the excursion and the package holiday, as if he was the only person involved, and ignoring other travel agents and organisers. This erroneous and misleading point of view assigns the role of passive consumers to large numbers of working people who travelled in the excursion trains and trips to the Great Exhibition and elsewhere and ignores the achievement of working-class organisations in the initiation of travel for the masses. This is not to belittle Cook's personal achievements as a radical campaigner himself, as an energetic entrepreneur and promoter of travel who passed on to his son, John Mason Cook, the basis of an international travel business. Thomas Cook though made no claim to having invented either excursions or inclusive tours himself. In his memoirs he clearly states that when he had that flash of inspiration on the road from Market Harborough to Leicester in 1841 he had in mind the trips between Leicester and Nottingham organised by the Mechanics' Institutes of the towns to each other's exhibitions.[66] This gave him the idea of running his own excursion from Leicester to Loughborough for a cause dear to his heart, a temperance rally. The Mechanics' trips were not the first excursions, either: since the inception of steam railways, excursions had been promptly organised. Even before steam trains there had been horse-drawn railway excursions and trips by boat. By the time the Great Exhibition was announced there was already a dozen years of excursion experience by steam train. The following chapter will look at the role of the Crystal Palace extravaganza in Hyde Park in providing a stimulus for longer excursions, involving stays away from home for a night or more for a reason not connected with employment. These visits fitted the modern definition of tourism.

Notes

1 Eric Hobsbawm, *The Age of Capital*, London, 1962, 1995 edn, p. 194.
2 R. A. Leeson, *Travelling brothers*, London, 1979.
3 E. J. Hobsbawm, 'The tramping artisan', *Labouring Men*, London, 1964.
4 *Ibid.*, p. 34.
5 *Ibid.*, p. 35.
6 Leeson, *Travelling brothers*, p. 215.
7 Hobsbawm, 'The tramping artisan', p. 47.
8 Leeson, *Travelling brothers*, p. 214.
9 Select Committee on Artisans and Machinery, 1824, pp. 295–6.
10 Hobsbawm, 'The tramping artisan', p. 36.
11 Leeson, *Travelling brothers*, p. 218.
12 The calico printers' circuit was between 1,000 and 1,400 miles and for compositors it could be 2,800 miles in distance (Hobsbawm, 'The tramping artisan', p. 36).
13 According to Hobsbawm (*ibid.*, p. 35), among masons it was valid for ninety-eight days.
14 Leeson, *Travelling brothers*, p. 218.

15 Piers Brendon, *Thomas Cook: 150 years of popular tourism*, London, 1996, p. 114.

16 Hobsbawm, 'The tramping artisan', p. 35.

17 G. C. Martin, 'Working-class holidaymaking down to 1947', M.A. thesis, University of Leicester, 1968, p. 6.

18 Centre for Kentish Studies, Maidstone (hereafter CKS), U3345/F1, Excursion into Kent from London, 18 September 1835.

19 Arthur Sketchley, *Mrs Brown at the seaside*, London, n.d. (*c.* 1860), p. 13.

20 *Ibid.*, p. 14.

21 *Ibid.*, p. 15.

22 *Ibid.*, p. 16.

23 CKS, U3345/F1, Excursion into Kent from London.

24 Sketchley, *Mrs Brown at the seaside*, p. 11.

25 John K. Walton, *The English seaside resort: a social history, 1750–1914*, Leicester, 1983, p. 26.

26 J. A. R. Pimlott, *The Englishman's holiday*, 1947, repr. Hassocks, 1976, pp. 77–8.

27 R. Marchant, 'Early excursion trains', *Railway Magazine* 100:638, June 1954, pp. 426–9, p. 426.

28 Susan Barton, 'The Mechanics' Institutes: pioneers of leisure and excursion travel', *Leicestershire and Rutland Archaeological Society Transactions* LXVII, Leicester, 1993, pp. 47–58.

29 *Nottingham and Newark Mercury*, 24 July 1840.

30 Thomas Cook, quoted by Christopher Hibbert, *The English*, London, 1987, p. 683.

31 R. J. Morris, 'Leeds and the Crystal Palace', *Victorian Studies* 13, 1970, pp. 283–300.

32 Marchant, *Early excursion trains*, p. 426.

33 J. Pudney, *The Thomas Cook story*, London, 1953, p. 53.

34 William Fraser Rae, *The business of travel: a fifty years' record of progress*, London, 1891, p. 23.

35 *Leicester Chronicle*, 25 July 1840.

36 A. Temple Paterson, *Radical Leicester: a history of Leicester, 1780–1850*, Leicester, 1954, p. 238.

37 *Nottingham and Newark Mercury*, 24 July 1840.

38 Toshio Kusamitsu, 'Great exhibitions before 1851', *History Workshop Journal* 9, 1980, pp. 70–89.

39 *Nottingham Review*, 24 July 1840.

40 *Leicester Journal*, 28 August 1840.

41 J. Simmons, *Leicester past and present* I, *Ancient borough to 1860*, London, 1974, p. 148.

42 *Leicester Journal*, 28 August 1840.

43 Barton, 'Mechanics Institutes', p. 49.

44 Toshio Kusamitsu, 'British industrialisation and design, 1830–1851', Ph.D. thesis, University of Sheffield, 1982.

45 *Leicester Exhibition Gazette*, 23 July 1840.

46 Walton, *The English seaside resort*, p. 28.

47 Douglas Reid, 'The "iron roads" and the "happiness of the working classes": the early development of the railway excursion', *Journal of Transport History*, 3rd series, 17:1, 1996, pp. 57–73.

48 Reid, 'The "iron roads"', pp. 60–1.

49 Alan Delgado, *The annual outing and other excursions*, London, 1977, p. 131.

50 Manchester Reference Library M6/3/10/1–60, Circular of the London Central Registry, London, May 1851.

51 *Cook's guide to Leicester*, Leicester, 1843, pages unnumbered.

52 Melanie Tebbutt, *Women's talk? A social history of 'gossip' in working-class neighbourhoods, 1880–1960*, Aldershot, 1995, p. 183.

53 Reid, 'The "iron roads"', p. 63.

54 Delgado, *The annual outing*, p. 131.

55 J. T. Staton, *Th'visit to th'greight Parris Eggsibishun of Bobby Shuttle un his woife Sayroh*, Manchester, 1867, p. 46.

56 *Ibid.*, p. 48.

57 *Ibid.*, p. 49.

58 *Ibid.*, p. 55.

59 Patricia Cline Cohen, 'Women at large: travel in antebellum America', *History Today*, 44:12, 1994, pp. 44–50.

60 Norbert Elias, *The civilising process*, 1938, repr. Oxford 1994, p. xii.

61 Delgado, *The annual outing*, p. 132.

62 Hobsbawm, *The Age of Capital*, p. 204.

63 *Leicestershire Advertiser*, 19 May 1855.

64 Present-day heritage centres and museums attempt to resolve this by attempting accurately to present and interpret the past but they also need to attract as many visitors as possible and compete with alternative attractions. They are therefore forced to provide amusement as well as purely serious education.

65 Delgado, *The annual outing*, p. 126.

66 Pudney, *The Thomas Cook story*, p. 53.

3

Workers and the Great Exhibition: the origins of the package holiday

In the last chapter it was shown that by the 1840s better-off working-class people in secure employment had become accustomed to taking excursions by rail or perhaps by boat as a leisure activity. These excursions to the coast or places and events of interest were usually of just a single day's duration, but in some cases they involved a stay away from home of several days, such as those from Birmingham organised by Friendly Societies, described in the previous chapter.[1] Whether or not these excursions combined with stays away from home were sold as an inclusive package or the components were purchased separately by travellers is a subject of speculation. It is, however, possible to identify clear evidence of arrangements for travel, accommodation and entertainment available as a package at a single price for visits to the Great Exhibition in 1851. This chapter will examine these arrangements for travel to the exhibition in detail as a key development in popular tourism. This event provided a focus for national interest and a common destination and motivation for visitors. The distances and time involved in travel to London made staying away from home overnight or for several nights essential. The usual length of stay was for three days to a week.[2] The railway network made the journey possible, in a reasonable length of time, from all around Britain. The exhibition took place between May and September 1851, providing a time constraint for those planning to visit and a defined period within which savings and travel clubs had to operate. The social and political background of 1851 needs to be explored, as this had a considerable effect on working-class behaviour, especially that of those active in the labour movement.

Plans to hold a Great Exhibition of the Works of Industry of all Nations, in London, were announced in 1850. The preparations and arrangements to enable large numbers of working people to travel to London, to stay there for a few days and visit the exhibition and other places of interest were of vital importance to the history of tourism. Trips to the exhibition showed many of the features of the modern inclusive tour, better known as the package holiday. The origins of the package holiday seem to lie in these trips and excursions, although the term 'holiday' was not used to describe the visits. The culture of the commodity, objects for their own sake, and consumerism, which includes the consumption of tourism, according to Thomas Richards, also seem to originate from this event.[3]

Before going on to discuss workers' activities around arrangements for the exhibition, it is necessary to describe what is meant by the term 'package holiday'. Essentially an inclusive or package tour is a combination or package of transport, accommodation and perhaps some other recreational services which is sold for a single all-inclusive price. That price is usually substantially lower than could be obtained by conventional methods of booking transport and accommodation separately with individual tariffs. Normally the tourist travels in a group with other travellers. The consumer has the convenience of buying a single ticket. Through bulk purchase of the components of the holiday, the tour operator is able to secure a lower price than that available to individual travellers. The volume of demand means transport providers can rely on a high load factor, that is, all or almost all seats on transport filled, allowing costs per passenger to be reduced.

In the twentieth century the need for marketers of tourism to be aware of the three fears that need to be overcome before mass tourism can take place was emphasised by Holloway and Plant.[4] These are fear of flying, fear of foreign food and fear of foreigners. Although in this context 'foreign' refers to people and places outside the United Kingdom, at the time of the exhibition London was a foreign place beyond the experience of many provincial travellers, used only to their own local customs. There are a number of features which form the components of package holidays and which help allay fears: advance booking, group travel, bulk purchase of transport; block booking of accommodation, advertising and brochures, the services of a tour guide or representative, entertainment, possible excursion opportunities and security for travellers.[5]

From the sources available, it emerges that all these features were present in the services provided by the exhibition travel clubs. The apparent need to overcome the three fears has been an underpinning factor in all trips organised for or by the working class. Fear of flying, in the days before popular aviation, was not a problem but fears of other travel technology would have been relevant. In the days when rail travel was a novelty, the effect on the human body of moving at speed was a cause of concern. For instance, in 1835 thirty miles an hour was considered a very high speed. A passenger in a letter wrote that his train was not very fast when it first started but soon was

> off like a shot from a gun. No sooner did we come to a field than it was a mile behind us, but this was nothing in comparison with meeting a long train of carriages from Liverpool. I was never so frightened in my life as at this moment; I shrank completely back, horrified, in my seat. We were going at a full thirty-four miles an hour.[6]

By the time of the exhibition trains were capable of reaching 60 m.p.h. and accident rates were high, frequently reported as being because of passengers' lack of fast travel experience. They jumped from moving trains pursuing blown-off hats, tried to board moving carriages, sat on top of carriages and were dashed against bridges or tunnels or fell out of wagons when drunk or jostling in arguments.[7] In 1851 anxieties about rail travel were justified and no less real than modern fears of flying. Even going through tunnels filled with smoke and steam could be a terrifying experience. 'You go through a dark, ugly, vile abominable tunnel three hundred yards long, which has all the horrors of banishment from life – such a hole as I never wish to go through again.'[8]

Over the decade between the early passenger trains and the exhibition, rail travel may have become commonplace for some people. A letter from a traveller from Scotland to the Great Exhibition, Alexander Frew, tells how he journeyed from Glasgow to London and stayed at Mrs McDonald's at 19 Addle Street. Perhaps the house where he lodged, 'which seemed a very respectable one', was advertised in Glasgow and chosen because it was superintended by a fellow Scot who would understand his needs and preferences. Showing how rail travel was no longer an alarming experience, Frew, in a letter home from London, wrote:

> We were seventeen and a half hours on the Railway, a pretty long drive – but after getting washed and dinnered here, was almost as fresh as tho' I had been in bed all night. The train was detained half an hour at Gartsherry waiting for the Aberdeen Mail train . . . but after that they went at a rapid pace and reached Carlisle within time . . . proceeding on to London . . . to this town I continued awake but had a very sound sleep from Carlisle to Lancaster, more than two hours.[9]

Excitement and apprehension had given way to recognition of the mundane, and a half-hour delay was worth mentioning. According to Wolfgang

Schivelbusch, this change in perception by rail travellers was part of the civil-ising process identified by Elias, when previously shocking experiences became commonplace.[10]

The nineteenth century's mid-point, as well as being significant as the time when England's population became mostly urban, was also of significance in the history of working-class politics. Only three years before, in 1848, there had been massive Chartist demonstrations calling for the extension of political rights, indicative of the Europe-wide revolutionary surge of nationalist and democratic demands. In Britain this movement had involved large numbers of artisans, independent tradesmen and skilled workers, precisely the lower-class groups most likely to visit the exhibition. From the peak of Chartist activity in 1842 and its resurgence in 1848 there was an apparent downturn in the class struggle. A newspaper report showed that the Financial and Parliamentary Reform Movement could not raise enough subscriptions for carrying on its campaign.[11] Sections of the mainstream press regarded this as a sign of 'the return of common sense to those classes who had hitherto been the dupes of a set of selfish demagogues'.[12] The organisation and contact between groups and individual activists probably remained but campaigning took on a different focus. It seemed that the demands of the People's Charter could not be met through traditional forms of struggle that often seemed like attempts to turn back the tide of industrial and capitalist development. It now appeared a more likely proposition that reform could be won by accepting the existing social order and any attempt to change it had to be done by constitutional means and incorporation into existing structures.

Events in Europe, and in the United Kingdom after the arrival in Britain of émigrés following the suppression of the 1848 revolutions, aroused a grow-ing sense of internationalism. Socialist and radical newspapers devoted large sections to international issues and the revolutionary movement overseas. Possibly the very idea of a world exhibition had been suggested by the senti-ments advocated and popularised by Julian Harney and other proletarian spokesmen. Writing in the 1920s, the labour historian and trade unionist Theodore Rothstein asserted that is was 'tolerably certain that the internationalist movement which arose among the liberal bourgeoisie about that time was greatly influenced by this proletarian propaganda and must be considered as a semi-conscious attempt at competition with it'.[13] The bourgeoisie of that period also began to court trade unions and the co-operatives, endeavouring by fostering Mechanics' Institutes and popular libraries, as well as the publication of cheap literature, to wrest working people from the intellectual influence of those 'agitators' who were still active. Other probable sources of inspiration for the Great Exhibition were the Mechanics' Institute exhibitions, held in several provincial towns and cities between 1838 and 1840, which themselves had been the inspiration for rail excursions.[14] The 'National Bazaar' of the Anti-Corn Law League held in Covent Garden in 1845 displayed products from all over Britain to celebrate a free-trade theme. Excursion trains to London from the Midlands and the North also contributed to the success of these events. The Royal Society of Arts had suggested a national exhibition a few years earlier, in 1845, but met with no popular response or support for the idea.[15] The Royal Society acknowledged that it was the French national expositions begun in 1798 that were the primary inspiration for all those later exhibitions.[16] The Royal Society itself had been using exhibitions to promote design and manufacture since the late eighteenth century. Patrons and commissioners of the Great Exhibition, such as Henry Cole and Digby Wyatt, had visited the Paris exhibition in 1850 and reported their impressions to Prince Albert, the enthusiastic promoter of London's own world exhibition.[17]

Hoping to emphasise social harmony, the Royal Commission set up to organise the Great Exhibition had initially recommended the establishment of a Working Classes Committee. This proposal was soon retracted. This short-lived committee had comprised two Members of Parliament, the Bishop of Oxford and the Chartists Lovett, Place and Vincent. It was Vincent who remarked that 'the working class regarded the Exhibition as a movement to wean them from politics'.[18] The idea, however, had caught on and working men went on to participate in the local groups that met to discuss regional contributions to the exhibition. Their functions included collecting financial contributions towards the cost, soliciting locally manufactured exhibits, promoting the event in their region, estimating the numbers likely to travel and liaison with the national organisers in London. Working men's committees were often set up as sub-committees of the official local ones. Many former Chartists were involved in these, as were Mechanics' Institute members and workplace representatives. However, of the leading Chartists who were involved it was usually those associated with the right wing of the movement, or the 'moral force' section, such as Place and Lovett.[19]

There were other Chartists who welcomed the exhibition not for its own sake but for the opportunity it would give them to advance their own ideas and the aims of socialism. At a large meeting of trade delegates in Glasgow, a number of men identified as Chartists, although disagreeing with each other on many issues, urged 'the necessity of union and energetic action amongst all shades of democrats and the importance of improving the opportunity afforded by the Great Exhibition of spreading their principles, and helping forward the Great European struggle for liberty'.[20] These people perceived the exhibition as a means of reviving the Chartist organisation through providing an oppositional focus.

Indicating the pervasiveness of this radical belief, a Central Committee of Social Propaganda was formed in London, with a number of local committees supporting it through fund raising. The congregation of so many visitors, including large numbers from overseas, presented them with a wonderful opportunity to spread the socialist message. 'What moment more opportune for promulgating these views so well calculated to make the world happy, than the time when the world is there to listen to you?'[21] The ageing but respected Robert Owen and 'others competent to develop the great principles of English Socialism' agreed to give a series of public lectures on the theme during the exhibition season. A series of tracts written by Owen in English with translations in French and German was proposed for distribution among their Continental brethren.[22] As pointed out in an address to the social reformers of Great Britain printed in the *Friend of the People*, 'as many come from countries where freedom of speech and press are almost unknown, such an opportunity for getting political and social information may be to them of double value'.[23]

The desire for international unity was not just a hopeful wish of the movement in Britain. The New York Industrial Congress passed a resolution in December 1850 that committed them to sending a delegation to London, 'to meet in convention the delegates of trade societies and labour associations from other parts of the world, during the Fair of 1851, for the purpose of interchanging opinions with each other in relation to the state of labour, and the condition of the labouring classes in the various countries they represent'.[24] In February 1851 Parsons E. Day was appointed US delegate to London, to where he travelled to meet inventors, clubs, trade societies and labour associations, in order to make the arrangements for the convention of mechanics to be held during the exhibition period.

The aim of unity between classes and educational improvement was attractive to members of Mechanics' Institutes. This should not detract from the recognition that instead of being merely dupes of a ruling elite, these working-class campaigners had their own political agenda; the fight for the franchise and for the consolidation and extension of the ten-hour day. Some class-conscious workers also promoted the idea of 'rational recreation' as a means not of social control but of self-improvement, a better quality of life and to use as propaganda

to get support for shorter working hours. Education was seen as a political necessity, a reform to be fought for in opposition to the ruling classes who 'well
know that Knowledge and Freedom go hand in hand, and therefore do they
attempt to stem her liberty-bringing torrents, fearful that they will sweep away
the pillars of Ignorance and Prejudice on which oligarchical power is based'.[25]
Many people believed that the exhibition would provide the ideal opportunity
for working men to demonstrate not just their skills and intellectual capacity in
the design and making of objects for display, but also their respectability and
responsibility through their good behaviour. It was not just the middle class
that despised drunkenness amongst the poor; class-conscious workers did too.

Other working-class militants were totally opposed to the exhibition and
the open class collaboration it seemed to involve. Julian Harney, writing as
'l'Ami de Peuple' in the Chartist paper the *Friend of the People*, described the
opening pageant which attracted crowds to watch the royal family's cavalcade
pass by as inspired by 'the spirit of flunkeyism'.[26] He went on to describe
the 'works of art and plunder wrung from the people of all lands, by their
conquerors, the men of blood, privilege and capital'. A truly worthy industrial
exhibition could take place only when workers from all fields of industry and
agriculture had renounced flunkeyism and substituted for the rule of masters,
and the royalty of a degenerated monarchy, 'the Supremacy of Labour, and
the Sovereignty of the Nation'.[27] Surprisingly the other major Chartist newspaper, the *Northern Star*, made no criticism in its coverage of the event but
merely related the description of its opening by Queen Victoria.[28]

In preparation, all round Britain there were public meetings presided over
by civic dignitaries. Local committees were formed in 297 different localities,
many of them with working men's sub-committees. In Leicester a meeting and
lecture at the New Hall, a building used by the Mechanics' Institute, heard a
speech from one of HM Commissioners, Highmore Rosser.[29] Advertisements
stressed that the meeting would be addressed to the 'working classes whose attendance was particularly invited on the occasion'. Sharing the platform were the
mayor and also a former mayor and hosier, William Biggs, a renowned radical in favour of franchise extension who was a Chartist supporter. Biggs had
demonstrated a pre-existing commitment to travel for workers and to the concept of exhibitions through involvement in the Leicester Mechanics' exhibition in 1840. William Biggs' brother John was vice-president of the institute.
John Matts was elected chairman of the Leicester working men's committee.

A second public meeting, specifically for the working classes, was held in the
town hall with William Biggs in the chair.[30] A typical radical, Biggs criticised

the Royal Commission's demand for local collections to finance the exhibition; he thought the government ought to pay, not the people! Prominent at this meeting was Francis Warner, who had been active as a 'physical force' Chartist but had split with the main group in the town in 1848.[31] Warner moved a resolution that a society should be formed called 'The Working Men's Provident Association' to allow the working classes of the town to visit the exhibition, which would be a symbol of peace and harmony between nations and classes.[32] The resolution was seconded by Mr Parker, probably the same Mr W. Parker who had been the Leicester Anti-Corn Law Association's working men's secretary.[33] In 1848 Parker had also been an active Chartist.[34] Although no women are explicitly mentioned as present at the meeting, Parker pronounced that he 'hoped that an equal number of the fair sex would go to London'.

The Leicester Working Men's Provident Association rules were read by Mr White; subscriptions were to be 6*d*, 9*d* or 1*s* a week. Like many other committee chairmen, John Matts had written to others, and the Leicester rules were therefore similar to those of other clubs, like in Bath, Bristol, Oldham, Northampton and Bolton.[35] The official club and committee secretaries formed a network that solicited each others' advice when it came to dealing with the working classes. The usual topics of correspondence related to the desirability of having working men on the committees and guidelines on the running of travel clubs.[36] The Bristol committee secretary wrote to Manchester's to ascertain what the effect of involving workers on the committee had been. The committee in Manchester also received at least ten other letters asking for information about travel club rules from such diverse places as Oldham, Runcorn, Bristol, Bath, Dundee, Salford, Sheffield and the Chapel Inn at Stalybridge. One man even wrote on behalf of men in his singing classes. Northampton's committee had supplied a copy of their rules upon which Bolton's were based. In Aberdeen a public meeting resolved that a committee of twelve, to be named by the working classes, should be added to the local committee; at Darlington a number of practical working men were invited to join the committee there; at Woolwich the foremen from the royal dockyard and the Royal Arsenal were added to the committee.[37]

For the Leicester committee John Matts, in common with other committee members elsewhere, calculated the approximate cost of the visit to London. Matts hoped that 5,000 or 6,000 working-class people from Leicester would visit London and the exhibition the following summer. Joseph Dare, a radical Unitarian working in Leicester, said, 'there was no reason why every working man and woman should not go'. Apart from Dare and Biggs, who was a prosperous hosier, the other speakers were all skilled working men from the independent tradition of the Leicester knitting and shoemaking trades. Their skill and confidence in public speaking to a large audience in the town hall are testimony to their previous political experience in the radical and Chartist movements.

In Manchester the proposers of resolutions to the town's Working Men's Committee were themselves all working men, employed as mechanics in the area. A handbill reporting a meeting held at the Mechanics' Institute records that resolutions passed were proposed by mechanics at Sharp Brothers, Fairburn's and W. & D. Morriss.[38] In their resolutions they stated that as working men they felt gratified to be consulted upon a matter of such importance to the world's industrious classes and pledged their exertions to further its objectives, so as to prove that the confidence of the commissioners was not misplaced. A committee of two men from each principal workshop and manufactory in Manchester was formed, meeting monthly to assist in carrying out the objects of the Great National Exhibition. The committee was to canvas among the artisans in the different machine shops and factories, to find out how many individuals or groups would prepare specimens of their skill for exhibition. Important in relation to the discussion about workers' travel and tourism was the objective to arrange a series of cheap trips, so as to allow all interested to visit the exhibition at the lowest possible cost.[39]

Using their letters, leaflets and quotations in newspapers as evidence, it seems that the committee members and those most active in the working men's groups were highly literate and would have been enthusiastic about an event that promised self-improvement. A chance to use their skills, to be taken seriously and to show responsibility would have been welcomed, especially if more overtly political activity was no longer a viable interest. Although they were creating the basis of future operations in popular tourism, this was not on their conscious agenda.

In Bolton J. R. Bridson donated a prize of £5 worth of books for the committee to award to the writer of the best essay by a working man with the title 'The advantages to be derived by the working man from visiting the Great Exhibition of 1851'. No further mention of this essay is made in the local committee's minute book but Audrey Short cited Thomas Briggs as the author of an essay with an almost identical title, published in Bolton in 1850.[40] Thomas Briggs was a millwright who in his essay expressed the hope that the exhibition of artisans' skills would lessen upper-class objections to the extension of the franchise. It could no longer be claimed that workers were an ignorant rabble. The text of a very similar essay by an unnamed writer appears in Thomas Cook's *Exhibition Herald and Excursion Advertiser*.[41] This was a magazine published by Cook to coincide with the exhibition and used by him to promote his campaign for cheap train fares for working-class visitors to the event. The article, entitled 'Why should working men visit the exhibition?', does not go into the political aspirations of the working class but romanticises the benefits to be gained by skilled craftsmen on the observation of the work of other skilled artisans.

> Friends and fellow countrymen – we live in strange times – in times when the different nations of the earth are called upon to wage war against each other; but not in deadly array – not in deluging our fertile fields and plains with the gore of our favourite sons – not in creating famine, pestilence and disease; but in multiplying, in a thousand degrees, every source and avenue of human enjoyment, happiness and social ties. A war . . . of love, concord and affection.[42]

Many other commentators predicted that once the world could witness the skill involved in producing exhibits the contempt shown by the upper classes for tradesmen and mechanics would end. Free-trade supporters believed that the exhibition would, through competition, lead to a general fall in prices that would benefit working people, although protectionists predicted an influx of foreign goods and workers that would undercut the British. An incident during the building of the Crystal Palace proved this idea partly true, because after a strike by English glaziers over conditions French workmen were brought in to finish the job.[43]

Piracy of ideas, models, machinery and design was also a worry that had to be assuaged for the exhibitors. A public meeting of the Leicester Working Men's Committee in August 1850 heard any doubts about foreigners counter-argued by Mr T. Goddard, another radical, who said 'that for every foreigner who got an advantage there would be a thousand Englishmen benefiting from seeing the works of foreigners'.[44] The *Stockport Advertiser*, though, complained that there had been no 'positive disavowal on the part of the Commission . . . that it may not be converted into a Great Foreign Bazaar'.[45]

> We will suppose that foreigners, having had the trouble, and being at the expense to send over certain articles for exhibition, will carry them back, and not sell them for what they will fetch in this country – although we do not believe they will do so, however stringent the rules may be on this.[46]

Free trade, assisted by growing economic prosperity, had led to a rise in living standards and greater numbers in secure employment, making the contemplation of a trip to London through regular savings possible for many working people. Evidence of higher living standards comes from Leicester, where in 1850 there was a scarcity of housing as former sharers and yard occupants were moving out to their own singly occupied homes.[47] The following month, under the headline 'Leicester under free trade', the *Leicester Mercury* announced there was not a single able-bodied pauper, male or female, in the Leicester Union workhouse. The guardians had to hire women to do the workhouse washing.[48]

Not everyone, though, was sharing in this prosperity. The *Stockport Advertiser* reported that manufacturing distress was common and that the existence of 'deep and widespread agricultural distress had ceased to be a point in dispute. The terrible retribution of the base principles on which free trade theory is built, is beginning to reach the very classes for whose alleged benefit the agricultural classes were so ruthlessly sacrificed.'[49] It is worth remembering that the left wing of the working-class movement had not been very enthusiastic about the corn laws' repeal, as they believed it to be a bourgeois move to keep wages down. About a thousand workmen in the clothing trade in Nottinghamshire were out of work, and as a consequence, when families were taken into account, 4,000 people were destitute as well as there being even more in only partial employment. In Nottinghamshire, Derbyshire and Leicestershire there were at least 3,000 framework-knitter glove makers, only 200 of whom were in full employment and hundreds more who were on very low pay of only between 2s and 4s a week.[50] Free trade was blamed for this hardship, and more distress was predicted because of the impoverished condition of landlords, farmers and the various classes dependent on them.

For political reasons, many working-class activists and spokesmen joined, or indeed chose not to join, the local committees established for planning the arrangements for the exhibition. As well as official committee involvement, the major participation of working people was in the workers' travel and savings clubs which were formed to enable those 'of moderate means' to visit the Crystal Palace on the cheaper 1s days during the summer of 1851. Many of these savings clubs were organised at community and workplace level.[51] A large number of them were supported by employers, some of whom granted financial contributions and time off, in a few cases with pay, to make the visit to London. Others perhaps negotiated with their employers for these concessions.

Workers' involvement was not unanimously approved. There had been political argument as to whether the entry fee of 1s would be enough to restrict entry to only the respectable working classes; middle and upper-class people were worried that the poorer and less desirable elements might be able to afford admission.[52] They were afraid of sedition and uprising, as well as of increased crime and unruly behaviour. Some of the middle classes feared that the descent on London by large numbers of working people would attract seditious elements not just from Britain but from abroad too, who would take advantage of the opportunity to stir up class hatred and rebellion among the congregated masses. The press started to campaign against foreign 'agitators' alleged to be planning a revolution. Even Feargus O'Connor thought it necessary to join in the outcry and, in the *Northern Star*, warned Chartists to beware of the foreign revolutionary crowd and spies,[53] to the indignation of other Chartist groups such as Julian Harney's Fraternal Democrats.[54] The French and other European revolutions of 1848 were still fresh in middle-class minds and the change in political tactics by many radicals was yet to be acknowledged. For the middle classes, fears of social revolution were linked with the general worry of lawless and criminal behaviour by the working class. This itself, they believed, was a result of the moral degradation inherent in industrial life. Lord Ashley, who succeeded to the title of Earl of Shaftesbury in 1851, was convinced that everywhere he looked there was a 'wild and satanic spirit' abroad.[55] He was particularly concerned with the ill behaviour of young people in the industrial areas, such as Manchester, Sheffield and the Potteries, and their involvement in violence associated with Chartist demonstrations. This idea has been given further credence by Charles Reith, the historian of the Metropolitan Police Force, who asserted that: 'The peaceably disposed citizens of England during the first decades of the nineteenth century visualised the overthrow of civilisation by mob violence more fearfully and acutely than their descendants feared its overthrow a century later by the violence of international war.'[56]

The barrackmaster at Canterbury wrote to those commissioners 'with a special interest in the arrangements for working class visitors' outlining a complicated set of proposals for organising workers staying in London for the exhibition. The commissioners, though, were 'indisposed to throw any restraint on individual plans or wishes of visitors who after all would be coming at their own expense.[57] The barrackmaster, Captain James Thomas, did not give up, sending to the Manchester committee his suggested rules for the guidance of those classes on their arrival in London, which 'demand most serious attention for the production of numerous advantages'. He suggested that a committee for working-class visitors should divide London up into neighbourhoods where, so far as possible, accommodation for the industrious classes should be in contiguous vicinities. These neighbourhoods were to be subdivided into districts corresponding with the counties and those districts would then be further divided into sections corresponding with their chief towns. The actual number of beds provided in each section and district was to be calculated. Local committees could then judge the probable number of working people proposing to visit and this total could be divided by the number of beds in each section so that groups could be allocated an appropriate area in which to stay. A leader appointed in each district would meet visitors from the trains and conduct them to their lodgings after explaining the rules of behaviour. As far as possible, apart from time at the Crystal Palace, working-class visitors should stay in their allocated area of London. Captain Thomas also thought it best if no carpets were laid in houses fitted up for working-class occupancy, nor any woollen furniture used except for bedding. Floors and stairs were to be kept clean by daily rubbing with sand and a dry scrubber. He calculated that London could accommodate 55,000 working-class visitors staying for two nights with a day allowed for turnover. He was convinced that the working classes would cheerfully fall in with these well intentioned plans for their comfort. One of his suggestions, however, was taken up by the commissioners, probably independently of his advice, and that was that single women were to be lodged by themselves, superintended by matrons or lodged with young families.

All the precautions to ensure good behaviour proved to be either unnecessary or very successful. Polite London society was pleasantly surprised by the good behaviour of the crowds, having feared the worst in drunken brawls from the invasion by the rough provincial masses. 'Public lavatories had even been invented for the occasion to head off the risk of an uncontrollable flood of indecent exposures.'[58] Sensitivities were respected and the toilets referred to as 'waiting rooms'. The use of urinals by men was not charged for but waiting rooms cost $1d$ to use in the central area of the exhibition and half that in the more peripheral locations. A profit of £1,769 18s 6d was made after attendance costs were deducted from the takings of £2,441 15s 9d. About 827,820 people, mostly women, 'spent a penny' or a halfpenny.[59] Not that many, compared with the overall total of 6 million visitors to the exhibition, only about 14 per cent of them. The number of men using the urinals is not recorded but would have been at least equal and probably higher in total. These figures show the importance of 'public conveniences' for any large event or tourist destination and the necessity of providing similar facilities whenever large numbers of people are congregated.

The excursions to London, like those organised by the travel clubs and Thomas Cook, were viewed essentially as uplifting educational visits. According to F. M. L. Thompson, these trips were largely for the 'respectable' working classes.[60] Altogether, 6 million people visited the Great Exhibition; not just artisans and their families made the visit to London, many factory hands and less skilled workers did so too. Not all the well behaved visitors would have fitted the 'respectable' categorisation.

Despite middle-class fears and anxiety about large groups of workers gathered together, the event passed off peacefully. Even the public opening ceremony, performed by Queen Victoria, went without incident. Initially it was planned to hold it behind closed doors because of the worry of an assassination attempt. A hundred and fifty policemen were recruited and extra troops were garrisoned to guard London, but their presence for counter-revolutionary purposes proved unnecessary.[61] To the authorities' surprise, according to the first report of the committee of the exhibition in 1851, crime actually decreased in London during the exhibition year from the figures for the previous year. More than half the arrests were for drunkenness. Incredibly there were only eleven reported thefts.[62] Crime figures showed remarkably few thefts around the exhibition site and in London during the summer of 1851, but these figures may not give a true indication of the actual number of crimes committed.[63] The police at that time kept details only of solvable crimes, even thefts were usually not recorded as such, the police preferring to list them as 'lost property' until the 1930s.[64] Good behaviour was also in evidence at all the other sites in London, such as the National Gallery and British Museum, where the masses also thronged as they made the most of their stay.

The workers' travel clubs were very successful. As well as organising the collection and saving of money, some of these groups also arranged travel and accommodation for their members. In some cases the travel clubs were organised under the auspices of the official local committees; some committee members, as prominent citizens and employers, were able to push the idea of the exhibition among their employees. Other clubs were independent working-class organisations, established spontaneously by enthusiasts. The many clubs operating from public houses would have been outside the sponsorship and control of employers.[65]

Accounts kept in Bolton give a good gauge of the enthusiasm for the exhibition in individual workplaces, as each contribution to both the general fund and the operatives' fund is recorded.[66] The general fund was used for subscriptions to be sent to London towards the exhibition's cost, after local expenses had been deducted. The operatives' fund was a separate local collection to enable people to prepare items for display by granting them the equivalent of wages for the duration of their projects and to pay for someone to go to London and assist in finding and inspecting lodgings and supervising the installation of exhibits.[67] These factory collections symbolise workers' commitment to the idea of the exhibition; at the time of the initial subscriptions there was no guarantee that the exhibition would even take place or that any travel clubs would be organised to allow the subscribers to go and see it for themselves. Criticism of the financial aspects of the event came from many radicals, like William Biggs, of Leicester, who berated the government and Prince Albert for expecting ordinary people to pay for the exhibition.[68]

The People's Club was founded to enable Bolton working people and their families to go to London. It intended to pay in advance to secure beds for its members. The ex-mayor of the town and Local Committee member, William Rushforth, was invited to act as its treasurer or trustee. People's Club representatives met the Local Committee of Bolton on 14 May 1851. From Bolton's records it is possible to deduce something about the People's Club representatives at the meeting. James Swift donated 6*d* to the operatives' fund and 1*s* to the general fund. He was employed by Benjamin Hicks & Son at the Soho Ironworks, where four other Swift family members worked. His companion was Joseph Kirkman, who worked at the same ironworks and contributed 6*d* to each of the funds.[69] Other subscribers called Kirkman worked locally at William Gray & Son and at the bleachers Ridgeway Bridges Son & Co. The surnames in the subscription list for Hicks's Ironworks show that the firm employed several members of a number of families. It had its own brass band advertising its concerts in the local newspaper.[70] The firm and its employees showed a high level of commitment to the exhibition. Entries in the Bolton Local Committee's accounts show that the firm itself gave £20 in January 1851, and from collections among the operatives £10 8*s* 3*d* was donated in February, followed by a further £2 in June. An even more generous donation of £18 17*s* 3*d* was given by workers to the operatives' fund on 20 February the same year. Benjamin Hicks's Ironworks won two medals for items exhibited in London.

Sunderland Local Committee took similar steps to those of Leicester and Bolton to involve the working classes, acting on the advice of the circular sent by the Royal Commissioners on behalf of Prince Albert. The initial step was to convene a public meeting to which the industrious classes were explicitly invited. In March 1850 the Local Committee resolved to make the public meeting about the exhibition known, using circulars distributed generally in large factories and advertised in local newspapers.[71] It also decided that a few workmen should be invited to work with the committee, and committee members who were employers were asked to promote this among their workmen. Two workmen, William Armstrong and George Rochester, were added to the

Sunderland Executive Committee very early in its existence, in March 1850. They were chosen because of their connection with the association for collecting subscriptions to allow workmen to go to London and see the exhibition. Presumably Armstrong and Rochester were two of the few workmen it had been promised to co-opt to the committee. Like Bolton's, Sunderland's committee seemed to be concerned with enabling working people to become involved in all aspects of the exhibition, including facilitating the production of exhibits through financial support. One of those to benefit from this was a Mr Hedley who received £6 for the completion of a model.[72] As early as April 1850 Francis Gray Ross approached the committee offering to make any medals that might be needed, his object being to earn enough to get to London to visit the Crystal Palace. The same meeting also heard a letter from someone who wanted to contribute a model of the bridge and a lifeboat but would not be able to complete them without some financial assistance. Later, in October, a local fund was set up to provide models of shipbuilding, Sunderland's staple industry. The accounts of Sunderland local committee show that a surplus left over was carried forward to a Paris Exhibition Fund in August 1851. The next Paris exhibition was not until 1855 but this forward thinking demonstrates a commitment not just to the idea of exhibitions but to the concept of travel.

In Southampton the local committee branched out to hold public meetings in the surrounding agricultural villages, where auxiliary committees were formed. At the first such meeting for Shirley, Millbrook and the surrounding area, crowded by an audience made up almost entirely of working-class men and women, 'a large number of both sexes enrolled their names and paid the weekly subscription of a penny'.[73] A collection of £10 was raised in the first few minutes by small sums. They were anxious to have a travelling fund connected with the Great Club in Southampton that had 700 members by May 1850. Other meetings were held at Whitehaven and Romsey, where the mayor hoped hundreds more would assist in 'this noble contest of mind over matter'. As well as Southampton's Exhibition Travelling Fund that entailed weekly subscriptions of 1d, there was an optional one called the Admission and Provision Fund whose members would be able 'to go to the door of the Exhibition with a silver key in the shape of a shilling'.[74]

Savings clubs also operated in many other places, including Bradford, Bridport, Bromsgrove, Northampton, Preston, St Austell, Stirling and Worthing, the Potteries, Carlisle and Glasgow, and Settle and Bramley in Yorkshire.[75] Money clubs were often established independently of the local committees, frequently on the premises of public houses. The use of such locations highlights the traditional role of pubs in working-class communities. Pubs had often served as trade union meeting places, landlords often looked after branch accounts as well as providing other social functions such as organising goose clubs. Newspapers were read aloud in pubs, which would have generated interest in the exhibition. Information about it would have been learned at these readings or through conversation, so it is natural that the pub should have been the focus of local interest for some, especially those working in small workshops or domestic industries rather than large factories. There was a club at the Chapel Inn in Stalybridge.[76] In Bradford, in March 1850, a club was formed at the Hope and Anchor and similar ones were formed at other inns in the town and neighbourhood. According to the *Journal of Design and Manufacture* the promoters of these clubs 'earnestly entreated all artisans who can make it convenient to become members, to secure the necessary funds to enable them to visit the Great Exhibition, which is so well calculated to improve the moral and intellectual condition of all classes'.[77] From Manchester a handbill and rule card show such a club based at the Feathers Inn, Deansgate.[78] Mr Hancock, the landlord, was treasurer of the club, whose shares were 1s a week. Copies of the club rules were sold at the bar of the house for 1d. Its committee met at the Feathers every Monday evening from 30 December 1850 to collect subscriptions. Members were charged 1d a week for expenses in addition to their 1s subscription. A penny fine was also imposed on shares not duly paid up. If a member wanted to withdraw his share a fine of 2s 6d was imposed and a 6d fee charged to transfer the shares to someone else. This was obviously a club suitable only for those in steady employment. The club would continue for seven months, until 30 July 1851, when members unable to go to London would get their money back.

Another Manchester organisation was the Albert Exhibition Club, whose fortnightly subscription was 5s for full shares until 30s had been paid, or 2s 6d fortnightly until 15s had been paid for half shares.[79] Full shares covered the cost of the journey, bed and breakfast for six nights, an exhibition catalogue and conveyance to lodgings, in effect a fully inclusive package. Half shares included only the cost of the train fare, members to make their own arrangements for accommodation. Membership cost 1s, which included a copy of the rules and a guide to all the free exhibitions and places of interest in London. This club offered a choice of lodgings in May according to priority on the books. The rest of the lodgings would be drawn for the week before going away. The Albert Club's headquarters was at 25 Abraham's Court, Market Street, the home of Richard Stanley, who styled himself 'manager and conductor'.

The Bristol Association in Connexion (*sic*) with the Great Exhibition of 1851 allowed members to pay in instalments of 6*d* at any convenient interval.[80] The secretaries and receivers of this club were all shopkeepers of some kind and included a salt store keeper, a stationer, two booksellers, three grocers, a linen draper, a brush maker, an oil and colour man and eight druggists. Bristol people could visit London for 9*s* 10*d* return by train and the Association would try to provide comfortable and economical accommodation for its members.

Salford Working People's Association had civic dignitaries as trustees, patrons and treasurer: the mayor, a Member of Parliament, several aldermen and councillors.[81] The honorary secretaries and half the trustees, though, had no title and were presumably working men. Like many others, this club had its committee room in a public house, the Albert Hotel in New Bailey Street, Salford. Members this time paid 2*s* 6*d* a week and at the appointed time received £2 9*s* together with a railway ticket allowing them seven days in London, leaving on the first Saturday in July. If membership were to exceed 250 a second train would be arranged for the following Saturday. It seems that Salford people had to make their own accommodation arrangements. This club did not charge any expenses or fines in the event of non-payment. Not all the travel clubs had enough members to meet the railway companies' requirement for groups to travel in parties of 200 or 250. Letters were sent to Manchester from Warrington, where only twenty people intended to travel, and from Glossop, where the club had only eighteen members.[82] These clubs in smaller towns with fewer members approached their local committee secretaries to see if they could combine with larger clubs of Manchester excursionists.

The People's Exhibition Club of Bolton charged £1 14*s* in June and £1 9*s* afterwards for transport and accommodation, club membership costing 1*s* 6*d*.[83] The Bolton committee claimed that if a person were to 'neglect to avail himself of the advantages offered, he will be in a worse position than his fellow workmen who embrace them', presumably in terms of intellectual stimulation. 'The Exhibition would thus injure him if he refused to benefit from it.' The Bolton committee estimated £4 as the sum required for a week-long visit to London: £1 for the journey, eight breakfasts at 6*d*, eight dinners at 1*s*, eight suppers at 9*d* each, making a total of £1 for food; six nights' bed at 1*s* 2*d* a night and malt liquor or tea budgeted at 1*s* a day, making 16*s*; admission to exhibitions and a steamer trip on the Thames added another £1, plus 4*s* extra for spending money. In order to enable savings to be made of this amount, the committee recommended an early start, saving 1*s* 6$^{1}/_{2}$*d* for a year. The committee's estimated prices were much higher than the 6*d* for accommodation guessed at by John Matts in Leicester.[84] The Mechanics' Home charged 1*s* 3*d* a night, so the Bolton estimate was not far out. The committee had printed blank savings cards, to be adopted by any club; it recommended that people of the same trade and of a similar age should join in groups of not more than twenty people to open savings accounts, sharing the interest.

Not all clubs would have needed the services of the railway companies. Groups from Scotland and near ports had the choice of steamboats at specially reduced fares to London. The Stirling Club collected 1*s* a week to include fare and lodging, so it seems that travel by steamer compared favourably with train fares, considering the extra distance involved to and from Scotland.[85]

Thomas Cook himself was one of several operators who offered assistance to the exhibition clubs, conveying as many as 165,000 people from the provinces to the exhibition.[86] In his published recollections he describes how for three months prior to the opening he visited the principal towns of the Midlands and the North for the purpose of assisting in the formation and furtherance of such clubs.[87] He was in touch with the 'gentleman at the Home Office', presumably Alexander Redgrave, with whom the registration of lodgings was entrusted. What is typical of Cook was his campaigning. He was a leading figure and probably the instigator of the 'great railway campaign' which inspired competition between the London & North Western Railway and the Great Northern Railway in a hot price war, with the campaigners in Yorkshire using the slogan 'Five shillings to London and back,' a campaign which was ultimately successful.[88] Like many others involved in the workers' clubs, Cook was a veteran campaigner for fair prices for bread, temperance and the charter.

Travel clubs offered members a large range of facilities that differed from place to place: some simply offered a savings bank; others bulk purchase of transport, accommodation, an exhibition ticket and catalogue, guidebooks and the help of an appointed person in London. In effect, some offered a fully inclusive tour or package, like the Albert Exhibition Club in Manchester, which arranged train travel, six nights' bed and breakfast, an Exhibition catalogue and conveyance to the lodgings on arrival.[89] These differences would have accounted for the different subscription rates, as would distance from London and the date the club formed giving a shorter or longer time in which to save. Train fares were also cheaper from July onwards, following the success of campaigning, and so date of travel would have had an effect on the costs.[90] Some savings may even have included an amount to compensate for loss of income while people were off work or perhaps some spending money.

So imperative was the need to provide suitable and respectable lodgings for working people that the Royal Commission appointed Alexander Redgrave, an inspector from the Factory Branch of the Home Office, to superintend arrangements by setting up an agency in London to correspond with the local committees.[91] This agency provided all the information about lodgings that was necessary, such as their quality and price, and regulated the dates for the various cheap trips from the large manufacturing districts, subdividing as much as possible the immense numbers converging on the capital. Accommodation providers had to register with the central agency. Every suitable street was canvassed by its officials and a complete registration of the amount of accommodation was produced and classified. As well as assisting visitors to find material comfort and security, the system of enquiry would 'prevent respectable persons locating themselves in houses of doubtful reputation'.[92] The registration form for lodging houses for artisans asked for details of whether the accommodation was for married couples, single men or single women. The regulations required different categories to be lodged separately: families and couples, single men and single women to be distinct. In no cases could single men and women stay in the same house. Lodgings for females had to be superintended by a married woman. Only the names of persons of good character were received, references were required before registration and a system of inspection was instigated. As well as a register of lodgings, Manchester's committee received from an estate broker, Pankhurst's, the offer of a register of erratic lodgers as a guide for prospective landlords, showing tenants who had previously not paid their rent.[93]

A range of accommodation was offered, even within the category designated for the working classes. One of the cheapest was H. Castle & Co. of Baltic Wharf, Westminster. For 1s a night 200 men at a time could stay in sleeping apartments fitted up in the style of emigrants' ships.[94] For this price each man had a berth to himself, a flock bed, a pillow, a blanket, two sheets and a coverlet – all clean. Breakfast cost 9d extra. Guests could bring their own cheese, biscuits, coffee and the like, as a store room was available. The decks of a ship lying beside the wharf made a good promenade where the men could go for a smoke. The advantage of accommodating no more than 200 was that it was the number likely to arrive at one time from a district or club. This would reduce the likelihood of disagreement which might result if several large bodies of men from different regions were lodged together, to prevent local rivalries developing into fights.

There were quite a few places like this. Two large houses were fitted up by Samuel Herapath in Holborn with eighty to 100 beds, to accommodate people of moderate means.[95] A carpenter and builder of Commercial Road East, John Parker, wrote to local committees offering accommodation for 150 artisans with dining, smoking and reading rooms in a fine, open and healthy part of London for half a guinea a week. Each guest would have a bed and washing facilities to himself, boots cleaned and hot water.[96] The Clarence Clubhouse for artisans and others offered a distinct apartment with bed, bedding, basin, soap and towels plus a box with lock and key for 2s a night for parties of at least ten.[97] This detached mansion had nearly an acre of grounds for the use of residents. Jones's of Rochester Row was advertised as being conducted on a similar principle to that approved by the central registry.[98] It could take in 100 guests a night but somehow this could be doubled if necessary. For 2s a night artisans could sleep in dormitories on a bedstead with a hair or wool mattress, sheets, blankets and a coverlet, and make use of a smoking and bagatelle room. The engraved picture on its advertising poster shows a smart building with hanging gas lanterns outside, headed by the name 'Jones, Wine and Spirit Merchant', showing how people in other businesses could benefit from the exhibition by taking in guests as a sideline. A list and information about other London attractions such as galleries, museums and Madame Tussaud's for prospective tourists bordered the poster.

The Mechanics' Home, Ranelagh Road, Pimlico, was run by Thomas Harrison. Harrison wrote to the Manchester committee including a prospectus for his new establishment, saying he would be taking bookings from 1 March.[99] The poster-format prospectus (plate 2) describes the accommodation as occupying two acres in a perfectly airy, well ventilated situation.[100] For 1s 3d up to 1,000 visitors a night could sleep in dormitories arranged so as to give privacy. In the smoking room where a band played in the evening, ale and porter could be bought. Despite the economies of scale, Harrison claimed to have made 'effectual provision for the comfort, convenience and discipline' of the large body of men resident there. In the dialect book *Tom Treddlehoyle's trip ta Lunnan* Tom's opinion of the Mechanics' Home is that its appearance makes it too much like a mechanics' home. 'It wor ta factoryfied ah thowt; a thing which t'mechanics owt ta hev aght a ther seet an aght a ther mind when tha go ta Lunnan.'[101] The inside is more to his liking, he claims: he 'wor better pleaz'd a good deal wit inside then t'aght'. His view of the thousand folks asleep at night was 'My wurd but wot an a snorin choras theal be abaght two o'clock it morning.'

All the accommodation for which a prospectus has been found was for single men. A special register of furnished lodgings and apartments produced

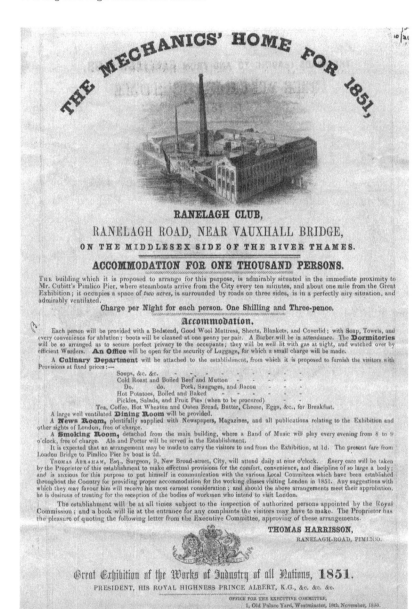

Plate 2 Ranelagh Club, the Mechanics' Home for the Great Exhibition, London, 1851

by the agents Eversfield & Horne listed rooms to rent in private houses, many of which would have been suitable for families. Lodgings or apartments were available in all price ranges from mansion houses with rooms for accompanying servants to shared bed-sits. Some seem to have been run like boarding houses, perhaps by less prosperous genteel families such as the lady and gentleman, without family, Mr and Mrs Buckland, of Euston Square. They lived in a comfortable and elegant home with seventeen large rooms that promised cheerful and good society. Terms were from £1 11s 6d to £2 2s a week in their highly respectable accommodation. The Bucklands were apparently well educated, as they advertised 'French and German spoken'.[102]

The central registry's circular had referred to 'temporary erections such as tents and Emigrants' Houses'.[103] Vast numbers of tents provided shelter for the poorest or those who did not book early. All lodgings were at a premium, with the massive influx not just from Britain but from all over the globe. Groups were expected from America, Belgium, Paris and Spain.[104]

The exhibition presented a golden opportunity for Londoners with initiative to improve their finances. There were those who feared not for London, with this influx of strangers, but for the safety of the visitors at the mercy of worldly Londoners. One reason claimed for the success of inclusive tours is the traveller's fear of foreigners, strange food and cultures. Fear of Londoners worried Rev. J. H. Morgan of Leeds, who thought the natives might trick the unwary visitor not familiar with London ways. He spoke of the need to protect them 'from the serious disadvantages which will at once occur to those who know what London is – what it is to be dropped from a railway train, a perfect stranger to the place and its ways, from a railway train in the middle of that vast wilderness'.[105] The story of the honest northern artisan wandering in London, pocket picked and baggage stolen, victim of the cunning Londoner, false friend, with his theatres, dens of vice and drink, was a common theme of the almanac and chapbook.[106] It also conjures up images of Oliver Twist and the Artful Dodger or Pinocchio and the fox and cat. In both stories the innocent arrival in an unknown town is taken in, led astray and exploited by worldly criminals posing as friends. The image is of the almost childlike innocence of workers, vulnerable to evil influences and ready to be led astray once away from the control of the middle classes and out on their own. Other potential visitors worried about the strange London food, contaminated milk and water. As late as 1877 the Local Government Board found that a quarter of the milk it examined contained excessive water or chalk; 10 per cent of bread and more than 8 per cent of butter was contaminated, and more than half of all gin had copper in it to heighten the colour.[107] This would perhaps account for visitors' desire to stay with people from their own locality and be served familiar food. Fear of foreign food and insecurity among strangers are factors that package holidays try to overcome.

All other attractions in London, including omnibuses and boat services, received a boost in business during the summer of 1851. Schweppe's soft drinks became a household name after being the sole provider of liquid refreshment at the Crystal Palace, where no alcohol was served.[108] Even the Mechanics' Institutes in London played their part by opening their doors free to members from the provinces and all foreigners during the Exhibition season.

For most of the working-class visitors this would have been their first experience of a 'holiday' away from home, although many would have been on excursions or works outings, or even Chartist rallies and camps.[109] Going to London and actually staying there for several days was quite an adventure, a completely new experience for the working-class travellers. The main obstacle to staying away from home would have been not just the actual cost but also the loss of wages whilst not working. Any time off had to be saved up for if normal household bills were to be paid. An article in Thomas Cook's *Exhibition Herald*, in typical campaigning mood, discussed the problem of time off for workers that posed the question 'how shall the people be spared from their employment with the least injury to business and the future comfort of the workpeople themselves?'[110] A Leicester working man, writing on behalf of a number of warehousemen and others, suggested that their employers should at least allow them wages for the time they would be absent, so that on their return they would not be destitute of the week's supplies. Some of the savings clubs with higher subscriptions may have taken this into account and included an amount for it. Some employers gave timeoff especially for the exhibition, encouraging their employees to go. Some even contributed to the cost, others even went so far as to give paid time off in what appear to be early examples of holidays with pay. In Leicester the firm of Berridge & McCauley gave its clerks £5 and leave to go to the exhibition, as did the bankers Parsons & Dain; clerks at Adcock & Dalton were also given leave. These all appear to have been white-collar workers but in what was undoubtedly one of the earliest examples of paid leave for manual workers Goodwin & Hobson, brewers, of Leicester, gave each man in their employ four days' holiday with pay and the train fare to London.[111] To allow them to visit the exhibition the Leicester watch committee gave policemen a week's unpaid holiday in turn to enable them to go in groups of ten.

Gentlemen and ladies, headed by the mayor, collected money towards the cost of the journey and leave for them and the other town servants. This arrangement was also made for the police in Hull. In the London area J. T. Christie & Co., a firm of hatters in Gracechurch Street, granted a one-day holiday on a Monday (probably a traditional day off work anyway) in May to the whole of its 600 or more work force. The company paid the cost of travel to the building and admission.[112] In June a coal merchant, Smith & Son, gave its 200 employees a day off on a Tuesday, paying the admission costs, providing refreshments, conveyance and, to round the day off, an evening supper.[113] The Great Western Railway gave its officers four days' leave to make the visit; Hodge's the distillers gave all men working for them a day's holiday and 5*s* towards their expenses; agricultural workers from several estate villages were also brought up.[114] Giving expenses seems to have been a compromise of the concept of paid leave.

Rail fares from the provinces to London became lower and lower with increasing demand and persistent campaigning. The fare from Yorkshire was eventually down to only 5*s*, showing the effect of high load factors on the price of transport, combined with competition between railway companies. This happened because of public and political pressure for as many working people as possible to have the opportunity to visit the exhibition. The railway companies clearly accepted that there was a highly elastic market and that, if they reduced the fare, even more tickets would be sold. The papers report that pawnbrokers were doing a brisk trade as poorer people scrimped and saved to scrape the fare together. A labourer from Huddersfield who could not afford time off work paid a forty-hour trip to London at a cost of 6*s*, according to contemporary newspaper reports.[115] He took an overnight train for 5*s*, sleeping on the way down. At the exhibition he paid 1*s* for admission, ate his own sandwiches and took no lodgings, so spent nothing while he was there apart from the entrance fee. He returned to Huddersfield that night ready for work the next morning.

It wasn't just the Crystal Palace that attracted hordes of visitors to the metropolis; many provincials saw the sights of London for the first time. Like modern package holiday destinations, the city provided a wealth of excursion opportunities. A letter from someone styled 'Mechanicus' appeared in the *Leeds Mercury* calling for the government to open up public buildings free of charge to all visitors during the exhibition season. Mechanicus also urged the Mechanics' Institutes and other working men's groups to give lectures to working people about the attractions and sights of London, giving them historical and other information to enable them to get maximum enjoyment and education from their visits to the capital. This would prepare them for not just a nine days' wonder but an experience the memory of which could give fulfilment throughout the rest of their lives.[116]

The opportunity offered for self-improvement through the event's enlightened message of material, cultural and moral progress and peaceful international competition was always emphasised as justification for the trip.[117] Arguments about the benefits to workers who might enhance their skills and craftsmanship through seeing examples of the best and most up-to-date products and techniques were used to persuade employers to grant time off to those wishing to go to the exhibition.[118] Despite the language of rational recreation and self-improvement, the visit to London was a tourist experience and not just an educational outing. All the lodgings described earlier emphasised in their publicity how conveniently situated they were not just for Hyde Park and the Crystal Palace but for steamboat trips along the Thames to other attractions; proximity to omnibus routes was also highlighted, and maps were supplied showing places of interest. Guidebooks were available as well as advice on the economical use of time. The character Tom Treddlehoyle certainly made the most of his time: he visited St Paul's Cathedral, Westminster Abbey, the Tower, the British Museum, the Coliseum, the Thames tunnel and Barclay's brewery.[119] This fictional itinerary is not entirely fantastic. In his diary, after winning the prize of a visit to the exhibition from Coventry Design School, William Andrews records that he spent the first day travelling, the second on a river trip to London Bridge and a walk round the Tower and the City (it was a Sunday, though, and other places were closed) and did not go to the exhibition until Monday, the third day of his visit.[120] Afterwards, on the same day, he went to see Buckingham Palace, the Serpentine and Kensington Gardens. On Tuesday he took a steamer trip to Gravesend. Next he visited a warehouse in Wood Street, the Guildhall, the Thames tunnel, St Paul's Cathedral, where he ascended the dome, Westminster Abbey, the National Gallery, the British Museum and the Zoological Gardens. He had obviously received and taken note of the advice on the economical use of one's time in London, outdoing even the exaggerated fictional exploits of Tom Treddlehoyle. On Thursday, his last full day in London, he went with his father to the exhibition again, returning to his Battersea lodgings by steamer. The next day he returned home to Coventry, having been to the Crystal Palace only twice in six days. William Andrews was a conscientious and educated artisan, keen on all aspects of self-improvement, but most of his time he spent on what must have been a mad rush around what was to become the London tourist trail. Maybe his hurry to see everything implies that he did not expect the opportunity to go back to London again. Andrews describes this in his diary as the longest journey he had ever undertaken. Later in the diary, for the year 1857, he described a visit to the Paris exhibition, so London was not destined to remain the longest journey of his life for long.[121]

Looking back in later life on the experience of visiting the Great Exhibition, another Coventry ribbon weaver, Joseph Gutteridge, related how his:

> delight and pleasure at seeing the varied collection of products from every part of the world was unbounded. However much the wonderful structure of glass and iron . . . might have been admired – it seemed almost a realisation of one of the gorgeous pictures of the Arabian Nights – the treasures it contained . . . surpassed anything previously conceived or read about and kept his mind in a state of continual excitement for some time.[122]

Visits to the Great Exhibition indicate various aspects of the development of tourism. Savings clubs, large venues, major national and international events and also package holidays can be demonstrated to have their roots in the trips arranged there. For many people in London for the exhibition it was the first time they had encountered foreigners. Contemporary accounts include comments that demonstrate curiosity, surprise and interest in people of other races and cultures. Charlie Rogers's Tom Treddlehoyle described how a friend he was with 'wor off like a lamp-leeter, in a throng starin' at a black man'.[123] All the nations that contributed to the exhibition had their own defined area in the Crystal Palace under their country's name. This and the overseas exhibits could have served as a stimulus to travel as the horizons of the visitors were broadened and they became aware of places and cultures beyond Britain.

It is from the Great Exhibition that the mass tourism of modernity, involving large numbers of people travelling and staying away from home for several days, derives. Accommodation at reasonable rates, providing familiar food, was needed. Transport, often provided by rail charter, was required for longer journeys. Thomas Cook was just one of a number of tour operators who met the demands of travelling workers. Some of the travel clubs and local committees made their own arrangements, others made use of the facilities offered by tour operators such as Cook and Henry Gaze. Some of the local groups made profits, although there were others that made losses. The Great Exhibition itself made a substantial profit that was used to finance many future educational projects. Some of the proceeds of local committees could have been put towards the cost of future trips. The accounts from Sunderland and

Bolton show that surplus funds were transferred in 1853 to a fund for facilitating exhibits and visits to the Paris exhibition.

After the exhibition had ended some people remained nostalgic about their experience, and the International Club was established near its Hyde Park site where former visitors and exhibitors could meet.[124] With a membership fee of three guineas a year no working people are likely to have joined but nostalgia for a happy time in 1851 is just as likely to have prevailed among them. Travel clubs themselves may have continued to function in form and to arrange further trips for members in subsequent years.

The working class's involvement in all aspects of the exhibition and its preparation showed that any risk of insurrection was over and an era of incorporation, collaboration and reformist politics commenced. By 1858 Friedrich Engels could describe with seeming despair how 'the English proletariat is becoming more and more bourgeois, so that this most bourgeois of all nations is apparently aiming at the possession of a bourgeois aristocracy and a bourgeois proletariat as well as a bourgeoisie. For a nation which exploits half the world this is of course to a certain extent justifiable.'[125] During unsuccessful campaigning later in 1851 for the 1852 Reform Bill a demonstration in Leicester on 11 October, the day after the exhibition closed, the gathering heard from Mr Thompson of the thousands who had visited the event in peace and behaved in a responsible manner. At 'yesterday's closing ceremony', he said, 'there were 107,000 people at the Crystal Palace and not one breach of the peace. This was in a country where there were only 850,000 voters and only 250,000 of those were independent.'[126] In total 6 million people had visited the exhibition during the summer; it had attracted more visitors than comprised the entire electorate at that time.[127] There was no justifiable reason why the majority of the people should be excluded from the franchise, as these people who had proved themselves to be respectable, sensibly behaved and thrifty posed no threat to the existing order, demonstrators were told. London had coped with the unprecedented influx of visitors; the visitors had coped with London, thanks to the innovative and resourceful combination of activities undertaken by organisations of the working class. The arrangements made by workers' travel clubs show elements of modern inclusive tours such as high load factors through advance booking and bulk purchase of transport and accommodation, the services of a guide, excursion opportunities and the provision of security and a sense of familiarity for travellers. The success of the operation and pleasure given to those who shared in the events meant that the memory of the trips would be an inspiration for years to come.

Notes

1 Douglas Reid, 'The "iron roads" and "the happiness of the working classes": the development of the railway excursion', *Journal of Transport History*, 3rd series, 17:1, 1996, pp. 57–73.

2 Alan Delgado, *The annual outing and other excursions*, London, 1977, p. 122.

3 Thomas Richards, *The commodity culture of Victorian England: advertising and spectacle, 1851–1914*, Stanford University Press, 1990, pp. 1–72.

4 J. C. Holloway and R. V. Plant, *Marketing for tourism*, London, 1988, pp. 6–8.

5 *Ibid.*, p. 112.

6 Charles Young, 6 August 1835, quoted by Christopher Hibbert, *The English: a social history, 1066–1945*, London, 1987, p. 650.

7 Railway Accident Returns, return of accidents to passengers from their own want of caution, trespass, etc., 1875 and 1876.

8 Hibbert, *The English*, p. 651.

9 Strathclyde Regional Archives, Glasgow, Alexander Frew, letter to his brother, London, 14 September 1851, Archive Notes, No. 21, September 1983.

10 Wolfgang Schivelbusch, *The railway journey: trains and travel in the nineteenth century*, Oxford, 1980, p. 158.

11 *Stockport Advertiser*, 31 January 1851.

12 *Ibid.*

13 Theodore Rothstein, *From Chartism to Labourism*, London, 1929, p. 158.

14 Susan Barton, 'Mechanics' Institutes: pioneers of leisure and excursion travel', *Leicestershire Archaeological and Historical Society, Transactions* LXVII, 1993, pp. 47–58, p. 48; J. Pudney, *The Thomas Cook story*, London, 1953, p. 53.

15 Scott Russell papers, II/218, A report to the Royal Society of Arts, 1849, quoted by R. J. Morris, 'Leeds and the Crystal Palace', *Victorian Studies* 13, March 1970, pp. 283–300, p. 284.

16 Paul Greenhalgh, *Ephemeral vistas*, Manchester, 1988; Toshio Kusamitsu, 'Great Exhibitions before 1851', *History Workshop Journal* 9, spring 1980, pp. 70–89.

17 R. J. Morris, 'Leeds and the Crystal Palace', p. 286.

18 Audrey Short, 'Workers under glass', *Victorian Studies*, December 1966, p. 195.

19 Short, 'Workers under glass', p. 194.

20 *Friend of the People*, 8 March 1851, p. 98.

21 *Ibid.*, January 1851, p. 59.

22 *Ibid.*, 19 April 1851, p. 168.

23 *Ibid.*, January 1851, p. 59.

24 *Ibid.*, 8 March 1851, p. 136.

25 *Ibid.*, January 1851, p. 51.

26 *Ibid.*, 10 May 1851, p. 189.

27 *Ibid.*

28 *Northern Star*, 3 May 1851.

29 *Payne's Leicestershire and Midlands Advertiser, Leicestershire Mercury*, 20 July 1850.

30 *Leicestershire Mercury*, 10 August 1850.

31 *Leicestershire Chronicle*, 17 June 1848; J. F. C. Harrison, 'Chartism in Leicester', in Asa Briggs (ed.), *Chartist Studies*, London, 1959, pp. 99–146, p. 118.

32 *Leicestershire Mercury*, 10 August 1850.

33 *Thomas Cook's guide to Leicester*, Leicester, 1843 (pages unnumbered).

34 *Leicestershire Chronicle*, 17 June 1848.

35 Letters from all these and other places to local committees elsewhere are held at Manchester Reference Library (hereafter MRL).

36 MRL, M6/3/10/32.

37 *Journal of Design and Manufacture*, London, 1851.

38 MRL, M6/3/10, handbill, 1850.

39 *Ibid.*

40 Short, 'Workers under glass', p. 198.

41 *Thomas Cook's Exhibition Herald and Excursion Advertiser*, No. 1, 31 May 1851, p. 2.

42 *Ibid.*, p. 2.

43 *Friend of the People*, November 1850.

44 *Leicestershire Mercury*, 10 August 1850.

45 *Stockport Advertiser*, 30 August 1850.

46 *Ibid.*, 30 August 1850.

47 *Leicestershire Mercury*, 20 July 1851.

48 *Ibid.*, 10 August 1850.

49 *Stockport Advertiser*, 20 June 1851.

50 *Ibid.*, 20 August 1851.

51 The *Journal of Design and Manufacture*, pp. 155–6, gives details of exhibition savings clubs reported to the commissioners in about thirty towns but this was only a small proportion of the final total.

52 Short, 'Workers under glass', p. 199.

53 *Northern Star*, 5 April 1851.

54 Rothstein, *From Chartism to Labourism*, p. 159.

55 Geoffrey Pearson, *Hooligan: a history of respectable fears*, London, 1983, p. 160.

56 Charles Reith, *Police participation and the problem of war*, p. 48 quoted by F. C. Mather, 'The railways, the electric telegraph and public order during the Chartist period, 1837–1848', *History*, February 1953, pp. 40–53, p. 40.

57 MRL, M6/3/10/46, letter to Captain James Thomas from Manchester Local Committee, February 1851.

58 F. M. L. Thompson, *The rise of respectable society: a social history of Britain, 1830–1900*, London, 1988, p. 261.

59 *Ibid.*

60 *Ibid.*

61 *Northern Star*, 3 May 1851.

62 Short, 'Workers under glass', p. 202.

63 *Ibid.*

64 Pearson, *Hooligan*, p. 218.

65 MRL, M6/3/10, Examples of clubs based in public houses include the Feathers Club and the Albert Exhibition Club in Manchester and the Chapel Inn, Stalybridge. The Salford Working People's Association was run from the Albert Hotel.

66 Bolton Metropolitan Library, Arts and Archives, FZ 39/1, Bolton Local Committee minute book, 1850–51, accounts. The Bolton account of subscribers gives a list of names and places of employment of the workers most likely to have visited the Exhibition.

67 *Ibid.*

68 *Leicestershire Mercury*, 10 August 1850.

69 Bolton Metropolitan Library, Arts and Archives, FZ 39/1, Bolton Local Committee minute book, accounts.

70 *Bolton Chronicle*, 6 April 1850.

71 Tyne and Wear Archives Service, 745/1, Sunderland Local Committee for the Great Exhibition minute book 1850–51.

72 *Ibid.*

73 MRL, M6/3/10/4, handbill, Southampton Local Committee.

74 *Journal of Design and Manufacture*, p. 156.

75 *Ibid.*, pp. 61–2; *Leeds Mercury*, 1 February 1851.

76 MRL, M6/3/10/32, letter from Stalybridge to Manchester Local Committee.

77 *Journal of Design and Manufacture*, pp. 61–2.

78 MRL, M6/3/10/40, handbill, Feathers Exhibition Club.

79 MRL, M6/3/10/40, handbill, Albert Exhibition Club.

80 MRL, M6/3/10/7, handbill advertising the Bristol Association in connection with the Great Exhibition of 1851.

81 MRL, M6/3/10/36, handbill, Salford Working People's Association.

82 MRL, M6/3/10/32.

83 *Bolton Chronicle*, 17 August 1851.

84 *Leicestershire Mercury*, 10 August 1850.

85 *Journal of Design and Manufacture*, p. 156.

86 Delgado, *The annual outing*, p. 121.

87 Thomas Cook, *Twenty years on the rails: reminiscences of excursions and tours in England, Ireland, Scotland, Wales, the Channel Islands and the Continent*, Leicester, 1860, p. 9.

88 *Thomas Cook's Exhibition Herald and Excursion Advertiser*, pp. 7–8.

89 MRL, M6/3/10/41, handbill, Albert Exhibition Club, Manchester.

90 *Thomas Cook's Exhibition Herald and Excursion Gazette*, p. 8.

91 *Journal of Design and Manufacture*, p. 192.

92 MRL, M6/3/10/58, circular of the London Central Register Office for house accommodation for visitors to the Exhibition of the Works of All Nations, London, 1851, p. 5.

93 MRL, M6/3/10/12, circular, Pankhurt's Estate Broker.

94 MRL, M6/3/10/53, handbill, H. Castle & Co., 1851.

95 MRL, M6/3/10/16, handbill, Samuel Herapath's lodging house, 1851.

96 M6/3/10/60, letter to Manchester Local Committee from John Parker, 1851.

97 MRL, M6/3/10/61, handbill, Clarence Clubhouse, 1851.

98 MRL, M6/3/10/51, handbill, Jones of Rochester Row, 1851.

99 MRL, M6/3/10/19–21, letter to Manchester Local Committee from Thomas Harrison, 6 December 1850.

100 MRL, M6/3/10/63. Either immediately before or after, or perhaps both, the site was used as the Thames Bank Depository for the storage of goods, although the site near Vauxhall Bridge is now occupied by Churchill Gardens and a school. See *Mechanics' Home Prospectus and Map*.

101 Tom Treddlehoyle, a.k.a. Charlie Rogers, *Tom Treddlehoyle's trip ta Lunnan*, published by Alice Mann, Rochdale and Leeds, 1851, pp. 54–5.

102 MRL, M6/3/10/59, accommodation list, Eversfield & Horne, 1851.

103 MRL, M6/3/10/58, circular of the London Central Registry Office, p. 5.

104 *Northern Star*, 10 May 1851.

105 Supplement to the *Leeds Mercury*, 1 February 1851.

106 *Ibid.*

107 A. S. Wohl, *Endangered lives*, London, 1983, p. 53.

108 *Stockport Advertiser*, 10 May 1851.

109 Harrison, 'Chartism in Leicester', p. 120.

110 *Thomas Cook's Exhibition Herald*, No. 1, p. 7.

111 *Payne's Leicestershire and Midlands Advertiser*, 5 July 1851.

112 *Northern Star*, 31 May 1851.

113 *Ibid.*, 28 June 1851.

114 *Ibid.*, 7 June 1851.

115 *Payne's Leicestershire and Midlands Advertiser*, 5 July 1851.

116 Supplement to the *Leeds Mercury*, 1 February 1851.

117 Thompson, *The rise of respectable society*, p. 261.

118 *Thomas Cook's Exhibition Herald and Excursion Advertiser*, p. 3.

119 Rogers, *Tom Treddlehoyle's trip ta Lunnan*, pp. 41–54.

120 William Andrews, 'The diary of William Andrews', in William Andrews and Joseph Gutteridge, *Master and artisan in Victorian England*, Coventry, 1893, repr. London, 1969, pp. 14–15.

121 *Ibid.*, pp. 21–2.

122 Joseph Gutteridge, 'The autobiography of Joseph Gutteridge', in Andrews and Joseph, *Master and artisan in Victorian England*, p. 142.

123 Rogers, *Tom Treddlehoyle's trip ta Lunnan*, p. 19.

124 MRL, M6/3/10/62, handbill, International Club.

125 Friedrich Engels, 1858, cited by A. L. Morton in *A people's history of England*, London, 1938, p. 377.

126 *Leicestershire Mercury*, 11 October 1851.

127 Short, 'Workers under glass', p. 202.

4

Holidays without pay

The arrangements made to allow workers to visit the Great Exhibition were to set a number of precedents for the future of working-class travel and holidaymaking. This did not herald an age of mass tourism; it was to be another century before the majority of working people were able to enjoy a holiday away from home of a week or more without the financial hardship of losing pay for the time they were absent. Even so, increasing numbers of workers managed to secure a holiday for themselves by a variety of means as the hundred years from the 1850s to the 1950s progressed.

The popular image of the seaside holiday evolved during the nineteenth century with the growth of the middle class. It became part of the routine of respectable life not just in Britain but in France and other industrial countries.[1] According to James Walvin, middle-class families did not like to admit to taking leisurely stays at the seaside. He uses the example of Clare Leighton, who, writing of her Edwardian childhood, said that her mother 'had profound contempt for people who took holidays. She dismissed them as having something common in their make-up.'[2] Lazy holidays were thought to belong to the lower orders. Clare Leighton's family didn't go to Lowestoft to enjoy themselves. They went there so that the children could benefit their health, and so that the mother and father could go on working with additional vitality. Time spent at the seaside in comparative idleness had to be justified on health grounds. Many middle-class families spent summer at the seaside while the fathers continued to work, perhaps joining them later. Servants accompanied the women and children so the mother would be ensured of relaxation with no worry about domestic chores. This middle-class diffidence towards the admission of pleasure for its own sake was also evident in the United States during the nineteenth century, where Cindy Aron noticed this attitude continuing to cause middle-class concern over the consequences of extended periods of idleness into the twentieth century.[3]

It was only during the twentieth century that the holiday ritual extended to the working-class majority in Britain. It became near universal only in the years following the Second World War. It would be a mistake, however, to imagine that the model middle-class holiday merely filtered down to the masses who have gratefully taken it up in imitation of their social superiors.

The roots of working-class holidaymaking can be traced back to the pre-industrial age when there was little division between work and leisure; leisure followed the annual routine of labour, allied with the religious calendar. It is probably no coincidence that the modern tradition seems to derive from the north of England, in the textile-producing areas of Lancashire and the West Riding of Yorkshire.[4] The explanation seems to lie in the industrial origins of these districts. Cotton and woollen textile production was at the leading edge of industrialisation. Because they were the earliest trades to undergo mechanisation their transformation incorporated many of the older cultural traditions of the recent pre-industrial past, including some paternalistic upper-class and religious sanction of community activities. This effect has also been noticed by Patrick Joyce, who in *Visions of the people* noted, 'a surprising amount of custom continued in place: this was so in the area of workplace and trade custom, particularly outside the factory, but was evident too in the area of leisure, for example, the persistence of wakes and fairs'.[5] Every village had its own traditional festivities, or wakes, commemorating the founding of its church or the saint to whom it was dedicated. These were opportunities for quasi-religious celebrations such as rush bearing, followed by religious services and afterwards games and sports, dancing and drinking.[6] Popular wakes entertainments were sports like climbing the greasy pole, eating scalding porridge, wrestling, cudgelling, smock racing by girls in their underclothes hoping to win the prize of a new smock, nude running races for men, chasing the greased pig and bull baiting.[7] On these days the whole village or town would come together, perhaps joined by visitors from neighbouring parishes with different wakes days. Of course, no everyday labour was performed on these occasions, but women would have had extra work to prepare the home for visitors. The wakes were celebrated as a community because the mills employed labour from within a specific locality or migrants from a particular nearby place; traditional communities and traditions therefore remained intact. Because everyone in the community celebrated at the same time it was impossible for the mill owners to impose a work discipline to suppress the holiday, as all the workers, as a collective action, ran off on wakes days.[8]

This seems at odds with Foucault's dichotomy discussed in the introduction, which divides the study of leisure into pre-industrial and industrialised societal forms.[9] No clear conceptual break or rupture occurred in the case of the Lancashire wakes; similar types of celebratory or festive activities were pursued throughout the transition to industrial society, albeit in different cultural contexts. The recognition that these celebrations were assigned different cultural meanings by different participants avoids the trap of anachronism, warned against by Foucault, when discussing continuity of a form of leisure from pre-industrial society into the industrial period. Whether or not the history of leisure is discontinuous, as Foucault claimed, is ambiguous. Although the activities enjoyed at the wakes and other celebrations before and during industrialisation were similar in form, they took place in different economic and social circumstances and therefore had different significance to participants.[10]

Pressure from the more puritanical elements in the Church of England, according to Robert Poole, had the most boisterous entertainments of the wakes and rush bearing moved from Sunday to Saturday.[11] The festivals became secular, with rowdy processions of decorated rush carts accompanied by drinking and dancing in local public houses, within many of which the communities' celebrations were actually organised in an early commercialisation of the leisure industry. Wakes Sunday became a popular day for entertainment in the home and Monday for fairs and more public forms of amusement such as bands, games and funfairs.

With secularisation and increased prosperity in the region throughout the century, apart from during the Cotton Famine, the wakes celebrations became more commercialised and extended to Tuesday and even, later in the nineteenth century, to Wednesday. Monday and Tuesday became the days for seaside excursions by rail to the Lancashire coastal resorts.[12] Although facilitated by the development of the railways from the 1840s onwards, there was a much older tradition in the west Lancashire towns of sea bathing. Visiting Blackpool in or before 1813, Richard Ayton found: 'Among the company are crowds of poor people from the manufacturing towns who have a high opinion of the efficacy of sea bathing, maintaining that in the months of August and September there is physic in the sea.'[13] This tradition was rumoured to have its roots in a long-forgotten pagan past, as did other forms of wakes celebration, albeit the meaning had changed within both the Christian and the industrial milieu. In 1838 William Howitt commented, in his *Rural Life in England*, on the growing number of operatives visiting the Lancashire seaside.

> The better class of operatives in the manufacturing districts consider it as necessary 'to go to the salt water' in the summer as to be clothed and fed for the rest of the year. From Preston, Blackburn, Bolton, Oldham and all those spinning and weaving towns, you see them turning out by the whole wagon and cartloads bound for Blackpool and such places.[14]

Whole communities would walk or ride in carts to the sea to indulge *en masse* in (often naked) bathing, outraging the sense of decency of their more respectable middle-class fellow tourists, who moved away to a safe distance in more remote, select resorts.[15] Others separated themselves in time, more genteel visitors preferring to go to Blackpool in October, when the wakes season was over.

By the end of the nineteenth century the wakes had become more commercial and lengthened to a full week in some places. Bolton's annual August holiday developed in the 1860s out of the trips run by the Operative Cotton Spinners' Association.[16] It therefore became imperative for the workers, mostly in cotton mills, to have the financial means to enjoy themselves on their trips. The seemingly frivolous extravagance of wakes week and the sacrifice of a week's wages was achieved only by thrift during the rest of the year. Wakes Saving or Going-off clubs became widespread in the last quarter of the nineteenth century; one of the earliest, other than those for the Great Exhibition, began in 1857 or earlier at Werneth Spindle Works, which had attained a week off by 1872.[17] As the wakes extended generally towards a full week, and seaside stays as opposed to day trips became common, these clubs proliferated. They were organised in factories, clubs, workshops, pubs, political groups and streets, and followed closely in structure and organisation savings clubs formed for the Great Exhibition.[18] The influence of trips to visit the exhibition was still felt at least eight years later, in 1859, as demonstrated by the Inspectors of Factories' report of that year, which referred in particular to free time and the consequent opportunities for self-improvement it realised for the working man, stating that

> It was by this, indeed, that they were enabled to realise the Exhibition of 1851 as a fact which they have never forgotten, and never will; for it lighted up a flame of observation in the minds of many, which has never dwindled; and it stirred up a spirit of inquiry, which has been of lasting benefit to the people as well as to the country at large.[19]

Whether or not the more recent wakes savings clubs were direct descendants of the exhibition clubs is not conclusively proved, though they were certainly very similar in form. The minutes and accounts of Sunderland's Local Committee for the Great Exhibition show that surplus funds were set aside towards trips to the Paris exhibition held a few years later.[20] It is possible that saving for the wakes or rush bearing antedates the Great Exhibition, although no evidence of specific savings clubs has been found from this earlier time. Describing the Middleton rush bearing of 1819 in his autobiography, Samuel Bamford, a dialect writer of descriptions of Lancashire life, wrote: 'Then lads and lasses would at all spare hours be engaged in some preparation for the feast. New clothes would be ordered and their quantity or quality would probably depend on the amount of money saved during the year, or on work performed during a certain time before the wakes.'[21]

Bamford referred to both saving and working extra hard in the preceding period to secure enough money to finance the 'holiday', showing that in 1819 wakes saving was not universal. Whether or not this saving was structured through clubs or individual thrift was not specified. It has even been proposed that the origins of the wakes saving clubs lie in the 'shaking clubs' of the 1830s.[22] These shaking clubs seem to have been a forerunner of modern lotteries: people paid in a weekly amount in the hope that they might win a payout decided on the shake of dice, although in many factories the throw of the dice decided the order in which contributors would be given the weekly pot to buy clothes or boots. In the going-off club at Werneth employees saved for fifty weeks at 6*d* a share for a 25*s* per share payout just before the wakes. The amount paid out by such clubs in Oldham rose rapidly, from £1,000 in 1871 to £10,000 in 1877, £60,000 in 1884 and £175,000 in 1900.[23] A Lancashire cotton worker remembered saving 6*d* a week in his youth during the 1850s, increased to 2*s* a week when he became an adult.[24] The number and importance of the smaller clubs grew relative to the large ones run by mills and other institutions. This was partly because of strikes in the engineering industry in 1885 and 1897 that set workers against saving with their employers.[25]

The clubs were not confined to the Victorian era; wakes clubs were still necessary until holidays with pay became general in the 1940s and 1950s. Although by the 1930s there were payouts to individuals of £25 to £30 the money was not spent entirely on frivolity.[26] While the mills were closed people were not earning but rent and bills still had to be paid and families fed. A proportion would also have been spent on new clothes and household items, many of which were traditionally purchased at the wakes fairs.[27] The cost of the visit to the fair and drinking during and afterwards also came out of this money. From later in the nineteenth century onwards the payout was used to pay for a seaside holiday as well as new clothing to wear whilst away.[28] The savings clubs made it possible for workers who received no paid holidays to enjoy a week off with little financial hardship by spreading the cost throughout the year.

These holiday clubs were not merely confined to the Northern textile manufacturing areas. The vicar of St Paul's in Finsbury, the Rev, Smith, claimed that in the 1880s his penny bank depositors withdrew money to pay for excursions.[29] The chemical company Brunner Mond in Northwich, Cheshire, had a savings club that had £26 in credit in January 1881.[30] This was three years before the firm introduced a week's paid leave for good attenders, illustrating that workers were already taking holidays when the employer introduced paid ones. Bournville works had a holiday savings club in the early twentieth century and Lever Brothers at Port Sunlight began a scheme in 1905.[31] At Lever Brothers in 1908 1,335 men and 935 women drew out savings and took holidays in such places as the Isle of Man, Blackpool, North and South Wales and even the Continent. Statistics show that 935 of those saving at Lever Brothers' were female, about two-fifths of the total number of savers. In Leicester in 1935 most big firms had a holiday fund.[32] In August that year £50,000 was paid out by thrift clubs to savers in Hinckley in Leicestershire.[33] How long these savings schemes had been established and whether they existed from as early as the Northern schemes is uncertain but during the late 1920s and 1930s representatives of Blackpool's holiday businesses had tried to market such schemes in other parts of the country in order to broaden their market.[34] There is no mention of any such clubs in Leicestershire in bank holiday reports in the local newspapers in 1919 or even as late as 1925, when record numbers of holidaymakers left the city for the seaside.[35] The earliest mention of Leicestershire clubs was in 1930 when voluntary savings clubs in Hinckley factories made holidays possible for many workers. One firm paid out £5,300 to workers in three factories in the town.[36] A former hosiery worker from the village of Stoke Golding near Hinckley recalled saving 2s 6d weekly during the working year, which gave her a holiday payout of £6.[37] She had her first holiday away from home as a young adult in 1937 and recalls that only about one family in her village ever went on holiday when she was a child in the years before 1920, which seems to indicate that the hosiery workers did not have savings schemes or 'Didlum clubs' at that time.[38] What the Leicestershire and Lancashire savings schemes have in common is that both areas had their major employment in branches of the textile industry, Leicestershire being a centre of the hosiery and knitted textile industry. A high level of female employment was characteristic of these areas, providing relatively high family incomes and women's influence over spending.

Mander Brothers, a Wolverhampton-based varnish and paint maker, had holiday savings administered by the firm's Welfare Club. Authorised collectors in each department took in payments each week and entered the amount on a card. The money was paid weekly into the Trustee Savings Bank with interest of 5 per cent every six months.[39] A subscription of 4*d* for adults or 2*d* for under-eighteens had to be paid to join the Welfare Club. Although a company-sponsored organisation, the club was run by elected members of the work force. It also offered a Christmas savings fund and sporting and social activities, open to both sexes.[40]

This small number of examples indicates that savings schemes were popular in industries employing large numbers of women. As well as contributing to a relatively higher household income than in areas with little opportunity for female employment, economic contributions may have given women more influence over expenditure, preferring saving for holidays and other consumer items to spending any excess income in the pub or on other local entertainments.

A full week away from the mill was common in practice long before it was officially sanctioned by the employers because of the collective action of the workers' 'running off' at the same time.[41] The extra days seem to have been gained during depression years when trade was slow and held on to through collective action in good years. This is because in a depression it is to the employer's advantage to limit production. It is also to the employer's advantage to have a week's closure rather than continued disruption caused by lots of odd days off here and there. Gradually the mill owners standardised the customary holidays by giving several consecutive days off in the summer. Many textile towns had regular week-long breaks by the end of the nineteenth century.[42] Darwen and Oldham had each acquired a full week by 1889, soon to be followed by Chorley, Nelson, Burnley and Blackburn.

The cotton employers and unions reached an agreement in 1906, giving an annual holiday equivalent to 116½ hours. Another agreement in 1914 increased the holidays to 136½ hours per year. This meant that as well as three days at Easter, three at Whitsun, a Saturday in July, Christmas Day and Boxing Day the cotton operative now had Wakes Saturday plus the whole of the following week off.[43] Although less usual, and outside the collective agreement, a fortnight's shutdown was becoming increasingly common, especially at limited liability companies, between 1890 and 1910.[44] Although no provision for payment during the break was made, the arrangement meant that textile workers had the time to take a prolonged stay of a week at the seaside.

Mass-Observation's study of Blackpool in the 1930s noted the central meaning of the holiday in the lives of Bolton people which was expressed not only in the rush to Blackpool but in the savings clubs and anticipations of mill families throughout the work year which were crucial to their self-esteem. The observers found a passion for holiday saving clubs and carefree holiday spending.[45]

Because the different towns, villages and localities had their wakes during different weeks through the summer, the resorts and travelling fair people could expect a full season of employment between Whitsun and September.[46] The 'lowbrow' activities of the fairground and seaside entertainments follow a cultural tradition evident in descriptions of the wakes. Towards the end of the eighteenth century a fair travelling from town to town came to Blackpool and from then on was there regularly.[47] The growth in popularity of the seaside holiday during the wakes weeks did not lead to the end of traditional wakes activities, they were merely relocated to the coastal resorts where bands, fun-fairs, donkey rides and rustic-type games abounded. Socialising within the community could still take place in Blackpool or some other resort if nearly the whole community had transferred there at the same time.[48] It also meant that travelling showmen and women and entertainers no longer needed to be constantly on the road, as now holiday revellers came to them and not the other way round. In the North-west of England the typical working-class holiday evolved from older pre-industrial traditions, nurtured by the particular pro-ductive relations, such as the communal nature of factory work and mill town life, prevailing in that region. This pattern of holiday development formed the prototype for working-class holidaymakers in the rest of the country, where the week away at the seaside for large groups of workers was slower to make its appearance.

Why had the holiday habit, which was ingrained among the North-western working class by the beginning of the twentieth century, not become so to such an extent elsewhere? After all, every part of Britain had its traditional festivals and feast days and every region was affected by the changes in pro-duction wrought by industrialisation. John K. Walton offers a hypothesis, confirmation of which he believes provides this explanation.[49] For a working-class presence at the seaside to develop beyond the day trip he proposes five conditions that had to be met: cheap and rapid access to the coastline; the ability to save; the existence of blocks of free time; adequate facilities in resorts; workers exercising choice in how they spent their wages.

Fast access was needed to resorts because the working-class holidaymaker had limited time as well as a limited amount of money to spend. However, from the 1850s all industrial areas were served by the railway network, which by now extended to the coast. This then cannot explain why not all communities made use of it for anything other than excursions. A significant proportion of the working-class population needed a sufficient income to enable a surplus to be allocated to the pursuit of health and pleasure. This income needed to be regular if savings were to be accumulated throughout the year. The textile trade, not offering especially high individual male earnings, could provide a relatively high family income as women were employed in jobs well paid by comparison with other common forms of female labour. Teenagers and young people had the financial independence to take holidays without the rest of the family. Of course there would be times in life when it was not easy to save for a holiday, such as when the children were too young to contribute to the family budget, or in old age when employment ceased. The cotton and woollen mills were also able to offer security of employment as employers preferred short-time working or wage cuts to laying workers off. From the 1870s average real wages in the textile districts rose, providing a surplus above normal budgeting that could be spared for savings.[50]

That the worker needed several consecutive days' holiday in the summer with the tolerance or approval of the employer was essential for working-class holidaymaking to take place. The textile workers were able to secure this time through their collectivity, as argued above, when they 'ran away' as a group from the mills on wakes days. It might also be argued that independent craftsmen in workshops could have achieved this through their relative independence but it was the textile workers who did so, thereby facilitating stays away from home extending beyond the day trip or the weekend.

In Lancashire, especially in the Oldham area, where the wakes habit was strongest and which had the largest number of savings clubs, there was a very early development of working-class consciousness as opposed to trade union consciousness. John Foster argues that this was based on a highly developed sense of community and social cohesion. Alex Callinicos, with reference to Anthony Giddens, describes these aspects of class consciousness as the difference between 'individual agents with a class identity based on a recognition of shared class membership and collective agents who co-ordinate their actions to effect change, in opposition to other classes'.[51] Oldham also had a history of radical politics and support for Chartism, led by weavers up to the 1830s and later, from the 1830s to the 1850s, by spinners.[52] Foster's comparative study shows that in the other areas he examined, Northampton and Shields, only a trade union consciousness had evolved by the 1850s. Oldham's strong and organised working-class movement was destroyed, following defeats at the hands of employers after 1850. However, this would still leave a group of workers with experience of organising independently and of collecting money in the past for subscriptions, strike and hardship funds, so it is likely that these people used their skills to more immediate ends, such as organising savings clubs for visits to the Great Exhibition in 1851 and later for wakes weeks. A number of former Chartist activists have been identified in workers' committees in Leicester and in Glasgow.[53] The attitude to time off may be, as in the case of Oldham workers, a good indicator of early collective organisation where there were the consciousness and structures for collective action to enforce the holiday.

The resorts needed to be able to offer sufficient and appropriate facilities to cope with working-class demand. In Lancashire Blackpool and Southport were able to offer and develop facilities for working-class visitors early compared with other parts of the country, stimulated by the existing local market. But despite the presence of these conditions the deciding factor was that working-class people were able choose how they spent their free time and disposable income when there was competition for it not just from holidays but from other things such as local entertainment and leisure activities throughout the year, new clothes, furniture or a bigger and better home. This exercise of consumer preference reinforces one of the primary suppositions, which is that working people were not passive consumers in a market place dominated by a few entrepreneurial individuals, anxious to imitate the classes above them in their holiday habits. They were instrumental in obtaining and in determining their own use of leisure. Consumerism as the convergence of economics and culture was recognised by Georg Lukács in 1922.[54] Thomas Richards goes further in this analysis, linking consumerism and commodities as the co-ordinating frame within which different forms of social life are grouped.[55] These forms do not just include economics and culture but represent a fusion of economic, political, cultural, psychological and literary influences.

In addition to the five conditions necessary for working-class holiday-making to become common, Walton identifies four main patterns of holiday observance other than in the textile areas. The first is the case of well paid craftsmen in workshops where labour discipline was loosely enforced who may have been able to enjoy seaside visits as part of a persisting pattern of casual holidays throughout the year.[56] These artisans could easily have met the conditions described above, being able to earn enough to put aside regular savings and being in a position to take time off if they wished. Many of them did, for example craftsmen in Sheffield contributed to the development of resorts like Scarborough, Bridlington and Cleethorpes. These steel and cutlery workers almost matched the demand for holidays among the Lancashire textile workers. However, where it differed was that although income could be relatively high in these craft-based occupations attendance was often irregular and labour discipline undeveloped. High living standards, including taking time off, were achieved by short bursts of hard work rather than by regular and disciplined habits of labour.[57] In the light trades of Sheffield, the Midlands and elsewhere in the country, workshops of independent artisans survived the coming of large-scale factory labour brought about by industrialisation elsewhere. Old traditions and patterns of leisure survived with them, such as a high level of absenteeism, taking time off when it suited, and the extended weekend through observance of St Monday.[58] Sheffield cutlers' long-standing cultural attachment to this lifestyle is illustrated in an eighteenth-century ballad:

> Brother workmen, cease your labour,
> Lay your files and hammers by;
> Listen while a brother neighbour
> Sings a cutler's destiny:
> How upon a good St Monday,
> Sitting by the smithy fire,
> We tell what's been done o' t' Sunday,
> And in cheerful mirth conspire.[59]

Most of the cutlers worked in establishments of up to five men or even in virtual isolation in domestic workshops. According to factory inspectors' reports there were 15,970 cutlery workers in 1901, making Monday important not just for leisure but for socialising.[60] This tradition survived until its final curtailment during the First World War.[61] Douglas Reid's study of Birmingham in the 1840s, discussed in Chapter 2, where most industries were also workshop or small factory-based, employing skilled craftsmen and artisans, shows that excursions of several days' duration were taking place at that time.[62] Monday was the most popular day for leisure activities of all kinds.

The Sheffield cutlers had a legacy of periods of time off work dating back at least to the sixteenth century. The earliest surviving ordinances of the trade, dated 1565, refer to 'ancient customs and ordinances', implying continuity with an older set of trade rules that have not survived. These ordinances provided for two annual holidays or cessations of work, a fortnight in summer from 15 August and four weeks in winter from Christmas Day.[63] This may have been for practical reasons: the grinders relied on water power, which was particularly unreliable in the drought of summer and during winter frosts. However, the wording of the ordinances says specifically that the closure was 'for the better relief and commodytie of the poorer sorte'. The enforcement of compulsory holidays may be partly attributed to the desire of these 'poor craftsmen for a period of leisure and recreation, a break from their arduous life'. This view gains some credibility from the voluntary adoption in 1689 by the scissorsmiths, also centred in Sheffield, of three annual holidays of one week each at Easter, Whitsuntide and Christmas and in order to 'check the physical disablement and bad workmanship resulting from excessive labour'.[64] The ordinances, though, date back to pre-industrial times and possibly reflect the pattern of work in rural communities. The dark winter months, while there was little agricultural labour, were a time when rest could be taken.

The assumption of the right to an extended break from work was also influential in other Sheffield industries. At the Sheffield Smelting Company, which employed 'men of good character' from the owners' place of worship, the Zion Chapel, unofficial holidays were taken. In 1824 the directors wrote in a letter to their London agent, 'next Monday being Whit Monday is a considerable holiday on account of the Sunday School Union celebrating its anniversary and as several of our people are concerned in it we are not at present sure whether we can attend to your samples on that day'.[65] These periodic breaks were not confined to Sheffield trades. Weavers in London stopped work for five weeks after Christmas, again reputedly for the sake of the workers' health and well-being.[66]

In the Sheffield trades most men preferred not to work on Mondays and Tuesdays, making up their hours at the end of the week.[67] A culture of irregularity of working habits prevailed in the city into the twentieth century, according to a writer in 1913 who argued, 'the custom of doing little work early in the week, and making up time by working long hours at the latter end of the week, still characteristic of the out-workers among the journeymen, became firmly established at an early date'.[68] At times when wages were particularly high, hours were short, workmen preferring leisure to income after reaching their normal earnings. This was not a trait peculiar to Sheffield artisans, and other examples of the preference were common.[69]

In large Sheffield factories with steam power the worker did not have the same level of control over working hours, as the wheels were powered from 8.00 a.m. to 5.00 p.m. at the beginning of the week, extending to 7.00 p.m. by Friday and on Saturday from 7.00 a.m. to 4.30 p.m., fifty-eight and a half hours in total. Reflecting the trend in the workshops, few grinders put in the full hours during the first two days of the week.[70] In these light trades, in 1850, the common holidays included ten or fourteen days after Christmas, one day each for Easter and Whitsun and a half-day on Shrove Tuesday and 5 November. A children's rhyme dating from the Victorian period shows the importance of collective tradition in enforcing holidays. Referring to Shrove Tuesday, the verse went:

> Pancake Day! Pancake Day!
> If you don't give us an 'oliday
> We'll all run away![71]

The Christmas holiday, used for stocktaking, was preceded by a few weeks of hectic work known in ascending order of intensity as 'calf', 'cow' and 'bull' weeks, to accumulate wages to last into the new year.[72] This demonstrates that workers in these trades were able to take time off if they chose but do not seem to have been particularly interested in breaks during the summer, at least not as early as 1850. The relative independence of this section of the Sheffield work force persisted and in 1906 working hours were fixed only in large works. The number of days off ranged from six to sixteen per year, with an average of 14.8 days.[73] The working day was still shorter on Mondays and Tuesdays, and St Monday and even Holy Tuesday remained popular. 'It is now Wednesday and five men in one department have not turned in yet', complained one manufacturer in 1907. This was so prevalent, although not officially sanctioned, that another manufacturer claimed that he 'lay awake at night devising ways of circumventing them and getting them to work'.[74]

Closely related to this first group of craftsmen working in small units, in organisation but not in terms of income, were those employed in the less prosperous kind of factory or workshop. Again in these labour discipline was lax and traditional communal holidays were observed which diverted free time and expenditure away from the seaside holiday habit. In the Potteries and the Birmingham hardware district St Monday continued to be venerated until the 1864 Factory Act Extension widened the scope of legislation on working hours beyond the large cotton factories, making it unattractive to lose pay on a Monday when limitations on the hours of young assistants meant that wages could not be made up at the end of the week.[75] The wakes of various towns in the West Midlands, held during different weeks throughout the summer and attracting revellers from neighbouring towns as well as local residents, continued to bring disruption through the 1870s and were subject to campaigns to consolidate them until the end of the century. The financial effect of these frequent breaks from labour meant that workers in these districts could not save up for holidays by the sea. Home and community-based entertainment and local excursions were the order of the day for all but a thrifty minority.[76] Savings clubs had no attraction for these workers, and no disposable income, if a person managed to attain one, could be accumulated, as it was spent on other forms of leisure. The Potteries and the Black Country exemplified this pattern, and when a thrift club among Stoke fitters was reported in 1900 it was treated as an unusual event, as such clubs were not common in the West Midlands until after the First World War. Even so, evidence that industrial workers from Birmingham and the surrounding towns spent time away from home before the mid-nineteenth century is provided by the example of the Cotswold Games. These were an annual event until the enclosure of the open fields around Dover Hill, where they were held. Writing in 1904, C. R. Ashbee related how, to his horror, industrial workers from the Midlands would gather for the festivities.

> The folk of Campden and the Wolds were wise in keeping the Industrial Revolution at arm's length. They must have seen it at its worst. To have the scum and refuse of the nearest great factory towns shot annually into Campden for a week's camping on Dover's Hill, two or three thousand at a time, with unlimited beer from unlimited booths and hooligans of the type of Tantiatopee; to have Kingcomb Lane a whistling pandemonium of roughs and the pleasant valleys of Saintbury and Weston tramped by armed bands of Birmingham yahoos was not a thing to be desired.[77]

In the Coventry ribbon trade too, traditional holidays persisted until well after the nineteenth century's mid-point. 'Coventry Fair begins today', recorded William Andrews in his diary on Friday 20 June 1862.[78] He noted that Cash's silk weaving factory was to be closed all the next week. Although mentioned in previous years, 1862 was the only time a full week's cessation of work for the Godiva procession was noted. The ribbon trade was beginning to experience a slump, prior to its eventual decline, so the reality behind the closure was possibly a lay-off of workers to avoid overproduction.

For the framework knitters concentrated in Leicestershire and Nottinghamshire work throughout the nineteenth century was subject to seasonal fluctuations in demand for their products. Before the application of steam power and factory production in the latter part of the century, work was ill paid and sporadic. Even so, the 1844 report of evidence given to the Hosiery Commission inquiry into the problems of the knitters, showing working conditions in the trade, indicates that some provision was made for holidays. In Leicester, for framework knitters in four of the best paid workshops, the total combined earnings of about 126 workmen in the week before Easter were £119 16s 4d (about 19s each) and during Easter week itself only £23 12s 8d was earned between them.[79] On average the knitters each earned about 15s 11½d a week, a combined total of £100 10s 4d in a normal week. These figures show that the knitters as a group increased their wages during the week before Easter and did little work during Easter week itself, presumably taking a 'holiday', which may not have been by choice if the workshops were closed. The report goes on to say that these earnings averaged out over a period of a few months during which one extraordinary workman varied his earnings from 8s 9d to 38s 4d in different weeks. During frequent lay-offs parochial relief was obtained. Even in the best paid areas of framework knitting no savings were available to be put away for old age or slack trade, let alone a holiday away from home.[80] As in the Potteries, savings clubs for holidays were not in evidence before the 1930s.[81]

Another pattern of taking time off work was found in areas of heavy industry and mining which offered fewer opportunities for the family budget to be enhanced through the contributions of working wives and children, although women who worked in the home could contribute to household income through taking in washing, lodgers and cleaning jobs.[82] These areas saw widespread observance of St Monday and traditional local celebrations and again offered little encouragement for extended seaside visits.[83] Workers in these areas did not develop a habit of saving up for their holidays but, when one was approaching, worked especially hard to increase output, according to which pay was calculated, in order to earn enough extra to cover their additional expenses. As in Sheffield, the week before was known as a 'bull' week.[84] Holidays away from home were not common, although a few South Wales and Tyneside resorts were attracting day trippers in the late nineteenth century, as were Weston super-Mare and Ilfracombe for South Wales steamer excursions patronised by colliers and their families. However, the demand for seaside holidays by working-class visitors in these areas remained limited even by 1900.[85]

Wide areas of southern and Midland England had lost their traditional holidays by the mid-nineteenth century. In his reminiscences, published in 1868, Thomas Wright, a journeyman engineer, wrote describing the London area:

> In some districts there are occasional holidays in connection with local customs. These, however, are but partial and accidental holidays, and the holidays proper of the unwashed are the three great festivals of Christmas, Easter and Whitsuntide. Of these, Easter, viewed purely as a holiday, is the greatest. Christmas is devoted more especially to the renewing of home associations and

the promotion of social intercourse; and Whitsuntide coming some weeks after the 'outing' season has fairly set in, the holiday zest that comes in with the spring is by that time somewhat toned down.[86]

Wright made no mention of holidays taken during the summer and went on to say, that in his experience, it was difficult for workers to put anything by for enjoyment at Whitsun, coming so soon as it did after Easter. The relatively long period of time between Christmas and Easter and the lack of other celebrations and opportunities for outings in the duration allowed surplus funds to be saved for a holiday at Easter but no other time.[87]

For large numbers in the southern and Midland areas of England work was ill paid and irregular. Until the Bank Holidays Act introduced the August bank holiday in 1871 there was no scope to develop or obtain an extended summer holiday. Even August bank holiday was initially slow to catch on, and in the first year passed by mainly unobserved.[88] From the second year following its inception the August bank holiday provided the opportunity for millions of workers, in the South-east and Midlands especially, to enjoy an extended weekend incorporating a seaside excursion.

As important as technological innovation in transport in facilitating holidaymaking for the majority not living in the textile-producing areas was the passing of the Bank Holidays Act in 1870 and, before that the generalisation of the Saturday half-holiday. The granting of these holidays was done for ostensibly improving reasons rather than to allow workers to enjoy themselves. In favour of the earlier payment of wages and ending of work at lunchtime on Saturdays it was claimed the half-holiday would:

> throw into the recreations of our working classes a number of the best and noblest of the working men; men who will not run into diversions upon the Lord's day, and, therefore, leave the diversions of the people who do take them upon that day without the tone and elevation and moral influence which the best of their own class would give if they were in the midst of them; but give them the working day, give them the Saturday, and then you will find that your most intelligent, your most religious, your most valuable working men will take their proper standing, and exercise their power of influence on the indoor and outdoor recreations which are resorted to by their fellow workmen.[89]

The gist of this argument was that without the Saturday half-day the only people who could take part in leisure and recreational activities were those who did not observe the Sabbath. Consequently the more respectable workers were excluded, leaving the less so without their moral influences and good example in their pursuits. Other advantages of the half-day on Saturdays, which would become the instigator of the modern weekend, was the belief that it would:

> be a powerful opponent of St Monday, which is a shiftless idler and a miserable demoraliser. Where the half-holiday already existed in 1856, piece workers did not lose out in wages but were able to find the means to subscribe to boat clubs, cricket clubs, musical unions and societies by which they recruit and refresh their minds and bodies, enabled to do more real work than if those hours were spent in drudgery or in pure idleness.[90]

The Saturday half-day had reached Sheffield by about 1840 but was not fully established there until about twenty years later.[91] The Jarrow Chemical Company acquired the Friars Goose Chemical Works in Gateshead, employing 1,400, in 1858 and became the first firm in the North-east to grant free Saturday afternoons.[92]

The idea of nationally observed holidays was not new to Lubbock's bank holiday Bill. In 1856, in addition to the Saturday half-holiday, a committee which included the Earl of Shaftesbury, who was also active in the Early Closing Association, campaigning for shorter working hours for shop assistants, advocated the sanction of four national holidays in the year, for which a Bill was being prepared in Parliament.[93] This proposal took until 1868 to be the subject of a parliamentary select committee reporting on the bank holidays Bill. This legislation, which came into force in 1870, had the seemingly innocuous aim of recommending that bills falling due on any holiday should not be payable until the day after, which would give bank clerks a day off on those days. The Bank Holidays Act, sponsored by Sir John Lubbock, introduced 26 December as a bank holiday and, as well as the traditional religious 'holy days' at Easter, Whitsuntide and Christmas, an additional completely secular day was also introduced on the first Monday of August. This was not at all unanimously supported. Many giving evidence thought that further holidays for bank workers were not required and it was strongly denied that clerks had any grievance on the score of holidays or hours of labour. It was the rule in the bank of Mr McKewan, a witness before the Select Committee on Bank Holidays, 'that all clerks were entitled to at least a fortnight's holiday'.[94] Another testified 'it was the right of every clerk in the London & Westminster Bank to a fortnight's holiday, whilst after twenty years' service the clerks were entitled to three weeks'; holidays were also given in individual cases under special circumstances'.[95] The debate focused around the claim that bank closures would lead to commercial damage and that increased work on the days following a holiday would cancel out any benefits to the bank workers. Of those in favour of the Bill, some thought a Wednesday in June or July would be the most suitable time for the new holiday.[96] The report discusses the effect of closures only on banking. Nowhere is a general holiday recommended. This seems to have passed into statute almost unnoticed as a consequence of the Act's provision that no one should be compelled to do on a bank holiday what would not be expected of them on Christmas Day or Good Friday.

The new holiday was not immediately taken advantage of by most workers, and little change was noticed in the first year after the Act was passed. Levels of observance of the first August bank holiday in 1871 varied around the country. In Liverpool it was celebrated almost as strictly as Christmas Day and Good Friday, while in Manchester most warehouses closed but the mills stayed open. 'The mass of the people did not seem to be aware that the day was a holiday.'[97] In London there were three or four times the number of excursion trains to Margate and other popular resorts. Crowds spent the weekend at the seaside but they were almost all middle-class City workers. Most working people did not seem to realise the full meaning of the Act. Perhaps that was just as well, as even this low take-up was seriously underestimated by the railway companies. Tens of thousands of would-be excursionists made for the London railway stations only to find that in many cases no trains were available. Posters had announced that steamers would return from Margate jetty to Thames Haven at 3.30 p.m. but the crowds struggling to board the boats were so great that it was four o'clock before they reached Margate.[98]

It didn't take long to catch on, and by the following year the August bank holiday had become as accepted by the public as the other traditional holidays at Whitsun and Easter. While the local papers in Leicester made no mention of the new holiday, apart from the usual advertisements for rail excursions in the 1871 and 1872 editions for the first week in August, by 1874 the papers reported that 'Sir John Lubbock's bank holiday is rapidly advancing in popularity'. In spite of an increase in fares the railway companies benefited from extra excursion traffic.[99] Leicester Town Council gave the day official sanction by recommending it as a general holiday. The number of shops opening decreased considerably from the previous year, those remaining open mainly ministering to the pleasure needs of their customers. The council even provided municipal entertainment in the form of a civic procession and amusements celebrating the laying of the foundation stone of the new town hall. In 1875 the Bank Holidays Extension Act extended the provision of the Act to the docks, customs houses, Inland Revenue offices and bonding

Plate 3 Visitors arriving at Clacton station, 1910. *Reproduced by courtesy of Essex County Council, Local Studies Department, Colchester Library*

warehouses, making it easier for other types of business to observe the bank holidays and advanced further the acceptance of holidays for the working classes.[100]

The new bank holiday took place at the beginning of August and so it was during high summer rather than the present-day arrangement of late in the season. In some areas, especially southern England, where traditional wakes holidays had been successfully suppressed and consequently there was no common focus for collective holidaymaking, the new bank holiday provided that focus. Bank holiday Monday became a time for seaside excursions (see plate 3) but it still took a little time for them to extend beyond the weekend. For that reason there was less expansion in the accommodation sector in the resorts serving the South and Midlands than there was for those serving Lancashire. In Southend in 1880 demand for accommodation for working-class visitors far exceeded supply when 11,000 mainly East End trippers tried to stay in the town over the weekend. The concentration of working-class holidays into bank holiday week created problems for the Southern and South-eastern resort towns, with overcrowding in that week alone but few people staying longer than a day or a weekend for the rest of the summer. This meant, at least until the 1890s, that it was difficult for towns like Southend and the Kent resorts to establish a summer season.[101] Such was also the case with places with a mainly Midland catchment area; Skegness was not established as a resort until the late nineteenth century.[102]

Although the events and activities described above relate to the development of holidaymaking, throughout the period under scrutiny only a minority of workers would have been able to indulge in the activity on a regular basis. This does not mean that poorer people, who were excluded from the growing market, never had a holiday away from home of any kind. Many urban industrial workers, especially first and second-generation proletarians, would have friends and relatives living in the country. Better rail links would help make visits and stays with family in the countryside accessible to many who thereby managed to maintain kinship connections with those they had left behind through migration. In her study of Banbury, Margaret Stacey showed how important kinship networks were to the community.[103] People who had migrated to the town in the nineteenth century maintained family relationships and so stays with family outside the town were integral to social life and encouraged future migration.

Visiting friends and relations was the only way many working-class people could get a holiday away from home. A Leicester woman remembered that as a child in the late 1920s she used to stay with friends of her father in North Kilworth, a village in the county. 'They had a thatched cottage and I had my own room there. At home I had to share with my three sisters.'[104] Another Leicester resident recalled that he was 'fortunate that some friends of the family were farmers'. He used to go and stay with them for his holidays.[105]

Joseph Gutteridge's autobiography of his life in Victorian Coventry describes two holidays staying with friends. The first, in the mid-1850s, was with farming friends at Smeaton, a Leicestershire village, accessible by train. Although it was not a resort, during his stay at Smeaton Gutteridge enjoyed some typical holiday pastimes. As this part of Leicestershire was geologically different from his familiar Coventry and Warwickshire haunts he was able to search for unusual stones and fossils with his small daughter. He made excursions by train into Leicester, where he visited the museum, Roman ruins and old churches. Gutteridge concludes his description with the words 'I cannot remember a time in which I so heartily enjoyed myself as during this visit to Smeaton. With renewed health I was better prepared for the struggle . . .'[106] As in so many descriptions of Victorian holidays, the emphasis in justification was clearly put on health and self-improvement. Gutteridge had recently been widowed and as a result was not in the best of health or spirits prior to his trip.

Another holiday was of a similar type, this time with friends in Northamp-tonshire in the late 1860s. Again Gutteridge enjoyed searching for specimens to add to his fossil collection. He visited Northampton and its museums and some of the stately homes in the area such as Althorpe as well as the local coun-tryside. Hobbies were important to Gutteridge, an intelligent and articulate man, whose class position gave him no opportunity for social advance. Ross McKibbin describes hobbies as giving pleasure through an activity emphasis-ing privacy and solitude within working-class domestic life and industrial life, which were all too collective.[107] They also permitted a socially acceptable level of intellectual activity in pursuits that involved mastery of a craft and knowledge, discipline and skill.

Visiting friends and relations remains to the present a substantial sector of the tourism market as, although the visitors may not be staying in commer-cially provided accommodation, they and also the hosts may take part in leisure activities and visits to local places of interest during the stay.

Temporary work in an area away from the usual place of residence, like hop and fruit picking, could give the opportunity of a 'change of air' and a chance to explore new surroundings. For the residents of the East End of London an annual September journey to Kent for the hop picking was an eagerly awaited break from routine in the fresh country air. Hop pickers and their families would reside in tents, barns and makeshift dormitories. Although the conditions and facilities were not at all luxurious, they welcomed the opportunity to have a couple of weeks in the country combined with the chance to earn some extra money. 'Hop picking was our holiday. It was brilliant to get away from where we lived. But, mind you, it was bloody hard down there, in the hopfields, but it was better down there, because you had the open air. We used to play a game of football, or play cricket on Sundays in the fields, there were plenty of open spaces.'[108] Picking the hop flowers is concentrated into a short period, usually the first weeks of September, and before mechanisation took over in the 1950s and 1960s the growers had relied for at least 200 years not only on casual labour from the surrounding towns and countryside but on mass migration of Londoners, poor people welcoming a chance to pick up a little money in the autumn sun. In the nineteenth century the beer consumption of a rapidly increasing population led to a huge increase in acreage devoted to hops. This and the expansion of the railway network turned hop picking into a vast Cockney holiday with its own traditions and rituals.[109]

The hop farmers gained by this attitude, as, according to George Orwell in his diary of his experiences as a hop picker in 1931, 'it was humiliating to see that most of the people here looked on it as a holiday – in fact, it is because hopping is regarded as a holiday that the pickers will take such starvation wages'.[110] The railway companies also took advantage of this annual exodus and ran 'hoppers' specials' with reduced fares from the 1850s right up to the 1960s. Initially cattle trucks were used and more trains were always needed for the return journey than the outward as many couldn't afford the fare and walked there, taking the train back as a treat with the money they had earned. Some parents were so poor they hid their children under the train seats to avoid paying for them. Special trains also brought weekend visitors, husbands, fathers and other relations to the hoppers' camps. In 1925 seventy-one 'hoppers' specials' were run by the Southern Railway into Kent and seventy-five back out.[111] They carried 34,448 hoppers and 33,950 friends on Saturdays, with another 13,850 on Sundays. Even in 1945 sixty special trains brought 30,000 hop-pickers to Kent.

The hoppers had to bring bedding and utensils from home, since few farmers would provide more than a hop poke for sleeping on, straw to fill it with and a tin basin for washing. George Orwell described his accommodation while hop picking in 1931:

> Most of us slept in round tin huts, about ten feet across, with no glass in the windows, and all kinds of holes to let in the wind and rain. The furniture of these huts consisted of a heap of straw and hop vines and nothing else . . . The farm gave us free firewood, though not as much as we needed. The tap water was two hundred yards away and the latrine the same distance, but it was so filthy that one would have walked a mile sooner than use it.[112]

The poor accommodation was not a deterrent to the hoppers, who described their attempts to make their temporary residences homely:

> A third of the hut was living area and the rest was a whitewashed wooden slatted bed like a big bench coming out from the wall. It had a hard trodden chalk floor, hard trodden chalk on earth, no floorboards or anything like that. We took our own rugs that we made, either knitted or made with hooks that you pull the wool through, to cover the floor area. The black box, my grandma's tin trunk, sat there like a bedside table. We didn't empty it because we had no cupboards, no nothing. We'd take a bit of wallpaper and a bit of net curtain to pin up to the door.

Some hoppers slept in a bed shared by the whole family made out of faggots formed from twigs tied in bundles that were delivered to the door. The faggots were separated and laid out. On top of the twigs went a mattress cover filled with straw. When the father and his friends came down to stay at weekends all the women slept at one end, and all the men at the other, with all their feet meeting in the middle. Sometimes families of ten or twelve slept in the huts together with pets. Families brought their own blankets and pillowcases were stuffed with straw. Candles or hurricane lamps provided lighting. Huts often had galvanised roofs, 'so if it poured with rain you never got no sleep. Rattled! It used to go like mad.'[113]

This was an improvement on earlier accommodation: in the nineteenth century farmers made up the hoppers' lodges from hurdles laced with straw and fastened together.[114] Later, on some farms, ex-army tents were provided. Many hop-pickers' homes in Poplar, Bermondsey and Southwark were almost equally poor, and some would use the hopping holidays to save rent and take all their belongings while 'flitting' from one landlord's room to another. An observer of 1883 cited by Colin Ward and Dennis Hardy makes the point that hop picking provided a healthy escape by giving a holiday in the sun: 'Imagine for a moment the change from a stifling court and room where the sun never shines, where pure air is never breathed, where cleanliness is unknown, to sudden transportation to one of these hop-gardens.'[115]

These sentiments regarding the health-giving properties of a period spent away from the city hop picking have been echoed in other testimonies. 'A hop picking holiday gave you health. The fumes from the hops did you a lot of good.'[116] Hoppers had to pick from seven in the morning until six in the evening. It doesn't seem much of a holiday but they valued the change of scenery in the country and enjoyed themselves despite the poor conditions.

> I think as time went on hop-picking wasn't regarded as a place to go and earn money. People loved doing it and still earned, but it wasn't anything like enough money to buy the children's things or something for yourself. There was never any difficulty of getting anybody to go to Whitbread's because it was a real holiday, it was still a holiday. They still went to the fields, they still picked, even when the urgent need for money had gone.[117]

At Whitbread's hop farm conditions were much better than at many of the smaller establishments. There was hot water available from a boiler in the field and simple showers. Up to a thousand people would live there for a few weeks, in the rows of huts on the 'common', the name given to the communal area where the hoppers' huts, fires and cookhouses were. Although facilities were very basic, the hop pickers usually had to pay for accommodation out of their earnings. Even if the bed was only straw the price of a bale, often at higher than normal cost, was deducted.[118]

The same families went hopping for generations. Some even had their regular huts which they would visit at August bank holiday to clean and decorate. During the hopping season there was music, dancing, community singing and impromptu entertainment. In the larger gardens a marquee was hired for the end-of-picking celebrations and a real holiday atmosphere prevailed. The festivities associated with the end of picking had their parallel in Harvest Home celebrations of the eighteenth and nineteenth centuries. This is indicative of the cultural continuity and conceptual change inherent in pre-industrial traditions evolving into a modern context, as discussed earlier. At the conclusion of the hop picking a feast was held. A king and queen of hop pickers were chosen and a procession was held between the hop yard and the farmhouse. Although recorded in the eighteenth century, the practice continued into the twentieth. According to a recollection of 1908, cited by Bob Bushaway, the participants saw no connection between their celebrations and earlier rituals, associated with the social cohesion of a pre-market economy. An elderly hop picker recalled that in these ceremonies 'the man had to be a smock-faced 'un. We chose a young man that 'ud make a nice gal, like, and a smart woman as 'ud make a smart boy', making no reference to any symbolic significance.[119] 'It was all a bit o' fun, you'd understand, and the king and queen opened the ball together.' George Orwell observed in 1931 that: 'On the last morning, when we had picked the last field, there was a queer game of catching the women and putting them in the bins . . . It is evidently an old custom, and all harvests have some custom of this kind attached to them.'[120]

Games and entertainment based on role reversal, such as men dressing in women's clothes, have survived from end of harvest rituals and celebrations for temporary agricultural workers beyond the twentieth century, remaining a feature of some holiday-camp and package holiday entertainment.[121] In the nineteenth century, harvest festivities and frolics took place in August, coinciding with what became the traditional holiday month. In the eighteenth century Harvest Home was 'still the greatest holiday in England: and it concludes at once the most laborious and most lucrative of the farmer's employment and unites repose and profit'.[122] Later, in 1827, Harvest Home was described as 'the great August festival of this country'.[123] The communal merrymaking ceased not because of mechanisation but because of the introduction of piece rates into agriculture, which broke the former relationship between farmers and labourers, who became concerned with profit and earning power rather than custom. These practices survived longest in the southern counties and perhaps contributed to the establishment of August as the preferred holiday month in that region just as the wakes had done in the North.

Hopping celebrations combined with the change of environment meant that hoppers regarded the picking season in Kent as a holiday. One former hopper described the experience thus:

> Hop picking's a glorified – no, reverse that: a caravan holiday is a glorified hop-picking holiday, without the fun. That's why they go in caravans, to pretend it was like down hopping. Well, it's not. The life, definitely, the life, made it fun. People have changed it. People have got so selfish and greedy. 'Cos everyone's trying to keep up with the Joneses. I wish we could go back to how it was. The holiday. The people. Lovely![124]

Hopping survived through the first half of the twentieth century until it ended owing to mechanisation in the 1960s.

It wasn't just hop picking that attracted families from industrial areas. Fruit pickers too were often city people working in the country for a few weeks a year, to get a change of air. The Select Committee on Holidays with Pay in 1938 heard in evidence that 'these people were obliged to undertake this work because otherwise they would not get a holiday, but if there was a legalised system of holidays with pay it would not be necessary for them to do this work'.[125] If the pickers were going to receive paid holidays and continue with the work, Sir Walter Citrine of the TUC didn't think that it would be 'a good thing for the country as a whole to subsidise cheap labour; to pay a man for a holiday so that he can work for anything a farmer may care to pay him'. Citrine acknowledged that the fruit and hop pickers' physical condition 'improved enormously during the time they were working in the country, but it would have improved much more if they did not work but simply enjoyed themselves for the holiday period'.[126]

Temporary work in a different environment did not have to be confined to agricultural work. A demolition worker born in 1903 in Shoreditch, London, describes how he did one job at a Leicestershire country house between long spells of unemployment in 1924. This, to him, was a holiday from life in the big city.

> I felt quite excited as we piled ourselves and our tools into the lorry and headed north – here I was, a young lad of 21, going for at least a fortnight's trip into the country. Last time I had been out of London had been for a trip to Leigh-on-Sea . . . I got more excited as we got near Tugby, because we saw a hunt, complete with red jackets, little black jockey caps, highly polished boots and crops – quite a sight for Cockney eyes.[127]

Temporary work did not have to be outdoors: free time during the course of the alternative working-week gave the opportunity for exploration and the pursuit of leisure activities. In 1870 Joseph Gutteridge took up an appointment to work a loom of six tiers of shuttles making beautiful pictures and bookmarks woven in silk at an exhibition near Bradford in Yorkshire.[128] He took this engagement so that he could visit Yorkshire and search for fossils in the area, as he had done on earlier holidays staying with friends. During his stay he also visited many places of interest such as Halifax, Kirkstall Abbey and the moors.

For children from poor families, charities, churches and youth organisations sometimes provided holidays. For young men who joined the Militia, Rifle Volunteers or Territorial Army, summer camps gave the opportunity of a week off work away from home under canvas. The Militia was a part-time form of army service dating from the Napoleonic Wars. From 1859 it became known as the Rifle Volunteers and provided a military 'hobby' for young men.[129] After 1881 these groups were attached to regular county infantry regiments, becoming the Territorial Army in 1921. The *Leicester Advertiser* reported on the local Volunteers' annual summer camp at Great Yarmouth in 1894.[130] Excursion trains took visitors to the camp from the Midlands throughout the week. This kept the camp full of visitors. Not only the lady and gentlemen friends of the rank and file but thousands of ordinary excursionists went to watch the Volunteers, regularly plying between the piers, amusements and the camp in large numbers.[131] The East Anglian Territorials' camp at Thetford in 1911 was reputed to have been the largest event of its kind in the eastern counties. Despite an early harvest, which prevented a number of men putting in an appearance, 12,000 were transported there, together with 1,100 horses, fifty guns and 150 wagons, plus tents, bedding, camping equipment and baggage.[132] The camps provided not just a change of environment for the part-time soldiers but a visual spectacle, attracting other holidaymakers and excursionists.

The temperance movement's efforts among workers and the poor were not just philanthropic but attempts to impose middle-class manners on the working class. Temperance societies offered picnics and excursions as alternatives to recreations involving the threat to morals of drunkenness and insobriety. These activities also had the ulterior motive of evangelism, to recruit new members to churches which also provided a weekly programme of voluntary pursuits such as mothers' meetings, mutual improvement groups, Christian Endeavour, cottage meetings, missions, Bible readings, choirs, Dorcas Clubs, sports clubs and plays.[133] In Charles Booth's survey of the 1890s a Presbyterian minister claimed that 'teetotal societies constituted the churches' fishing ground for more regular membership – from younger age-groups through the Band of Hope, and from lower social levels through the teetotal experience meeting'.[134] However, teetotalism was not popular with the working-class public. The famous Baptist, temperance campaigner and excursion organiser Thomas Cook was among a persecuted minority when living in Market Harborough in the 1830s.

> Harborough ranked in the estimation of the public as one of the most discordant and riotous of all anti-teetotal populations. My house in Adam and Eve Street was violently assailed, and brickbats came flying through the window to the imminent danger of Mrs Cook and myself. On one occasion a horse's leg bone, taken from a cartload of bones standing in . . . the street, was thrown at me with such violence that, striking me on the back of the neck, I was felled to the ground, and it is strange how I got up and gave chase to my assailant.[135]

Cook caught the attacker, who was brought before the magistrates and fined. This fine and others were probably paid by a notorious Market Harborough drinking club known as the Tenth. The unpopularity of militant teetotalism among adults led the campaigners to look to the future generation and in the mid-1840s they set up the Band of Hope, an organisation that worked with six to sixteen-year-olds. By March 1849 the Leeds Band of Hope had pledged more than 4,000 children.[136] The aim was to raise children in sobriety rather than concentrate on reclaiming adults. The children were encouraged to sing temperance songs and, of course, to influence their parents. The pledge was not very onerous to children who had not yet experienced temptation. By 1860 there were 129 Bands of Hope in London. Manchester and Salford had ten groups in its union when established in 1863, a number which quickly rose to 166 by 1871. By this time there were several hundred thousand child members of the Band of Hope. Meetings of the Bands of Hope usually took place fortnightly and included prayers, music, recitations and, of course, pledge signing. Occasional picnics, tea meetings and outings provided extra motivation for attendance. The Band of Hope was a respectable institution from the start. The large membership of the organisation should not give the impression that children were empty vessels into which middle-class notions of respectability could be poured. The notion of submissive and regimented children is misleading. According to Stephen Humphries, many older children and youths viewed the proceedings at meetings with humorous detachment and would gain comic relief by inverting the oaths and pledges that they were requested to make. When chanting the pledge one man recalled that he and his friends would change it to 'I promise not to abstain from alcoholic liquor'.[137] The promise of outings and tea parties made membership of the organisation by working-class youth instrumental rather than demonstrative of any commitment to teetotalism or religion.

In Leicester the Ragged School Mission was responsible for arranging the activities of Pearson's Fresh Air Fund. This was a charity designed to give poor urban children a taste of the countryside. Each year a 'treat field' was hired at the village of Thurmaston, only a short distance from the city. Every Saturday for three weeks 500 children and helpers would travel there by train from a poor district of Leicester. Recalling her childhood in the 1920s and 1930s, a woman reminisced of the Fresh Air Fund trips, 'very few children today could realise the wonder and sense of adventure these ragged, underfed children felt. First the train ride into what – for them – was the unknown ... For those 1,500 children, that single day in the country must have been a vision of near heaven.'[138] They disembarked at Rothley, from where they marched crocodile-fashion to the Treat Field, singing as they marched, the little ones being carried piggyback. Once there, the wonders had only just begun. Inside marquees were mounds of sandwiches and cakes, to be washed down with l emonade. For those who wanted it, games were organised. For others there was the delight of paddling in the stream at the bottom of the meadow, or climbing trees, or just daydreaming in the tall, sweet-smelling grass.

Recalling a camping holiday in the late 1920s, arranged by the Ragged School Mission in Leicester, a man related that transport to 'Skeggy' (Skegness) was on the back of a lorry loaned by the local coal merchant. He enthused that being 'crammed on to the lorry with a marquee and all the other apparatus required for a week's camp was the highlight of the year for us'.[139] One of the camp leader's employers donated sacks of potatoes for it, so it was a real community initiative.

The Country Holiday Fund was another philanthropic scheme, started by Lady St Hellier, to give poor children a break from urban life. A schoolteacher, who worked in Hackney between 1916 and 1923, recalled taking girls in her class to Tongham, near Farnham, for a fortnight. Those who could not afford it were helped financially by the Country Holiday Fund but the trip was already subsidised and cost only a minimum amount, she recollected.

> Most of the children had never seen the country; it was the only holiday they had. They didn't wear anything special for the holiday. They came in what they'd got – they all had to pack their own parcels, nothing very special, but all clean. Everybody at the school had the opportunity to go at some time ... The girls

slept in a conservatory which was set out like a dormitory . . . We had to make calico hats for the girls to protect their heads. We went for walks in the country and they had never seen anything like it. They did some school work while they were there, as well – a sort of educational holiday.[140]

The Scouts and Guides and other church youth organisations also held camps and took their young members on holiday. A Leicester man remembered when he joined the Boy Scouts he was asked if he would like to go on holiday. The Scouts saved up all their pennies and went to Clovelly. The boys 'had a wonderful time there . . . it was beautiful'.[141]

Oral reminiscences suggest that sport, the band and the annual camp were the activities which most attracted members to these voluntary youth associations. The prayers, drilling and military manoeuvres of the uniformed organisations were usually regarded as tiresome concessions to authority, to be avoided whenever possible.[142] The respectable ethos of these movements was often viewed with cynical detachment by working-class young people.

The co-operative movement also had its own youth organisation, the Woodcraft Folk, established to offer an alternative to the perceived militarism and religious indoctrination of the uniformed companies of Boy Scouts, Girl Guides and Boys' Brigade and Church Lads. The Woodcraft Folk encouraged socialisation into a culture of co-operation based on the ideals of the movement. Camping trips were a significant part of the organisation's activities with children and young people, offering an alternative to the inculcation of dominant cultural values of other youth movements.

A guaranteed national, or potential, tourist market could not depend on charity or individual thrift and initiative, which, as we have seen, for cultural and organisational reasons tended to be regional or dependent on membership of a particular club, organisation or occupational group. Lack of paid time off was obviously a disincentive to the development of working-class tourism, although ways and means of enjoying a holiday could be found by those who were determined. For a real mass market to develop, holidays with pay were essential.

Notes

1 Anne Martin-Fugier, 'Bourgeois rituals', in Michelle Perrot (ed.), *A History of Private Life* IV, *From the Fires of Revolution to the Great War*, Cambridge MA and London, 1990, pp. 289–307.

2 James Walvin, *Beside the seaside*, London, 1978, p. 94.

3 Cindy S. Aron, *Working at play: a history of vacations in the United States*, Oxford, 1999, p. 183.

4 John K. Walton, 'The demand for working-class seaside holidays in Victorian England', *Economic History Review* 34, 1981, pp. 249–65.

5 Patrick Joyce, *Visions of the people: industrial England and the question of class, 1848–1914*, Cambridge, 1991, p. 149.

6 Robert Poole, 'Oldham wakes', in J. K. Walton and J. Walvin (eds), *Leisure in Britain, 1780–1939*, London, 1983, pp. 71–98.

7 John K. Walton and Robert Poole, 'The Lancashire wakes in the nineteenth century', in Robert Storch (ed.), *Popular culture and custom in nineteenth century England*, Beckenham, 1982, pp. 100–24, p. 112; Douglas A. Reid, 'Interpreting the festival calendar: wakes and fairs as carnivals', pp. 125–53 in *ibid.*, p. 129.

8 Walton, 'The demand for working-class seaside holidays', p. 254.

9 M. Foucault, *The order of things*, trans. A Sheridan, London, 1970, p. xxii.

10 Peter Burke, 'Viewpoint: the invention of leisure in early modern Europe', *Past and Present* 146, February 1995, pp. 136–50, p. 139.

11 Poole, 'Oldham wakes', p. 78.

12 Walvin, *Beside the seaside*, p. 35.

13 Richard Ayton, *Voyage around Great Britain*, 1813, cited by Morris Brooke Smith, 'The growth and development of popular entertainment and pastimes in the Lancashire cotton towns, 1830–1870', M.Litt. dissertation, University of Lancaster, 1970, p. 130.

14 William Howitt, *The rural life of England*, cited by Morris Brooke Smith, 'The growth and development of popular entertainment', p. 132.

15 Harold Perkin, 'The social tone of Victorian seaside resorts', in *The structured crowd*, Brighton, 1981, pp. 70–85, p. 73.

16 John K. Walton, *The English seaside resort: a social history, 1750–1914*, Leicester, 1983, p. 28.

17 Stephen G. Jones, 'The Lancashire wakes, holiday savings and holiday pay in the textile districts', *Eccles and District Local History Society*, 1983, pp. 27–39, p. 30; Poole, 'Oldham wakes', p. 88.

18 Jones, 'The Lancashire wakes', p. 29; Poole, 'Oldham wakes', p. 88.

19 Report of HM Inspectors of Factories, 1859.

20 Tyne and Wear Archives, 745/1, Sunderland Local Committee for the Great Exhibition Minute Book.

21 Samuel Bamford, *Early days*, 1848, Cassell, 1967, chapter XV.

22 Poole, 'Oldham wakes', p. 88; Jones, 'Lancashire wakes', p. 30.

23 Poole, 'Oldham wakes', p. 88.

24 From parliamentary debates, fifth series, vol. 338, col. 1570 cited by G. C. Martin, 'Working-class holidaymaking down to 1947', M.A. thesis, University of Leicester, 1968, p. 44.

25 Poole, 'Oldham wakes', p. 88.

26 *Ashton under Lyne Reporter*, 20 August 1932, p. 8, Minutes of evidence before the Select Committee on Holidays with Pay, 1932.

27 Poole, 'Oldham wakes', p. 89; Stephen G. Jones, 'The British labour movement and working-class leisure, 1918–1939', Ph.D. thesis, University of Manchester, 1983, pp. 148–9.

28 Minutes of evidence of before the Select Committee on Holidays with Pay, 1932.

29 Martin, 'Working-class holidaymaking', p. 44.

30 *Ibid.*, p. 45.

31 *Progress*, Lever Brothers' magazine, February 1905, cited by Martin, 'Working-class holidaymaking', p. 45.

32 *Leicester Mercury*, 2 August 1935.

33 *Ibid.*, 3 August 1935.

34 John K. Walton, *The Blackpool landlady*, Manchester, 1979, pp. 38–9.

35 *Leicester Mercury*, 2 August 1919 and 1 August 1925.

36 *Ibid.*, 2 August 1930.

37 North Warwickshire and Hinckley College, Hinckley College library, ERDF, Arqueotex Textile Heritage Project, Nellie Skelton, oral reminiscence, interview cassette-recorded by Rhianydd Murray, 6 June 1998.

38 Su Barton and Rhianydd Murray, *Twisted yarns: the story of the hosiery industry in Hinckley*, ERDF Arqueotex Textile Heritage Project, North Warwickshire and Hinckley College, 1999, p. 72.

39 G. le M. M., *The history of Mander Brothers, 1773–1953*, London, 1953, p. 250.

40 *Ibid.*, p. 249.

41 Poole, 'Oldham wakes', pp. 90–2.

42 Jones, 'The Lancashire wakes', p. 29.

43 Edwin Hopwood, *A history of the Lancashire cotton industry and the Amalgamated Weavers' Association*, Manchester, 1969, p. 125.

44 Jones, 'The Lancashire wakes', p. 28.

45 Gary Cross (ed.), *Worktowners at Blackpool: Mass-Observation and popular leisure in the 1930s*, London, 1990, p. 9.

46 Walton, *The English seaside resort*, p. 256.

47 Cross, *Worktowners at Blackpool*, p. 99.

48 Poole, 'Oldham wakes', p. 92.

49 Walton, 'The demand for working-class seaside holidays'.

50 Jones, 'The Lancashire wakes', p. 30.

51 Alex Callinicos, *Making history*, Cambridge, 1987, pp. 134–5.

52 John Foster, *Class struggle and the industrial revolution: early industrial capitalism in three English towns*, London, 1977, pp. 125–49.

53 *Leicestershire Chronicle*, 17 June 1848; *Leicester Mercury*, 10 August 1850; *Friend of the People*, 8 March 1851.

54 Georg Lukács, cited by Thomas Richards, *The commodity culture of Victorian England: advertising and spectacle*, Stanford CA, 1990, repr. London and New York, 1991, p. 14.

55 Richards, *The commodity culture of Victorian England*, p. 14.

56 Walton, 'The demand for working-class seaside holidays', p. 258.

57 *Ibid.*, p. 259.

58 Douglas Reid, 'The decline of St Monday, 1766–1876', *Past and Present* 71, 1976, pp. 76–101.

59 G. I. H. Lloyd, *The cutlery trades: an historical essay in the economics of small-scale production*, London, 1913, p. 181.

60 *Ibid.*, p. 182.

61 John Lowerson, 'Brothers of the angle: coarse fishing and English working-class culture, 1850–1914', in J. A. Mangan (ed.), *Pleasure, profit, proselytism: British culture and sport at home and abroad, 1700–1914*, London, 1988, pp. 105–7, p. 124

62 Douglas Reid, 'The "iron roads" and the "happiness of the working classes": the early development of the railway excursion', *Journal of Transport History*, third series, 17:1, 1996, pp. 57–73, p. 61.

63 Lloyd, *The cutlery trades*, p. 110.

64 Leader, *History of the Cutlers' Company*, n.d., p. 63, cited by Lloyd, *The cutlery trades*, p. 111.

65 Ronald E. Wilson, *Two hundred precious metal years: a history of the Sheffield Smelting Company, 1760–1960*, London, 1960, p. 75.

66 Lloyd, *The cutlery trades*, p. 111.

67 Sidney Pollard, *History of the labour movement in Sheffield*, Liverpool University Press, 1957, p. 61.

68 Lloyd, *The cutlery trades*, p. 180.

69 For example, match factory workers and piano workers, described by Booth in *Life and labour of the people of London* IV, *The trades of east London connected with poverty*, London, 1989, 1902 edn.

70 Pollard, *History of the labour movement in Sheffield*, p. 61.

71 Rhyme recited by Mr Fred Dunkley of South Wigston, Leicestershire, born 1906.

72 Pollard, *History of the labour movement in Sheffield*, p. 62; Lloyd, *The cutlery trades*, p. 181.

73 Pollard, *History of the labour movement in Sheffield*, pp. 61–2.

74 *Ibid.*, p. 211.

75 Reid, 'The decline of St Monday', p. 101.

76 Walton, 'The demand for working-class seaside holidays', p. 261.

77 C. R. Ashbee, 'The last records of a Cotswold community', quoted by Bob Bushaway in *By rite: custom, ceremony and community in England, 1700–1880*, London, 1982, p. 246.

78 'The diary of William Andrews', in William Andrews and Joseph Gutteridge, *Master and artisan in Victorian England*, London, 1969, pp. 57–8.

79 W. Felkin, *An account of the machine-wrought hosiery trade, its extent and the condition of the framework knitters, being a paper read at the statistical section, at the second York meeting of the British Association, held September 18 1844, together with evidence given under the Hosiery Commission inquiry*, London, 1845, pp. 19 and 20.

80 *Ibid.*

81 *Leicester Mercury*, 2 and 3 August 1935.

82 Andrew Walker, 'Pleasurable homes? Victorian model miners' wives and the family wage in a nineteenth-century South Yorkshire colliery district', *Women's History Review* 6:3, 1997, pp. 317–36, p. 323.

83 Walton, 'The demand for working-class seaside holidays', p. 258.

84 John Benson, *British coal miners in the nineteenth century*, Dublin, 1980, pp. 56–7.

85 Walton, 'The demand for working-class seaside holidays', p. 262.

86 Thomas Wright (The Journeyman Engineer), *The great unwashed*, London, 1868, repr. 1970, p. 235.

87 *Ibid.*, p. 236.

88 J. A. R. Pimlott, *The Englishman's holiday*, London, 1947, p. 148.

89 Rev. William Arthur, M.A., 'Saturday half-holidays and the earlier payment of wages', speeches delivered at the Exeter Hall meeting, 24 April 1856, p. 24.

90 Andrew Spottiswoode, 'Saturday half-holidays and the earlier payment of wages', speeches delivered at the Exeter Hall meeting, p. 26.

91 Lloyd, *The cutlery trades*, p. 181.

92 Peter J. T. Morris, Colin Russell and John Graham Smith (eds), *Archives of the British chemical industry, 1750–1914: a hand list*, British Society for the History of Science, monograph 6, Faringdon, 1988, p. 114.

93 George Hitchcock, 'Saturday half-holidays and earlier payment of wages', speeches delivered at the Exeter Hall meeting, p. 31.

94 Index to the report of the Select Committee on the Bank Holidays Bill, House of Commons, 22 June 1868, p. 5.

95 Index to the report of the Select Committee on the Bank Holidays Bill, p. 5.

96 *Ibid.*, p. 19 .

97 Pimlott, *The Englishman's holiday*, p. 148.

98 R. Marchant, 'Early excursion trains', *Railway Magazine* 100:638, June 1954, pp. 426–9, p. 429.

99 *Leicester Journal*, 2 and 9 August 1872; *Leicester Daily Mercury*, 4 August 1874.

100 Pimlott, *The Englishman's holiday*, p. 149.

101 Walton, 'The demand for working-class seaside holidays', p. 264.

102 Skegness holiday guide, Skegness Tourist Office, 1989.

103 Margaret Stacey, *Tradition and change: a study of Banbury*, Oxford, 1960, p. 128.

104 Cynthia Brown, *Wharf Street revisited*, Leicester, 1997, p. 90.

105 *Ibid.*, testimony of Mr Britten, p. 90.

106 Joseph Gutteridge, 'The Autobiography of Joseph Gutteridge', in Andrews and Gutteridge, *Master and Artisan in Victorian England*, London, 1969, p. 207.

107 Ross McKibbin, *The ideologies of class: social relations in Britain, 1880–1950*, Oxford, 1994, p. 164.

108 Reminiscence of Stanley Rose in Age Exchange Theatre Trust, *Our lovely hops: memories of hop picking in Kent*, London, 1991, p. 7.

109 Colin Ward and Dennis Hardy, *Goodnight, campers*, London, 1986, p. 8.

110 George Orwell, 'Hop picking', *Collected essays, journalism and letters of George Orwell* I, *An age like this, 1920–1940*, London, 1968, p. 66.

111 Ward and Hardy, *Goodnight, campers*, pp. 9–10.

112 Orwell, 'Hop picking', p. 63.

113 Reminiscence of Marjorie Balcombe in *Our lovely hops*, p. 23.

114 Ward and Hardy, *Goodnight, campers*, p. 10.

115 *Ibid.*, p. 11.

116 Age Exchange Theatre Company, *Fifty years ago: memories of the 1930s*, London, 1983, cited by Christopher Hibbert, *The English*, London, 1987, p. 687.

117 Reminiscence of Kathleen Ash in *Our lovely hops*, p. 62.

118 Select Committee on Holidays with Pay, evidence of Sir Walter Citrine, p. 44, paras 261–7.

119 Bushaway, *By rite*, p. 137.

120 Orwell, 'Hop picking', p. 67.

121 A 'beauty contest' where men dressed in their partners' clothes on an Airtours holiday in Tunisia was observed in 1994. On the Costa Brava in 1997 hotel staff dressed up to entertain guests, involving some role reversals.

122 David Hoseason Morgan, *Harvesters and harvesting, 1840–1900*, London, 1982, p. 168.

123 *Ibid.*, p. 167.

124 Gilda O'Neill, *Pull no more bines: hop picking memories of a vanished way of life*, London, 1990, p. 127.

125 Select Committee on Holidays with Pay, evidence of Sir Walter Citrine, p. 44, para. 268.

126 *Ibid.*, p. 44, para. 262.

127 Reminiscence of John Welch, 'demolition labourer', *Working lives* I, *1905–1945*, Hackney, 1975, p. 45.

128 Gutteridge, 'Autobiography of Joseph Gutteridge', p. 211.

129 John Cannon, *Oxford companion to British history*, Oxford, 1997, p. 642.

130 *Leicester Advertiser*, 12 August 1894.

131 *Ibid.*

132 *Great Eastern Railway Magazine* 1:8, 1911, p. 274.

133 Brian Harrison, *Drink and the Victorians: the temperance question in England, 1815–1872*, London, 1971, p. 24.

134 Charles Booth, *Life and labour in London*, third series, V, 1902 edn, p. 155, cited by Brian Harrison, *Drink and the Victorians*, p. 171.

135 Thomas Cook, unreferenced source cited by Robert Ingle in *Thomas Cook of Leicester*, Bangor, Gwynedd, 1991, p. 5.

136 Harrison, *Drink and the Victorians*, p. 192.

137 Stephen Humphries, *Hooligans or rebels? An oral history of working-class childhood and youth, 1898–1939*, Oxford, 1981, p. 133.

138 Brown, *Wharf Street revisited*, p. 89.

139 Testimony of Dorothy Rayson of Leicester, cited in *ibid.*, p. 89.

140 Reminiscence of Ida Allison, *née* Rex, in *Working lives* I, *1905–1945*, p. 24.

141 Reminiscence of Mr Ernie Martin, cited by Brown, *Wharf Street revisited*, p. 91.

142 Humphries, *Hooligans or rebels?* p. 134.

5

Collective bargaining for holidays with pay

The efforts discussed in the last chapter secured holidays away from home, or at least a change of air, for only a small minority of the working class, but their demands led to the development of resorts and amenities for visitors in seaside towns like Blackpool, which by the 1930s was supposed to have had 7 million visitors a year, and Southend, which annually attracted 5.5 million.[1] It was not so much the number receiving paid holidays that was important as acceptance of the principle. Pimlott argued in 1944 that the preferential treatment of salaried and a few black-coated workers was resented by manual workers, who seem to have regarded pay without work as a contradiction in terms. 'A man should be well paid for the time he is at work and lose time for holidays,' the Sheffield Engine Drivers' and Stokers' Society told the 1894 Royal Commission on Labour. 'A man that wants paying without working is a drone to his fellow men.'[2] George Potter of the London Working Men's Association told the select committee on the Sale of Liquors on Sunday Bill in 1868, anticipating the Bank Holidays Act, that there should be less work on weekdays and instead of Sundays being spent in recreation there should be some sort of national holidays on which working people could enjoy a change of air. Potter did not foresee that these holidays might be taken with payment. 'I should anticipate that before such things are adopted a man will have more money for his labour, in order that he may be able to afford to lose his time.'[3] Payment for not working was anathema, and paid holidays had to be accepted into working-class culture as an antidote to summer shutdowns and layoffs. Some felt payment for holidays an attack on their independence. The Royal Commission on Labour reported no cases of unions asking for paid time off but was concerned that in the textile industry people would go on strike in order to get a break. In the nineteenth century paid leave was not a necessity; having adequate income to cover necessities and then allow saving was. The attitude of manual workers to those paid for time off changed from the belief that it was unreasonable to resentment that they were denied equality. A signalman's letter to the Great Central Railway's staff magazine in 1906 testified, 'it "bites" very hard to hear the office boy with a few months' service jubilantly assert that he is taking his six or ten-day holiday with perhaps "passes" to any part of the country whilst men with five to forty-five years' service are limited to four days and passes over the company's system only'.[4]

It now remains to examine how payment for holidays was achieved, at first by a minority of workers in organised sections of the labour force and eventually by almost all those permanently employed. Before exploring how workers achieved their employers' sanction and later payment for their holidays it must be acknowledged that, before the predominance of large-scale mechanised production, workers in small workshops without motive power were able to control the hours they worked and have time off when it suited them. In his London research of 1889 Booth found that even among the poorest, as well as among well paid workers, unauthorised holidays were prevalent. He found it not uncommon for saddle tree makers to go 'on the booze' for weeks at a time. Pianoforte workers did not want to work all year round. Booth said, 'hard work and large earnings succeeded by idleness and hard drinking make exactly the life that suits them'.[5] He also noted that for some casual workers it was this spurious independence that compensated for their precarious existence.

Motive power and large-scale production made the earlier control over working hours untenable. Before holidays for the working class could be redeveloped, it was imperative for both time and financial resources to be available. Those in occupations with a high degree of trade union organisation were in the strongest position to secure these resources.

When looking at how workers achieved more leisure time and paid leave from work through collective bargaining it must be remembered that by the time of the Holidays with Pay Act most clerical and non-manual workers already had holidays taken into account when calculating pay, an arrangement which derived from their status through established custom and practice.[6] Examples can be found dating back to the early nineteenth century. This presented no problems, as the pay could be calculated on the basis of fifty weeks but divided into fifty-two or twelve instalments. In 1875 the Civil Service Enquiry Board discovered the usual allowance for office workers was a fortnight or more for long service.[7] At Pilkington Brothers' glassworks in 1876 both production and office staff enjoyed three days' holiday a year, including the Friday of Newton race week in June, showing the continued importance of local custom. This changed to Whit Monday about 1880. August bank holiday was not taken until 1882. Departmental managers sometimes had a week's paid holiday but the employers did not encourage it. When one manager, who earned £5 10s a week, was away his work was covered by a deputy earning only £3. The board decided to deduct the difference between the two wages from his holiday pay and added the note, 'last year we paid him in full but holydays (*sic*) are becoming more the fashion and it behoves us to check the tendency'.[8] At the Sheffield Smelting Company staff had a paid fortnight off in summer from 1882 plus all the general holidays. Manual employees were paid only for two days.[9] In the public sector, local government officers and civil service clerks had negotiated leave of at least two weeks by 1919.[10] By 1920 the Whitley Council for the civil service gave holidays ranging from twenty-four days for the lowest grades to forty-eight for the highest. The Civil and Public Servants' Association in 1921 was pressing for the minimum leave to be extended to include typists and shorthand typists, who had been excluded from previous arrangements. Its conference passed a resolution asking for twenty-four days' holiday for all, rising to twenty-eight days for those with over five years' service and thirty-six for those with over ten years'. This was still not fully achieved by 1932 when the arrangements concerning holidays were extended.[11] The expectation of paid leave by white-collar workers had become the norm even in the private sector by the 1930s. Herbert Elvin, General Secretary of the National Union of Clerks and Administrative Workers, in 1932 was able to write to the TUC, 'in regard to clerical and administration workers, paid holidays are the rule rather than the exception'.[12] White-collar workers were in a privileged position regarding working conditions compared with most manual workers.

It has already been shown that workers in the cotton textile industry were able to secure a full week off work for the wakes by the last quarter of the nineteenth century. The textile workers made financial provision for this themselves through their savings clubs. The process of recognition by employers of the operatives' right to a holiday through negotiation began in the middle of the century. A delegation representing textile workers in 1850 asked the main employers to extend the July holiday from one day to two. This was agreed, 'an indulgence for which the operatives . . . warmly expressed their thanks'.[13] Following a successful wage campaign in 1890 by spinners in the Cotton Workers' Association, the union merged with the Card Room Workers in 1893. The resulting closed shop was strongly organised and when mill owners refused to improve holiday arrangements operatives took them unilaterally.[14] Lancashire weavers were covered by a county-wide agreement between the Cotton Employers' Parliamentary Association and the United Textile Factory Workers' Association from December 1906. This provided for 116½ working hours or eleven and a half days' annual holiday. In June 1914 holidays were extended to 136½ hours following a ballot. As well as breaks at Easter and Christmas, the cotton workers ceased work from the Friday before wakes week until the Monday following. These breaks were unpaid, financed by the workers' savings. Twenty-three years later, giving evidence before the Select Committee on Holidays with Pay, employers claimed that it was 'understood that the earnings of the workers in fifty weeks allow ample provision for holidays'. On behalf of the unions the TUC disputed this and emphasised that in negotiations it was never recognised that holidays had to be provided for out of the earnings of the weeks of employment.[15] Employers believed that workers were satisfied with these arrangements and were able to put by a good deal more than a week's wages for their holiday, as they appeared well dressed, seemed to have plenty to spend and came back to say what a grand time they'd had. They did not think that workers made sacrifices to save, as 'they did not notice them walking about miserable saving up for their holidays'.[16] Walter Citrine of the TUC responded to the committee, 'this is the real danger of thrift, the employers count it up and use it as evidence against the workmen'.[17] The TUC found it impossible to believe from the weekly earnings figures that normal earnings were enough to enable workers in many large industries, including textiles, to save in the course of a year's employment enough for a sufficiently protracted and attractive holiday.[18] Employers' evidence was misleading to people who might not realise that Lancashire people saved in clubs not only for holidays but for clothing, furniture and old age. Some clubs even provided borrowing facilities. This implies that, rather than having money left for saving for holidays after paying for life's necessities, clubs were used by the low-paid to acquire essentials. In textile work, women frequently worked full-time after marriage out of economic necessity. Men's wages were often low compared with those in other areas, which encouraged married women to work. The lives of women workers, and by implication those of the rest of the family, were stressful and demanding in the extreme. 'It was bed and work all the time,' was a common complaint.[19] Housework had to be fitted in before work started at 6.00 a.m. or afterwards from 6.30 p.m., involving the whole family in a ceaseless round of toil. No wonder textile communities valued the change of routine and relaxation of the wakes so much they developed collective methods of ensuring a holiday.

As the mills tended to close during wakes week, though, saving was a necessity not a choice. Mass-Observation's evidence highlighted the problems caused by unpaid holidays. As well as excitement at the prospect of going away there was always a certain strain because of the discomfort of the ever-present awareness that next week there would be no wage packet. One Bolton worker told an observer that when his holiday was over he was generally spent up. It took a few weeks to get back on the financial level.[20] The communal aspects of saving reflect what Patrick Joyce saw as a local and regional identity of popular values in Lancashire.[21]

Similarly, in other older industries based around particular communities, established local traditions influenced patterns of holidaymaking. Bull, cow and calf weeks, described earlier, allowed coal miners, Sheffield steel workers and framework knitters and others to take time off. Originally this reflected workers' control of the production processes but this style of working became essential as mechanisation gathered workers together into larger workplaces where production stopped for the whole work force, who had no choice but to take time off. As holidays for manual workers became more acceptable to employers after the First World War, those employed in these and other trades secured negotiated unpaid leave. To finance this, savings schemes were adopted. Some of them were voluntary, run by the workers themselves, as in Lancashire, but many of the newer schemes were administered by employers. Some firms made a small contribution as a 'gift', in exchange for good conduct and attendance. In the boot and shoe trades, paid holidays became a demand in 1914 when Leicester workers called for equality with office staff who received seven days' paid leave and bank holiday payment.[22] Although unanimously carried by the union the concept contained in this resolution was treated with derision by the trade papers. Changes in previous conventions and values that came about during the Great War allowed the claim to appear more realistic. By the middle of the war some shoe operatives were receiving holidays with half-pay. In 1918 workers in the co-operative movement shoe factories were granted six days' paid leave a year. That same year Bostock & Co. of Leicester circulated details of a contributory holiday savings scheme. In this for every 4d saved by operatives the employer would donate an additional 1d. The footwear industry's Joint Industrial Council drew up a savings scheme recommended to all employees in 1919. The employer paid into a Holiday Savings Fund a sum equal to the worker's minimum weekly wage. The worker made the same contribution in weekly instalments, creating two weeks' wages in a pool to be drawn on at holiday time throughout the year. The system was widely adopted

and in some factories employers saved clerical expense by not taking contributions from the workers.[23] The scheme also had a disciplinary effect, as
contributions had to be made weekly. Absenteeism could count against a
worker who might not be eligible for the employer's 'gift'. Not all firms
welcomed the scheme and in 1935 a strike occurred in Hinckley as a result
of employers reneging on the agreement. Operatives should have been paid
non-contributory holiday money accumulated between Whitsun and the
August break, the workers being responsible for their own contributions.
When the holiday came round no money was forthcoming but the ensuing
strike was quickly victorious and the employer's share promptly paid out.[24]

Building workers benefited from a similar scheme, which was more complicated to administer because of the frequent changes of employer from job
to job.[25] In coal mining, too, where there had been a tradition of voluntary
absenteeism, savings schemes were introduced in the twentieth century to provide for loss of earnings during enforced or negotiated holidays. In 1842 the
only recognised holidays were Christmas Day, Good Friday and a day or two
at Whitsun. Miners, though, did not work continuously the rest of the time.
Absenteeism was particularly noticeable among those who had working wives
and in periods of prosperity when hewers could earn enough to live on relatively easily. In South Wales they usually took the first Monday off in every
month, known as St Mabon's Day after a miners' leader. This ended after defeat
in a five-month dispute in the 'Great Lockout' of 1898 at the Powell Duffryn
colliery.[26] It was abolished officially in 1905 in the Coalfield Conciliation
Board agreement.[27] As a legacy a South Wales Miners' Federation was born
amid increasing militancy. *The Miners' Next Step* was published in 1912 by
the unofficial reform committee of the federation in reaction to the conciliatory policies of the main organisation from 1900 onwards. One of the aims of
this syndicalist group was that 'mankind shall have leisure and inclination to
really live as men and not as the beasts that perish'.[28]

Nationally miners continued to uphold and even extend unpaid holidays,
supported by bull weeks. During the First World War they agreed to limit the
number of days they took off each year. In 1920 employers refused a request
from the Derbyshire Miners' Association for a fortnight's paid holiday,
included with their wage claim.[29] Miners' demands for increased leisure time
continued. Charles Markham told the Samuel Commission that 'too much time
is taken by the colliers on holidays. The average time worked by colliers when
trade is good is only about 230 days a year.'[30] Colliery owners saw the demand
for holidays with pay as absurd, as it would put production costs up. When a

paid holiday was proposed to the employers in South Wales in 1934 the response was 'one can only regard this proposal as far too Utopian to be within the range of practical politics as far as we in this coalfield, or any coalfield in the country, are concerned'.[31] Despite time off, low wages meant that few miners at that time could actually afford to go away on holiday. Only a few piece workers on exceptionally high wages could afford to take their families for a week at the seaside in the 1930s.[32] It was a savings scheme similar to the ones described already that enabled miners to make the transition from unpaid holidays to paid leave. As colliery closures regulated periods of leave, savings schemes were administered by the employers into which miners paid weekly and to which the employer made an additional contribution. The Bolsover colliery began closing the pits for a week in summer and giving the miners gifts to help them to enjoy a holiday. As the payments were gifts the miners could also claim Unemployment Benefit. The company paid men from a fund to which the miners themselves had contributed most of the money, owners and men subscribing to it in the ratio of 15 : 85.[33] The Durham Miners' Association and that of Nottinghamshire also had similar schemes subsidised by 15 per cent.[34] To describe these savings systems as arrangements for holidays with pay would be a mistake, as 85 per cent of the money belonged to the miners themselves. What made it attractive was the added bonus of Unemployment Benefit on top of the savings pay-out. A number of test cases countering the unemployed status of miners were brought before the Court of Referees in 1938, some of which were successful. The Derbyshire Miners' Association argued it was a savings scheme, since the men contributed 85 per cent of the fund, but the court decided they were getting deferred wages and were therefore not entitled to Unemployment Benefit.[35] The Derbyshire Association urged its branches to continue with the savings scheme and supplemented savings with unemployment benefits from its own funds.[36] A development of this scheme was the building of the Derbyshire Miners' Camp near Skegness. Negotiations with railway companies led to the arrangement of cheap fares from Derbyshire to Skegness that enabled many miners and their families to have a week at the seaside for the first time.[37]

Genuine paid holidays where employees received fifty-two weeks' wages every year without having to save up or contribute to it themselves, outside the clerical sector and civil service, were first achieved by manual workers providing essential public services or who were highly organised in trade unions, although there were isolated examples for the Great Exhibition. Antedating 1851, the South Metropolitan Gas Company granted wages on Good Friday and Christmas Day. From 1860 it was paying workers in constant employment for a week's holiday.[38] This advance was a form of discipline to encourage good attendance and loyalty. However, it did not apply to gas workers in other companies and it was 1920 before holidays with pay applied to the industry nationally.[39] This gain corresponded with the short boom following the First World War, when British trade union membership reached a record high of about 8.25 million, before the sudden and rapid decline commencing the following year.

At Brunner Mond & Co. in Northwich paid holidays were also an incentive to encourage regular attendence. Only 42 per cent of employees qualified for paid leave in 1884, a figure that rose to 98 per cent in the early 1900s, showing a change in workers' attitude to unauthorised absence as well as the effectiveness of the firm's strategy. In 1902 just two days' absence could lose someone their holiday pay but the firm paid two weeks' money for only one week's leave.[40] A savings club existed at the works from 1881 showing holidays were already an important aspect of working life. Brunner Mond also reduced its shifts from twelve to eight hours without loss of pay in 1890. At the Metal Box Company, where modern personnel methods began to be adopted between 1906 and 1912, a week's paid holiday became available, depending on good timekeeping. Even those with only a month's service qualified for four bank holidays off without loss of wages.[41] Once entitlement to paid leave was on the agenda, the wording of some agreements still made it clear that paid holidays were not an automatic right but a privilege related to good conduct. The Chemical Joint Industrial Council in 1930 negotiated criteria for annual holidays. A week's holiday on full pay was to be given to every worker who fulfilled conditions relating not just to continuity of employment but also to the fact that 'he must not have lost without reasonable excuse . . . more than five days in the case of day men or six shifts. Additionally his work and conduct generally must have been satisfactory.' Only the basic wage without overtime was paid, so chemical workers might still be financially disadvantaged despite paid leave.[42] As late as 1953 disciplinary processes were still sometimes being linked with paid leave. Mander Brothers' workers received a maximum of two working weeks, provided that lost time did not exceed six normal working days. For seven days' work lost one week's holiday was forfeited, with another day lost for each day of absence above seven. Fortunately what counted as lost days was not too stringent. Certified sickness and unavoidable absence due to unforeseen circumstances were not held against the employee.[43]

Railway workers, too, were able to achieve holidays with pay through the collective bargaining process from 1872, when three days were granted by the Great Northern Railway to the Amalgamated Society of Railway Servants' members with at least a year's service. Public opinion had a role to play here. Rail workers' fatigue was recognised as a contributory factor in accidents, as publicised in 1870, when companies overworking men to the point where their senses were numbed were blamed for the high accident rate.[44] After the Second Reform Act of 1867, extending the franchise to include some of the artisan classes, aspiring politicians had to respect the opinion of better-paid railway employees, not all of whom were manual workers. The London & North Western Railway from 1890 gave a great proportion of the men a week off with pay. This too was discretionary, a reward for good conduct and attendance.[45] Not all railway servants were able to benefit from paid holidays. Stationmasters and signalmen on the Great Central Railway complained in letters to the company magazine in the first decade of the twentieth century that they did not get the holidays they were entitled to. Correspondence from a signalman described the longing of men in his occupation for their annual leave.[46] Bells and telephones ringing all day with no margin of error allowed made the job extremely stressful. Sadly the man complained that because demand for their work was so high, he and other signalmen could not be spared until the winter, when they were compelled to stay by the fireside. A stationmaster in 1907 claimed he had had no holiday at all the previous year although it had been repeatedly pressed for. He was required to be at his station between 6.30 a.m. and 10.30 p.m. and had had no Sunday off for eight months.

The picture was less bleak for workers with some other railway companies. Any employee with the Great Eastern Railway received three days' paid leave, rising to four days for those with over five years' service. These workers were given an unlimited number of 'privilege tickets' by means of which a railwayman and his dependants could travel anywhere in Britain at quarter-fare. Twice a year they were granted free passes, one of which had to be used at the August holiday, for travel on Great Eastern trains. Many of the Great Eastern's employees worked at Stratford in east London. As hardly any of them failed to make use of their passes the August exodus of about 8,000 railway workers and their families from Stratford was quite an event. The works closed down completely just before the bank holiday. Most popular destinations accessible by free pass were Yarmouth, Southend and Clacton. Some went farther; to get to Scarborough (on another company's system) a GER worker could travel to York free of charge and then complete the journey with a privilege ticket costing only 1*s* 9*d*.[47]

A demonstration of the change in attitudes to paid holidays during the First World War was the demand for fourteen days' paid leave made at the railway union's 'After war matters' conference in Leicester in November 1917. Peace brought many industrial disputes after the wartime ban. Andrew Bonar Law, deputising for Lloyd George, agreed to make concessions to the Association of Locomotive Engineers and Firemen as the government couldn't afford a show-down while simultaneous volatile negotiations were going on with the miners. Bonar Law agreed to guaranteed pay for a guaranteed working week and a week's holiday with pay after one year's service, with extra payment for working nights and on Sundays, an important recognition of the right to leisure time.[48] These terms were not offered to members of the National Union of Railwaymen, who would have suffered pay cuts as a result of the offer made to them. After the victory of ASLEF Lloyd George's government wanted an end to the industrial crisis. The well prepared government believed it could crush the NUR in a sectional dispute, having already settled with ASLEF. Troops were called out, alternative transport was arranged and local authorities were asked to enrol a citizens' guard. The NUR was totally unprepared for action. Ignored pleas to the Prime Minister for more time to negotiate forced it into strike action.[49]

Nothing, it seemed, had been overlooked to make certain that the NUR would be routed and trade unionism taught a lesson. But in fact one thing had been overlooked – an intangible quality which Lloyd George and his colleagues were incapable of understanding – the solidarity of industrial workers in crisis.[50] The government had misjudged the situation. ASLEF came out on strike in support. In solidarity the co-operative movement made food and supplies available to the strikers.[51] The strike was victorious after just a week, the cuts were abandoned and ASLEF's agreement, including holiday pay, was extended to cover all sections of the railway work force. This proved to be the last major victory of the trade union movement in the immediate post-war period. Not everyone was satisfied, and in July 1919 the Railway Clerks' Association and the Amalgamated Society of Railway Servants agreed a programme of demands, including, unsuccessfully, twenty-one days' paid holiday. The Depression and later the Second World War delayed any further improvements in holidays.

Organised workers in the printing industry also secured paid holidays through negotiation. When trade was booming and prices were rising in the 1850s the Typographical Association won successive wage rises and reductions in hours but not the Saturday half-holiday until the 1870s. In 1891 the

Manchester branch secured an annual week's holiday with pay for all compositors on newspapers as part of a settlement on wages and hours, claiming that many other print employees already received this concession.[52] Dissatisfaction with the wages and hours agreement of 1911, which secured a fifty-one-hour working week, led to calls for a forty-eight-hour week and also paid holidays. The outbreak of war prevented any progress along these lines but the demands became Typographical Association policy and set the precedent for the post-war settlement.[53]

Until 1918 conditions of employment in all industries tended to be set through local agreements but the war brought a move towards national agreements and the standardisation of conditions throughout large-scale industry. During the short post-war boom the Printing and Kindred Trades' Federation negotiated the Hours and Holidays Agreement, applying across the different graphical trades. This set the standard working week at forty-eight hours, 5 per cent piece rate rises and one week's holiday paid for at the ordinary 'stab' rate or average weekly earnings for piece workers. Time-and-a-half rates were paid to those who had to work on bank holidays, plus time off in lieu.[54] The boost in confidence this gave increased the union membership of PKTF affiliates from 75,000 in 1914 to 190,000 in 1920. In the 1930s the PKTF unsuccessfully pressed for a fortnight's paid holiday.

After the short post-war boom, coupled with growing union confidence, had secured paid holidays for workers in large-scale, stongly organised industries, workers in a less favourable bargaining position were unable to secure similar concessions for almost two decades because of the ensuing Depression. Other organised trades made no progress regarding paid holidays until the mid to late 1930s. One such industry was pottery, where there was no pay rise between 1931 and 1937. The revival of the trade in 1937 was enough to give pottery workers in the Ceramic and Allied Trades Union confidence to campaign for a rise for the first time in five years. That spring, not only did they secure a rise of 2.5 per cent but holidays with pay given on a fixed scale with different rates for boys, adult males and women and an influx of new members.[55]

Foundry workers, too, had to wait until after the recession for any progress regarding holidays. The situation here shows the relationship between union organisation, economic circumstances and holidays. Wages were reduced during the Slump in the 1920s and then again between 1929 and 1932. The Iron Workers' Association was the first foundry union to join the campaign for holidays with pay in 1934. In 1938 came the winning of six days' paid holiday, although there had long been unpaid traditional holidays, regarded as unemployment without dole. Within two months a similar agreement was reached between the Iron and Steel Trades Employers' Association and the National Light Castings and Iron Founders' Union. The situation in engineering was similar to that in the foundries. In the early 1930s paid holidays were virtually unknown and the summer shutdowns 'known as lockouts'. The issue of holidays was not taken up by the Amalgamated Engineering Union until 1935. The employers conceded the principle of paid holidays during the 1937 negotiations. The engineers were offered half their rise in higher wages, the rest in paid holidays. All firms federated to the union were to inaugurate holiday funds into which one-fifth of the value of each week's wages was paid.[56] The steel industry too was a prominent industrial sector where no paid leave was received until the late 1930s when the Holidays with Pay Act appeared imminent. Steelworkers received a paid holiday for the first time for the King's silver jubilee in 1935. The following year a conference was held at Swansea to consider wage issues. This meeting heard a report showing that progress was being made towards holidays with pay and that generally the principle was accepted. A bonus of £2 was given for August bank holiday week in 1937 to workers over twenty-one and £1 given to those younger. In Sheffield a scheme was agreed providing a week's paid leave for smelters in Siemens open-hearth and electric furnace plants. Later this agreement was extended to cover all Sheffield's rolling mills, forges and press shops.[57] Steelworkers outside Sheffield had to wait for the outcome of the Select Committee on Holidays with Pay.

Some industries made no progress regarding holidays despite efforts to win them in negotiations. The hosiery union demanded paid holidays before 1920, when the concession seemed just weeks away. The Slump hit the industry and the demand was not actually achieved until after the Second World War. Weakened, the union was unable to maintain existing wages and conditions, let alone press for paid holidays. The subject was not raised again until 1937. Members felt cheated when negotiators dropped the demand after employers pointed out that a compulsory scheme was imminent. The war delayed a holiday agreement until 1948, when modest interim wartime arrangements ended. The agreement was updated in 1951, when a new settlement was reached.

Convinced of the justice of the issue, the Trades Union Congress was urged by its constituent members to make the issue of paid holidays an aspiration of the entire labour movement. This meant that the campaign would be undertaken on behalf of the whole working class, not just members of particular trades and industries in a favourable bargaining position. When the TUC first debated the proposal in 1911 it had met with little serious consideration. As has been shown, some well organised unions had achieved payment for periods of annual leave in the years immediately after the First World War. Workers employed by the co-operative movement also benefited from such agreements early compared with other manual workers. In Lancashire, the Manchester and District, Bolton and District and Co-operative Wages Board and Journeyman Butchers' Federation Agreement on Holidays in 1922 gave holidays ranging from three days for employees with less than six months' service and six days for all others.[58] No deductions for bank holidays and other recognised holidays were made either. This agreement combined with the mill workers' tradition of saving for holidays to cover thirteen and a half days off at this time, would have made an annual period of leave practically universal in the textile-producing region of Lancashire, not just in the cotton industry itself. In 1925 approximately 1.5 million workers nationally were covered by collective agreements, usually giving six days' paid holiday after a year's work.[59]

This period also saw a rise in concern about health and safety issues, particularly industrial illness and accidents. Hoping to create better health conditions in industry the TUC, at its 1926 congress in Bournemouth, decided on a campaign for two weeks' holiday with pay as well as statutory holidays and May Day.[60] A circular from the TUC General Council to all affiliated union branches gave the text of the resolution, requesting it to secure for all workers an annual summer holiday of two weeks with full pay, payment for all statutory holidays and May Day as an additional statutory holiday.[61] The resolution had been a composite one, promoted by several organisations. The call for a national campaign had come from the National Union of Building Trade Workers, with the National Union of Distribution and Allied Workers (NUDAW) also contributing to the wording of the resolution. Walter Citrine wrote to these unions asking how they thought a national campaign could be undertaken. NUDAW's general secretary, Hallsworth, wrote back saying that as far as his union was concerned the first step would be for the General Council to send a circular letter about the policy to all unions, asking them, when entering upon negotiations with their employers, to place in the forefront of their demands the request for fifty-two weeks' wages for every member every year. They could also table resolutions at their various delegate meetings demanding that the securing of this condition should be one of the declared objects of their union. In addition Hallsworth suggested that the General Secretary should arrange for articles to appear in the *Daily Herald* promoting the policy.[62] Walter Citrine also wrote to the National Brass and Metal Mechanics'

Union, based in Birmingham. Arthur Gibbard, the union's general secretary, replied that his committee thought that a national movement could be started like the local one created by his union in the Birmingham area. Some little time after Congress had met at Bournemouth the Brass and Metal Mechanics' Union approached the Birmingham and District Brassfounders' Employers' Association on this subject. The employers viewed the question more favourably than expected, and they went so far as to say that if the principle was generally adopted, then they would readily consider the application of such a claim to the industry in the Birmingham area. If this course was taken by all societies it was felt it would give some indication of the likelihood of getting the claim brought into operation.[63]

Paid holidays were an issue not just to the English trade union movement; the International Federation of Trade Unions (IFTU) began to formulate policies covering a much wider area. In response to a questionnaire distributed by the IFTU to the TUC General Council, the research department reported that the only legislation regarding holidays in Britain applied solely to shop assistants and made provision for a week's or a fortnight's leave, which was given as compensation for working longer hours than the normal working day, or as an alternative to the half-holiday.[64] Using information such as this, gathered from labour organisations around the world, the IFTU was able to draft the Taylerle resolution at its General Council meeting in Prague in May 1929. This resolution concluded that the economic and hygienic conditions under which employees worked entitled them to a regular holiday. 'The trend of the modern technique of production, towards unbroken acceleration of pace, systematically exhausts the body and mind of the worker and renders it absolutely imperative that he should have an annual holiday of some considerable duration'. As it was closely associated with the question of working hours and the distribution of work and rest, both of which formed the basis of the rationalisation of production and human activity, a minimum paid annual holiday should be guaranteed, not merely by collective agreements, but also by social legislation.[65] Whether their work was physical or mental, workers ought to have a paid annual holiday of at least fourteen days, or longer for under-eighteens, older workers and those in heavy industry. The International Labour Organisation was to initiate an inquiry and to compile a draft international convention through which the minimum holiday recommended could be secured by legislation. Individual trades were to give special attention to the holiday question and to use appropriate means to secure it through their collective agreements while national bodies should inaugurate action for statutory regulations. To promote these endeavours, the IFTU published the results of these inquiries in order to gauge progress. The Taylerle resolution concluded that the holiday issue was closely associated with the efforts made by the ILO regarding the 'utilisation of spare time and the wise use of holiday by young workers'. To this end unions were told they should establish holiday homes with the aid of state and other public bodies.

The IFTU's Taylerle resolution reflected the position of many British unions. A letter from the National Union of Stove Grate and General Metal Workers in June 1929 told the TUC of a policy it had recently adopted. It demanded 'that the TUC General Council press for legislation to make it compulsory for every employer to pay all employees at least one week's summer holiday with pay each year.[66] Walter Citrine read similar sentiments from Gorton United Trades and Labour Council in September 1929. It forwarded the resolution that 'this Council requests the TUC General Council to press the government to institute a national annual holiday with pay for all workers'.[67] Congress met in Belfast later that year and reaffirmed its commitment to annual holidays with pay by passing a motion saying that 'the time was opportune to press for payment for holidays for all workers, such payment to be made on the basis of wages earned, whether on piecework or on timework'. Holidays to be paid for should be all statutory and customary holidays in addition to two weeks' annual holiday. Congress called upon the whole labour movement, both political and industrial, nationally and locally, to use its utmost power to ensure the practical application of this resolution as soon as possible.[68]

Following the Belfast resolution, the British labour movement took up the campaign as advocated by the Taylerle resolution. In 1929 a Labour MP, Ernest Winterton, supported by other parliamentary colleagues, introduced a Private Member's Bill, supported by the TUC and a number of affiliated unions. It reached a second reading and went before a standing committee on 15 November that year. The TUC accepted that as it was a Private Member's Bill, and of course controversial, the chances of its becoming law were remote, even though the discussion in committee would be of great value. An important aspect of the Bill was 'a provision rendering it penal for an employer to attempt to evade the provisions of the Bill by dismissing or suspending an employed person, the penal liability being in addition to any civil liability'.[69] At the time there was a Labour government, which may have given the unions and workers more confidence to press for reforms. The Amalgamated Weavers' Society wrote optimistically to the TUC in February 1930, resolving to secure paid holidays for its members and all workers.[70] More letters describing branch policies in accordance with the Bill were sent to the TUC General Council from the Barge Builders' Union,[71] the Typographical Association, the National Union of Railwaymen,[72] the National Union of Blast Furnacemen Ore Miners Coke Workers and Kindred Trades[73] and the National Society of Electrotypers and Stereotypers which declared unanimous support, saying that only 7 per cent of its members were not already getting a fortnight's holiday with pay.[74] Another letter sent by the National Asylum Workers' Union stated that holidays were general among its members, who were municipal employees, but it hoped the practice would become popular among private employers.[75] These responses in support of the Bill appear to have been from unions not requiring debate because of existing policy on paid holidays. Samuel Fisher of the Cardiff Penarth and Barry Coal Trimmers' Association wrote to A. S. Firth of the General Council, saying, 'the management committee of the union are all in favour of workmen being paid for holidays and we are doing all we can to create a demand for the above'.[76] This wording implies a hurried response to a request to union branches for support for Winterton's Bill received between scheduled branch meetings, as the letter refers to the management committee's position, not that of the branch as a whole. With two months longer to organise a discussion, a letter in August from W. Allington, secretary of the No. 2 Barrow in Furness branch of the Electrical Trades Union, told Congress of its resolution 'that the government be urged to proceed immediately on the above vexed question, Holidays with Pay for all Workers'.[77] After serious and lengthy discussion, the Barrow Trades Council passed its own policy on the issue. Its secretary, W. Spencer, sent the text of its motion 'that we ask the TUC and TUCGC, and also the MP for the borough, to bring pressure into Parliament in respect to Payment for Holidays for all workers, as in our opinion this is long overdue'.[78] Portsmouth Trades Council too, was organising around the slogan 'Holidays with pay for all workers'.[79]

All these letters of support and resolve from union branches show that the demand did not represent the view of a few members or even of a few isolated branches. It had become a general demand of the union movement that could now develop a united campaign for its achievement. Even so, no communication so far had been addressed to employers' organisations. The Minister of Labour at the time, Margaret Bondfield, a founding supporter of the Workers' Travel Association, felt that no good purpose would be served except by allowing the action of the department to be determined by the trade union view. Leggett of the TUC, in a memorandum to Firth, said he had pointed out to Winterton the sort of reply which would have been received from the national confederation of employers and that it seemed highly desirable to avoid creating a position at that time in which there would be clearly defined hostility between the employers and trade unions on the subject, seeing that if the matter was handled patiently the two sides might be led to co-operate in its objective consideration, for which there was considerable sympathy even on the employers' side.[80] The position of Bondfield and Leggett was that formal action of the kind Winterton seemed to expect would probably do more harm than good. Failure to approach employers, however, does not seem to have been in the spirit of the Belfast or Taylerle resolutions and can be interpreted only as lack of confidence of the ultimate success of the campaign at that stage.

The TUC's commitment to securing holidays with pay was again reaffirmed at the Nottingham Congress of November 1930. The resolution this time suggested that the General Council should take steps to give effect to the unions' claim and urged all trade union and labour organisations to bring the matter before their members and thus assist the General Council in its efforts.[81] Again in 1931, at the Bristol Congress, the demand for compulsory holidays with pay was reiterated, in a resolution moved by the National Union of Clerks and Administrative Workers and seconded by the National Union of Textile Workers.[82] Information about the Bristol Congress policy was sent out to the secretaries of all constituent unions.[83]

To assist unions in the ongoing campaign, copies of agreements reached in other branches and trades were circulated to all those affiliated. When progress was made in negotiations for paid leave the TUC was informed and details were sent out to other unions, where copies of agreements acted as blueprints in the deliberations of others.[84] Where agreements had not yet been ratified it was normal practice to supply information to branch officers only, with the caution that the details should not be made public in case they jeopardised the conclusion of the bargaining process through pressure on the employer from other employers.

By the time of the 1933 Congress the composite resolution calling for paid holidays had been strengthened in its wording. In a motion moved by the National Federation of Insurance Workers and seconded by the National Union of Sheet Metal Workers and Braziers, previous resolutions were reiterated.[85] Its conclusion showed heightened confidence and expectation; this time the text ended with the words 'the Congress *instructs* the General Council to take all necessary steps in an endeavour to achieve this object'. The previous resolutions had asked the General Council only to 'urge' unions and labour organisations to bring the matter before their members and assist it in its efforts.[86]

At the International Labour Organisation Conference (ILOC) thirty-five governments had voted for an international convention on holidays with pay but the British National Government and four others voted only for a recommendation to industry. By 1936 the whole labour movement was taking up the demand and campaigns for paid holidays were part of the general social trend towards more intervention by the state in industrial and employment matters. The TUC passed another resolution calling for two weeks' paid holiday in September 1936 and a fortnight later another Private Member's Bill was sponsored by the Labour Party, which would have given every worker in the same employment for twelve months or more eight days' paid leave in addition to existing entitlement.[87] When the Private Member's Bill reached the committee stage before being defeated, a Tory amendment said it should apply only when a Minister of Labour was satisfied that wages were such that employees could not make their own provision and where such holidays would not harm trade or industry. Twenty-two nations by that time, including Brazil, Portugal, France, Poland and the Soviet Union, had holidays with pay, but not Britain. The government did, however, concede a committee of inquiry, and the TUC plus representatives of particular industries presented evidence before it.

The Labour Party initiated a summer campaign in seaside towns to arouse public interest in 'Labour's Immediate Programme', and the proposals for paid leave in particular, canvassing support from people on holiday.[88] Party branches and trades councils in resorts such as Scarborough and Southport organised this. In that year, too, the TUC again reaffirmed its policy at its Norwich Congress when a resolution calling for a fortnight's paid holiday was moved by the Amalgamated Weavers' Association, seconded by the National Union of Tailors and Garment Workers.[89] This campaigning pressure was instrumental in achieving the establishment of the Select Committee on Holidays with Pay, chaired by Lord Amulree. Even so, the steelworkers' union, the Iron and Steel Trades Confederation, in its magazine *Man and Metal* felt 'it would now appear that the hope is likely to be disappointed as the organised employers are adopting their time-honoured delaying tactics and propose to offer evidence in sections instead of as a body through the employers' central organisation'.[90]

Much of the debate surrounding paid holidays centred not on their desirability but on how they would be financed. The main contending proposals were a contributory scheme in which the employer, worker and state each contributed similar amounts like the health insurance scheme, a contributory scheme paid into by both workers and employers, or schemes financed entirely by the employer, either out of wages or out of gross profits. The latter proposition was favoured by the TUC, insisting that the idea of a holiday scheme should be to ensure that taking a holiday would not leave a worker materially worse off. To allow this, payment should be secured at the normal rate of pay, excluding overtime. The TUC objected to a state contribution, as that would mean taxpayers, working people, still paying for it. They were also concerned that it would encourage the state to 'poke its nose in' and prescribe conditions that could be objectionable. Any other form of contributory scheme would also mean the worker paying for his or her own holiday. Ideally the TUC wanted legislation laying down the principles to be adhered to but wherever possible maintaining collective bargaining and negotiation procedures between employers' and workers' organisations intact. They aimed to have the force of law behind any arrangement for holidays while leaving the actual details as flexible as possible. This would give scope for some unions to secure better terms while giving unorganised workers minimum legal entitlement.

Arguments presented from the employers' side were uncharacteristically in favour of collective bargaining, and derided the TUC witnesses, as the employers wished to avoid any state interference in industry. The anomaly of this argument was pointed out by the TUC representatives, who found it odd that the employers should support what from the unions' point of view meant strike action, as that was usually the only way workers were able to coerce their employers into the collective bargaining process and win any advance. The TUC disagreed that all agreements should be achieved through voluntary collective bargaining, believing that any necessary flexibility and variety could be secured by making the law only in general terms, giving the Ministry of Labour or some other appropriately constituted authority power to give legal force to agreements between employers' organisations and workpeople. It favoured a scheme whereby employers and workers in each industry or trade should be required to submit a draft proposal for the approval of the Minister of Labour. Failure to do so or cases where no proper negotiating machinery existed would result in the Minster drafting a scheme in consultation with industry representatives. Without some legal compulsion all working people could not be guaranteed a paid holiday.

As was to be expected, industry claimed not to be able to afford to make such a concession, especially those export industries where there was international competition from countries with lower-paid work forces. The additional costs, the unions calculated, would not be excessive, only a matter of 1s 5½d a week for weavers and 1s 4d for miners and agricultural workers. The TUC countered the argument that it would be detrimental to industry by challenging the committee to give an example of any of the industries where there were already paid holidays being adversely affected. Furthermore, it declared, where holiday payment had been granted 'the employers themselves attested that the effect of the holidays had been greatly to improve the physique and the power of the operatives, and in some case actually increased output despite the holiday period'.[91]

As speed of production increased and changes in production methods occurred in industry the skill of the individual craftsman was replaced by repetitive tasks, making the need for a break from the continual strain vital. The cost of not giving an annual break ought properly to be taken into account, Citrine submitted. 'It was no longer a question of leisure or of wages, it was a question of ensuring that those people in a position where they might suffer from the strain of nerves incidental to certain industries may not be allowed to become what they would become if nothing was done.'[92] Citrine declared to the committee that 'if a 4 per cent increase in costs would break British industry there was no hope for labour nor any future for the country!' If holidays with pay were extended to the whole of the work force, the additional payment made from their expenditure on leisure would compensate the economy. It would circulate more money over a much wider field, and consequently business would improve.

The TUC's efforts to secure the advantage of paid holidays for members of its constituent unions were undermined by workers in some places choosing additional wage rises rather than a holiday. In North Wales slate quarries men were offered a choice between a week's holiday with pay (which would have cost the company about $2^{1}/_{2}d$ a day per man) plus $3d$ increase on daily wages or, alternatively, a straight $5d$ a day rise. After consideration in the quarrymen's lodges they turned down the first offer that included the holiday. In a ballot on the second option they voted about 1,825 in favour and 336 against.[93] The select committee also brought up hypothetical cases where one industry might accept a straight holiday with pay in negotiations while another might choose to have half its increase in wages, the rest in holidays. What would happen if, as a result of legislation, the first group came back and claimed the holiday after having already had the pay rise? The issues of wages rises and holidays needed to be separated, which was difficult, as both were payments made to workers for the same amount of production.[94] It was likely that only the same amount overall in funds would be forthcoming; whether it was divided up over fifty or fifty-two weeks during the year would make little difference to the individual worker.[95] If required to save for a holiday, at least the employee would have a choice in what was done with the money. Criticisms regarding paid holidays as an attack on thrift were also aimed at the TUC, which correctly pointed out that 'even with paid holidays the workers would still need to save up to be able to go away. It was thereby more likely to encourage thrift among even more people.'[96]

On 21 October 1937, in the House of Commons, the Minister of Labour estimated that there were between 2,500,000 and 2,750,000 people covered by collective agreements providing for paid holidays.[97] Agreements providing paid holidays for manual workers had existed in at least thirty-four separate industries and services by June that year. Some individual firms also introduced such schemes and there were already a large number receiving paid leave through custom and practice. Altogether, by the time of the select committee, the TUC calculated, there were probably about 5,025,000 employed persons, excluding salaried staff, in receipt of paid holidays in one form or another. This demonstrates the rising demand and force for change in society, as only the previous June the total had been estimated at around 4 million, exclusive of the salaried sector; only about half were manual workers. Of these hardly any received a holiday of more than a week's duration. This still left about three-quarters of the work force outside the scope of such provision.

The Holidays with Pay Act, passed in 1938, was essentially a compromise between both sides of industry, based on the select committee's report. Out of line with the committee's recommendations, the Act did not apply to all employees. The TUC's view that workers should pay nothing towards their own holidays prevailed. The Minister of Labour would have authority to help bring about voluntary schemes under collective agreements. Although two weeks' holiday was not seen as unreasonable, it was thought judicious to proceed with caution at first, with one week as the immediate goal. The Holidays with Pay Act was not a strong piece of legislation and in some cases it retarded existing arrangements. The Act itself proposed no more than three days' consecutive holiday.[98] The committee agreed that holidays were a condition of employment and should be removed from the sphere of remuneration but they decided to allow industries the opportunity of dealing with this before applying compulsion. A probationary period was recommended so that as much as possible could be achieved through collective bargaining. This period was also needed to enable the details of how the legislation would work to be devised and also to enable steps to be taken, such as staggering of holidays, to provide for the number of people taking holidays away from home that would undoubtedly vastly increase.

To promote to workers their new rights and entitlements, emphasising its own role in the campaign, the TUC produced two booklets, *Holidays for all*, which sold at 2*d*, and *Holidays with pay: the TUC policy*, priced at 3*d* each.[99] These materials were intended to be purchased by union branches for distribution to members, as they could be ordered at twelve copies for 3*s* or fifty copies for 11*s* or 100 copies for £1, post free.[100] Sickness, proneness to accident, absenteeism and other factors, the TUC claimed, were part of the cost to industry that could be set off against the cost of introducing a general and comprehensive system of annual holidays with pay.[101] Trades' councils like that in Loughborough spread the news to non-members through advertisements and notices in local publications.[102]

The effect of holidays with pay was not simply confined to payment of wages whilst on leave. Another important issue was the payment of contributions towards health and unemployment insurance. A number of test cases from Morris Motors and Pressed Steel Company went before the Court of Referees in August 1938. After a three-hour session the court decided that neither group of workers was entitled to Unemployment Benefit during the holiday period, no matter how small the holiday payment received. Although the Ministry of Labour ruled that the men concerned were on holiday, and therefore in employment, no health or unemployment stamps were put on their cards for two weeks.[103] The Oxford Trades and Labour Council urged the TUC to take action immediately on this important question. People could find themselves ineligible for Unemployment Benefit or a full pension if their contributions were not fully paid up. Another weakness of the Act was that it applied only to industries covered by trade boards and agriculture and road haulage.[104] Nearly 10 million workers were still without paid holidays in 1939, according to a letter from the Resources and Economic Department of the TUC, in answer to a question from Gloucester Labour Party.[105] The Holidays with Pay Act, 1938, did not give effect to the recommendation of Lord Amulree's Committee on Holidays with Pay that 'during the Parliamentary Session of 1940 to 1941 legislation be passed making provision for holidays with pay in industry'.

For the more fortunate quarter of the working population the right to a paid holiday was won mainly in two periods: immediately after the First World War during the industrial crisis and rise in militancy which led to demands for improved conditions and the willingness in a number of occupations to take action to secure them; and in the 1930s as the long slump came to an end and workers regained confidence in their ability to win reforms through their own activity in trade unions. As the threat of unemployment subsided, workers were willing once more to fight to improve their working conditions and pay. This improvement in their bargaining position allowed unions, through the TUC, to initiate a national campaign culminating in the Holidays with Pay Act. The statute did not apply universally to all workers, most of whom achieved paid leave through negotiation and agreement with their employers. Any success of this limited legislation, to enable working people to have a holiday away from home, was dependent on the prior existence of an adequate supply of affordable, appropriate accommodation.

Notes

1 Elizabeth Brunner, *Holiday making and the holidaymaking trades*, Oxford, 1945, p. 8.

2 J. A. R. Pimlott, *The Englishman's holiday*, London, 1947, repr. Hassocks, 1967, p. 232.

3 *Ibid.*, p. 156.

4 *Great Central Railway Journal* 2:4, 1906, p. 107.

5 Charles Booth, *Life and labour of the people of London* IV, *The trades of east London connected with poverty*, London, 1889, 1902 edn, repr. 1969, p. 286.

6 Minutes of evidence taken before the Select Committee on Holidays with Pay, 1937, p. 126, para. 6.

7 Pimlott, *The Englishman's holiday*, p. 154.

8 T. C. Barker, *Pilkington Brothers and the glass industry*, London, 1960, p. 176.

9 Ronald E. Wilson, *Two hundred precious metal years: a history of the Sheffield Smelting Company, 1760–1960*, London, 1960, pp. 166 and 124.

10 Civil and Public Servants' Association, Annual Report, 1919, p. 10.

11 *Ibid.*, 1921–22, 1931–32.

12 Modern Records Centre, University of Warwick (hereafter MRC), MSS 292/114/1, letter to Mr Tracey of the TUC from Herbert Elvin, General Secretary of the National Union of Clerks and Administrative Workers, 28 January 1932.

13 *Blackburn Standard*, 3 July 1850.

14 Alan Fowler and Terry Wyke, *The barefoot aristocrats*, Littleborough, 1987, p. 100.

15 Select Committee on Holidays with Pay, Sir Walter Citrine, p. 403, para. 5200.

16 *Ibid.*, p. 137, para. 1552.

17 *Ibid.*, p. 47, para. 303.

18 *Ibid.*, p. 349, para. 36.

19 Elizabeth Roberts, *A woman's place: an oral history of working-class women, 1890–1940*, Oxford, 1984, p. 143.

20 Gary Cross (ed.), *Worktowners in Blackpool: Mass-Observation and popular leisure in the 1930s*, London, 1990, p. 57.

21 Patrick Joyce, *Visions of the people: industrial England and the question of class, 1848–1914*, Cambridge, 1991, p. 314.

22 Alan Fox, *A history of the National Union of Boot and Shoe Operatives*, Oxford, 1958, p. 409.

23 *Ibid.*

24 *Leicester Mercury*, 20 August 1935.

25 H. S. Hilton, *Foes to tyranny: a history of building trade workers*, London, 1963.

26 Andy Croll, 'Coal without dole', *History Today* 49:2, 1999, pp. 14–16, p. 14.

27 Select Committee on Holidays with Pay, evidence from South Wales Miners' Federation, para. 11.

28 Unofficial Reform Committee, *The miners' next step*, Tonypandy, 1912, p. 23.

29 J. E. Williams, *The Derbyshire miners*, London, 1962, p. 628.

30 *Ibid.*, p. 648.

31 Select Committee on Holidays with Pay, evidence of the South Wales Miners' Federation, para. 14.

32 *Ibid.*, para. 4175.

33 *Derbyshire Times*, 5 November 1937.

34 MRC, MSS 292/114/2, Walter Citrine, letter to John Swann of the Durham Miners' Association, February 1938.

35 Williams, *The Derbyshire miners*, p. 792.

36 *Ibid.*, p. 792.

37 *Ibid.*, p. 629.

38 H. A. Clegg, *General union: a study of the National Union of General and Municipal Workers*, Oxford, 1954, pp. 151–4.

39 *Ibid.*

40 G. C. Martin, 'Working-class holiday making down to 1947', M.A. thesis, University of Leicester, 1968, p. 47.

41 W. J. Reader, *Metal Box: a history*, London, 1976, p. 29.

42 MRC, MSS 292/114, Chemical Trades Joint Industrial Council, regulations for the workpeople's annual holiday in 1930, 19 December 1929.

43 G. le M. M. *The history of Mander Brothers, 1773–1953*, London, 1953, p. 231.

44 Philip S. Bagwell, *The railwaymen*, London, 1963, p. 66.

45 Select Committee on Railway Servants (Hours of Labour) Bill, 1890–91.

46 *Great Central Railway Journal* 2:4, 1906, p. 106.

47 *Great Eastern Railway Magazine* 1:8, 1911, p. 272.

48 Bagwell, *The railwaymen*, p. 559.

49 Associated Society of Locomotive Engineers and Firemen, *ASLEF, 1880–1980*, 1980, p. 30.

50 Francis Williams, quoted in *ibid.*, p. 30.

51 A. L. Morton and George Tate, *The British labour movement*, London, 1956, p. 282.

52 A. E. Musson, *The Typographical Association: origins and history up to 1949*, London, 1954, p. 156.

53 *Ibid.*, p. 163.

54 John Child, *Industrial relations in the British printing industry*, London, 1967, p. 228.
55 F. Birchall and R. Ross, *A history of the potters' union*, Stoke on Trent, 1977, p. 185.
56 Richard Croucher, *Engineers at war, 1939–1945*, London, 1982, p. 103.
57 Iron and Steel Trades Confederation, *Men of steel, by one of them: a chronicle of eighty-eight years of trade unionism in the British iron and steel industry*, London, 1951, pp. 531–5.
58 Modern Records Centre, University of Warwick (hereafter MRC), MSS 292 114/1, Manchester and District, Bolton and District and Co-operative Wages Board and the Journeyman Butchers' Federation agreement on holidays, 1922, sent to the TUC.
59 Select Committee on Holidays with Pay, p. 1, para. 4.
60 MRC, MSS 292 114/1, TUC General Council circular No. 34 (1926–27).
61 *Ibid.*
62 MRC, MSS 292 114, letter to Walter Citrine, General Secretary, TUC, from J. Hallsworth, General Secretary, National Union of Distributive and Allied Workers, Manchester, 27 January 1927.
63 *Ibid.*, letter to Walter Citrine from Arthur H. Gibbard, General Secretary, National Brass and Metal Mechanics, Birmingham, 9 March 1927.
64 *Ibid.*, International Federation of Trade Unions (IFTU) questionnaire, Holidays with pay, R292262, TUC General Council, Research Department.
65 MRC, MSS 292 1114/1, Taylerle resolution, draft resolution on holidays for workers and salaried employees, for the TUC Executive meeting of 22 May 1929.
66 *Ibid.*, letter to TUC General Council, from the National Union of Stove, Grate and General Metal Workers 12 June 1929.
67 *Ibid.*, letter to Walter Citrine from W. Wooley of Gorton United Trades and Labour Council, 19 September 1929.
68 *Ibid.*, TUC General Council, Finance and General Purposes Committee 10/1, 1929–30.
69 *Ibid.*
70 MRC, MSS 292 114/1, letter to TUC from the Amalgamated Weavers' Society, 3 February 1930.
71 *Ibid.*, letter from Thomas Challis, Barge Builders' Trade Union, 23 May 1930.
72 *Ibid.*, letters from the Typographical Association and the National Union of Railwaymen to the TUC General Council, May 1930.
73 *Ibid.*, letter to the TUC General Council from the National Union of Blast Furnacemen, Ore Miners, Coke Workers and Kindred Trades, 13 May 1930.
74 *Ibid.*, letter to the TUC General Council from the National Society of Electrotypers and Stereotypers 9 May 1930.
75 *Ibid.*, letter to the TUC from the National Asylum Workers' Union, 9 May 1930.
76 *Ibid.*, letter to A. S. Firth from Samuel Fisher, Cardiff, Penarth and Barry Coal Trimmers' Association, 2 June 1930.

77 *Ibid.*, letter to TUC General Council from W. Allington, Branch Secretary, No. 2 Barrow in Furness branch of the Electrical Trades Union, 29 August 1930.

78 MRC, MSS 292 114, letter from W. Spencer, Barrow Trades Council, 1930.

79 *Ibid.*, letter from R. S. Ball, General Secretary, Portsmouth Trades Council, to Walter Citrine, 21 July 1930.

80 *Ibid.*, memorandum to A. S. Firth, TUC General Council, from F. W. Leggett, 25 November 1930.

81 'Industrial news for the use of the press', No. 224, issued by the TUC General Council Publicity Department, 23 December 1930.

82 MRC, MSS 292 114, Bristol Trades Union Congress Resolution 1931, Composite 3, Holidays with Pay, p. 333; TUC General Council circular No. 38 (1931–32).

83 *Ibid.*, TUC General Council, circular No. 69, 8 May 1930.

84 MRC MSS 292 114/1, letter to the Amalgamated Furnishing Trades' Association from TUC, 11 November 1932.

85 MRC, MSS 292 114/2, Trades Union Congress Resolution 1933, Composite 13, Holidays with Pay, p. 277.

86 'Industrial news for the use of the press', No. 224.

87 H. J. Fyrth and Henry Collins, *The Foundry Workers*, Manchester, 1957, p. 221.

88 MRC, MSS 292 114/2, letter to TUC General Council from Southport Trades Council and Labour Party, 1937.

89 *Ibid.*, Trades Union Congress resolution, Norwich, 1937.

90 Iron and Steel Trades Confederation, *Men of steel*, p. 532.

91 *Ibid.*

92 Select Committee on Holidays with Pay, p. 37, para. 139.

93 *Ibid.*, p. 400, paras 5159–60.

94 *Ibid.*, p. 404, para. 5232.

95 *Ibid.*, p. 402, para. 5186.

96 *Ibid.*, p. 43, para. 242.

97 *Ibid.*, evidence of the TUC General Council, p. 22, para. 16.

98 Stephen G. Jones, *Workers at play: a social and economic history of leisure*, London, 1986, p. 19.

99 MRC MSS 292 114/3, TUC booklet, *Holidays for all*, 1938; *Holidays with pay: the TUC policy*, 1938.

100 *Holidays for all*, p. 3.

101 *Ibid.*, p. 3.

102 MRC MSS 292 114/3, Loughborough Guide, No. 236, Thursday 3 August 1939.

103 MRC, MSS 292 114, letter to Sir Walter Citrine from L. J. Bush, Secretary, Oxford Trades and Labour Council, 30 August 1938.

104 MRC, MSS 292 114/3, letter to R. Coppock of the National Building Trade Operatives from the Assistant General Secretary of the TUC, 12 August 1940.

105 *Ibid.*, letter to J. E. Walsh, Gloucester Labour Party, from TUC Resource and Economic Department, 10 August 1939.

6

Accommodation for working-class visitors

In the preceding chapters we have seen how throughout the years from about 1840 to the Holidays with Pay Act of 1938 a growing minority of workers had managed, by various initiatives, to obtain a break from the routine of work.[1] In ever increasing numbers they enjoyed a stay away from home, typically at the seaside. The Holidays with Pay Act and the ensuing rush by employers and unions to get holiday arrangements in place by voluntary agreements, to pre-empt legislative interference, meant that from 1938 onwards the number anticipated to seek accommodation by the coast was expected to exceed all previous records, perhaps doubling the existing figures.[2] In 1938 a large proportion of the 11 million people who as yet had no entitlement to paid leave and their families was expected to join the 15 million holidaymakers of 1937 very soon.[3] In this chapter the changing features of holiday accommodation for working-class visitors, in response to their changing tastes and expectations, is examined. The type of accommodation used by workers was both culturally and economically determined: visitors needed to feel at ease and pay a price for rent or board that they could afford. For the middle-class tourist the choice of accommodation was no less determined socially, although cheapness and accessibility from home were not the main considerations. Social distance was maintained even on holiday. The different classes rarely rubbed shoulders, segregation was upheld through physical distance and pricing. As the working-class presence grew in existing resorts like Blackpool, visitors of the middle class based their holidays in the more select North Shore development or in Lytham and St Anne's.[4] Even in places of entertainment, such as theatres and music halls, segregation was maintained through higher ticket prices in certain seating areas.[5] More distant coastal areas, such as Devon and Cornwall, began to be favoured by the middle classes, away from the trippers and less affluent holidaymakers, who could afford neither the travel and accommodation costs nor the time involved in travelling to more distant places. Along the coast of North Wales the prices of accommodation as well as the 'social tone' of resorts rose in progression from Prestatyn, through Rhyl and Colwyn Bay to the dignified Llandudno.[6]

This relationship between social tone and physical distance from the urban, industrial towns is not entirely simplistic. Harold Perkin, discussing the 'social tone' of Victorian seaside resorts, gave as examples Scarborough and Skegness, both a similar distance from the West Riding, yet very different in the class of visitor they attracted.[7] Skegness and other 'lower' status resorts provided cheap amusements, beach entertainers, street traders and, by the end of the nineteenth century, cheap, spectacular entertainment for a mass market, financed by large capitalist enterprises.[8] In contrast Scarborough provided genteel entertainment such as theatres and concert halls, in keeping with its earlier status as a spa, and also parks, gardens and beaches where admission was free and not plagued by hawkers. In themselves, these differences do not explain why a resort offering peace and relaxation, not a commodity prone to commercialisation and additional expense, should be less popular with those with least spending power than a place with countless trivial amusements to fritter away hard-earned cash. The providers of cheap entertainment did not create the demand for their products or coerce working people to choose that kind of holiday over another. Many working-class visitors may have actually preferred to congregate in resorts frequented by other people from their own background and community, whose tastes in entertainment and accommodation were similar to their own, but they may not have had much choice, being compelled by economic circumstance to go to the nearest and cheapest resort. Mass-Observation's study of Bolton people in Blackpool in the late 1930s cited examples from people's letters entered into a press competition on the theme 'How I would like to spend my holidays'. Many of the writers say they would love to go to places like the Cornish Riviera, Wales, Oxford, Buxton, but most acknowledged that these were but dreams; Blackpool was where they would end up, if they went anywhere at all.[9]

The development of working-class holidaymaking, with the number travelling and staying away from home increasing throughout the period under discussion, was matched by a corresponding development of the accommodation sector to meet workers' needs and demands. The major expansion of working-class holidaymaking anticipated after the Holidays with Pay Act could never have been a viable proposition without the existence of suitable places for the tourists to stay. At the beginning of the period under study, in the years immediately preceding the Great Exhibition, accommodation for the poorest travellers was in 'low and filthy lodging houses', where both sexes were huddled indiscriminately together. Manchester police statistics for 1846 recorded 109 lodging houses where men and women slept together and ninety-one mendicant lodging houses. This kind of low-quality accommodation was not peculiar to Manchester but was even more common in London, Liverpool and Glasgow and in the lodging houses frequented by the travelling poor along the main roads of England.[10] This sort of place would have been used only as a necessity when travelling or newly arrived in a town as a migrant. Residents of these lodging houses, the very poorest section of the working class, would not have regarded themselves as guests or on holiday and so would have been looking for the cheapest possible arrangements. However, the name lodging house may have created a particular image and put off the more respectable holidaymaker from accommodation bearing this description in the seaside towns. In response, many providers of seaside lodgings distinguished their premises from the common lodging houses by calling them company houses.

A description of holiday accommodation offered to working-class people in 1813 is given by Richard Ayton in his *Voyage round Great Britain*. After walking from Manchester, bringing their own tea and sugar with them, visitors paid 9*d* a day each for their lodgings in Blackpool.

> A single house here, and not a large one, frequently receives a hundred and twenty people to sleep in a night: five or six beds crammed into each room, and five or six people in each bed; but, with every art of packing and pinioning, they cannot all be stowed at one time: those, therefore, who have the places first are roused, when they have slept through half the night, to make way for another load – and thus everyone gets his night's rest.[11]

At Southport, accessible from Manchester after a canal was completed to only five miles away in 1821, hay lofts were let out at 1*s* a head as sleeping rooms without any bedclothes except horse cloths or straw.[12] Many poorer workers' own homes may not have been much better.

Apart from these lodgings and descriptions of houses of call for tramping artisans, advertisements for visitors to the Great Exhibition provide some of the earliest insights into the commercial provision of temporary accommodation for the working class. These were lodgings associated with and servicing the tourism industry rather than travel as a necessity. Although hastily provided at short notice, this accommodation possessed many of the features prevailing in the accommodation sector of the tourism industry ever since, particularly within that section catering for the working-class market. These features included an attempt through the Royal Commission's sub-committee, at setting minimum standards and matching supply with demand, rather like a modern local tourist office.[13] Other features offered in various combinations by some of the accommodation providers in 1851 included a fixed or inclusive system of pricing; communal activities and entertainment, giving help to guests with orientation in their temporary surroundings, offering advice and information on local attractions, ensuring the provision of familiar foodstuffs, providing a host or representative to assist and help with any difficulties caused by unfamiliar local ways, keeping costs down through the bulk purchase of accommodation; and organising some form of staggering or regional segregation. This paternal consideration was linked with concern to maintain and promote respectability among the lower classes. Even so the heavy demands were met and a range of places to stay, calculated to meet the needs of working-class visitors, was made available. For most of these people it was the first time they had been anywhere as a tourist and so they would have had no prior expectations or existing standards of what boarding accommodation ought to be like, except for the common lodging houses already discussed. Even for the middle classes, hotels were a new concept, associated with rail travel just as inns were associated with journeys by road, rather than tourism or holidays, although this was to change during the next decades. The upper classes preferred to stay as guests in private houses rather than lower themselves by staying at an inn.[14]

At the end of the exhibition season the temporary hostels and boarding houses reverted to their former or intended uses. They were the first experience of being a paying guest for the majority of working people visiting London. The type and standard of accommodation available would have influenced future demand and expectation of what boarding ought to be like in seaside lodgings. This has been the case in more recent times when British boarding houses have found the need to provide en-suite facilities for working-class guests who have experienced this standard of provision on Mediterranean package holidays and then expected and demanded to find facilities of equal quality when taking holidays in Britain.[15] These experiences and demands have also led guest houses to install radio and television, central heating and fitted carpets in even the most basic of accommodation. The type of accommodation demanded and expected is a reflection of the social and cultural environment of the working class.

The descriptions of early working-class lodgings clash remarkably with the expectations of the middle classes. For them, holiday arrangements were indicative of a completely different social and cultural milieu – one that reinforced the nuclear family rather than the extended one or the wider community. Exclusivity, not collectivity, was important. Locations were not chosen for their cheapness or proximity to home. As the railway opened up and expanded existing resorts to the inhabitants of the urban industrial hinterland wealthier tourists preferred to make longer journeys to quieter, more 'select' seaside towns and villages beyond the reach and pocket of the working class. Even so, the middle-class family on holiday would not have been a group made up exclusively of that class. Household servants were part of the group, maintaining the mother's freedom from domestic labour and child care at the seaside just as at home. This could have an effect on future working-class holidays, as when servants married and left service they would have had a template of what a respectable family holiday ought to be, creating higher aspirations for some individuals in this sector. In the 1920s Winifred Feltwell, a teenage domestic servant and later housekeeper to a middle-class family in Leicestershire, travelled to genteel resorts such as Sidmouth with the family she worked for, as a companion and carer for the children. In her own holidays she took her younger sisters, Agnes and Joan, to the seaside. They had never been on a seaside holiday with their own parents: it was behaviour learned in service.[16] Some middle-class families rented an entire house for several weeks during the summer, run by their own staff. An upper middle-class girl in the early years of the twentieth century, Esther Stokes, travelled every year to Cornwall by train in a carriage her family had to themselves. 'We were very excited about the journey for two reasons, one was that we always had tongue sandwiches . . . and the other was it was the only time we saw the maids without their caps. All the maids went with us and the caretakers would move into the London house.'[17] Travelling with servants meant that those hotels housing affluent holidaymakers needed to provide basic rooms for the household staff as well as more luxurious ones for family members. Children often stayed in cheaper, nearby boarding houses with their nannies and governesses, seeing their parents only a little more on holiday than they did at home.[18]

In the early years of the working-class presence at the seaside, in the nineteenth and early twentieth centuries, the expectations of accommodation were not high. For just one week of the year people were prepared to rough it in shared rooms and even shared beds during the busy August peak periods. Even in 1859, before the expansion of the resort's accommodation facilities, there were times when Blackpool was so crowded that, according to the *Preston Chronicle*, railway carriages and the station were placed at the disposal of persons to sleep in, but in addition to this a great number had no option but to walk the beach all night.[19] For the working-class holidaymakers whose culture centred on immediacy, hedonism and collectivism this was not such a major hardship, as the point of the holiday was to be out enjoying oneself and having fun with the family or extended family or a group of friends.[20] The accommodation in itself was not especially important and provided merely a place to sleep. The seaside landladies themselves usually demanded that their guests should be off the premises all day, returning only for mealtimes and, of course, bedtime.

Already, by 1870, a stereotype of the landlady or company house keeper had begun to emerge. Joseph Gutteridge, a Coventry ribbon weaver, described his landlady in Bradford, where he was sightseeing in the area as well as working temporarily at an exhibition:

> Lodgings were found at the house of a middle-aged person. She was not the ordinary vulture type of landlady, but had a kind and sympathetic face, and owing to lameness was unable to labour beyond household duties. I was so glad to find a place so much like home. She was a kind-hearted and cheery woman, towards whom I felt grateful for the many acts of kindness received while under her roof.[21]

He seemed pleasantly surprised that the woman did not live up to his prior expectations of 'a vulture type of landlady'. As there is no reference to his ever having stayed in lodgings in England before, his preconception can have been based only on stereotyping and not on experience.

In the fictional account of a mid-Victorian seaside holiday in Margate, Arthur Sketchley's *Mrs Brown at the seaside*, the leading characters were less fortunate in their landlady. The house was described as 'a washywoman-lookin' sort of place'.[22] Mrs Brown 'never did see a bigger sloven than the woman as come to the door'. Still, as rooms were in short supply she 'was glad to ketch at the one she'd got, tho' at the top o' the 'ouse and bakin' 'ot, just under the slates, as was suffocatin''. The bed they got was ''ard as pavin'-stones, and not so even'. There were lumps like cannon balls in it, and it was too short for Brown, and 'full narrer'. It was a tent bed that Mrs Brown would not have had as a gift. She did not sleep well, although her husband was snoring before the light was out. After half an hour Mrs Brown struck a light and claimed that never in her days did she see such a sight as that tent bedstead. The bed was covered in bugs, which she referred to as 'tigers': there must have been millions, she said. 'As to killin' 'em, it was not thought on, so I gets up and put on a shawl, and set a-dosin' with the light a-burnin' till daylight'. When she woke she felt more dead than alive.[23] Mrs Brown was much taken aback when the landlady accused her of having brought the bed bugs with her. As fiction intended to amuse this account is likely to be promoting the stereotype lodging house. Nevertheless, there must have been some truth in the image, as readers needed to recognise something of reality in the story to be able to identify with the characters and laugh with them.

Board in company houses for much of the period under study was usually provided in what was known as the apartment system. This type of lodging predominated in the late nineteenth and early twentieth centuries and survived as a minority provision until the 1950s, when it was superseded by boarding-house facilities, which were growing in popularity throughout the period. Guests would have a bedroom and service would be a cross between self-catering and half-board. Holidaymakers described this as 'board yourself' with bedding and attendance at a low price, around 4s a night in the 1920s. 'The woman of the house would cook the meat and so on. That was the attendance.'[24] The guests, normally the wife, would buy food, which the landlady would prepare and cook. This meant that even on holiday women were not free of domestic duties. This imposition on the leisure time of working-class women was a result of the lack of domestic labour-saving technology which would have given the landlady time to shop, combined with the inability of working-class families to afford the dearer rates of staying at hotels or boarding houses with servants to do the additional work. According to John Walton, for the proprietor of the cheaper class of company house the expense of a servant's wages could make a considerable dent in the season's income and make the difference between economic survival and bankruptcy.[25] Hard-pressed and hard-up company house keepers would provide basic items such as bread, milk and potatoes and hot water for making tea at an additional charge. Sometimes charges were even imposed for the use of the cruet.[26] 'Mother went out after breakfast to shop. The landlady always supplied the vegetables . . . That's where she made a bit of profit. She charged about sixpence or a shilling a week for vegetables each day.'[27]

Although the apartment system infringed the holidaymaking woman's free time it could also, especially in the busy peak period, be extremely hard work and stressful for the landlady, especially one keeping costs to a minimum who couldn't afford a servant. The working day could be from five or six o'clock in the morning and often wouldn't end until after midnight. Guests could bring in food to be prepared and cooked at any time and doing the washing was a particularly arduous task. The landladies' efforts did not go unappreciated, as other oral evidence, this time from a woman, shows:

> I don't know how those women did it! They advertised apartments, so much a
> night for the bed, and you bought your own food and you had a section of the
> sideboard to put it in. And the woman would have a full house and she'd pro-
> duce a nicely cooked meal. You know, there's Mrs So-and-so's beans and lamb
> and Mrs So-and-so's beef and Yorkshire pudding. How on earth they did it! It
> was very reasonable. There was your fare and I think it was about five shillings a
> night for a double bed and a shilling for the cruet.[28]

Fortunately for the landladies, most working families followed a routine gov-
erned by factory hours, with set meal times which didn't vary very much even
on holiday. The social environment of working-class life affected the timetable
of daily life even away from work and the local community.

When catering for working-class visitors it was important to emphasise the
homeliness and familiarity of the establishment. Accommodation had to
reflect cultural preferences. Gutteridge's remark 'I was so glad to find the place
like home' is indicative of this desire to feel at ease in unfamiliar surroundings.[29] If guests felt comfortable then they might return to the same house year
after year. Repeat trade is important in the tourism business, which can then
rely on some guaranteed business as well as new, attracted by word-of-mouth
recommendation.[30] For this reason proprietors preferred the term company house
keeper, with its connotations of friendliness, warmth and even respectability,
compared with the term lodging house keeper, which conjured up images of
accommodation for the poor and transients.[31] John Walton has highlighted
the centrality of the landlady in the creation of the working-class holiday: 'They
offered a welcome to working-class people on their own terms, and which was
indeed increasingly provided by people whose culture was firmly grounded
in the working class of the industrial towns, this eased the path for new holiday makers and encouraged the return of established ones.'[32]

Despite its shortcomings, the apartment system survived in most resorts
oriented to a working-class clientele until the 1950s, when it was finally
replaced by boarding houses that were fully catering, with fixed meals and fixed
rates. The main reason for the system's survival, as well as cheapness and lack
of domestic technology, was that it was popular. Guests liked the freedom to
choose their own food and to decide when and where to eat.[33] As already noted,
familiar food was important to working-class travellers. Gradually, however,
the apartment system gave way to boarding houses. Making their appearance
in the late nineteenth century, they were initially slow to catch on; in 1912
Scarborough had only about fifty and there were probably even fewer in
Blackpool, the major resort of the working class, although some company houses

offered optional full board. This would have been the preference for married women in families that could afford it, who particularly wanted to get away from the routine of domestic work if not child care.[34] In the inter-war years, apartments were most popular in the North of England but in the Midlands and South full board was preferred.[35] Boarding houses were the norm by the Second World War but apartments survived into the 1950s as a minority taste.[36]

By the 1930s most providers of accommodation for the working-class visitor would have had access to labour-saving domestic appliances which would have given the landlady more time to plan meals, purchase food and service the rooms. The number of households with electricity had risen from only one in seventeen in 1920 to one in three by 1930.[37] In December 1927 *Good Housekeeping* carried advertisements for thirty-four different lighting, cooking and heating companies, in addition to various firms selling washing machines and vacuum cleaners and other 'labour saving' devices.[38] Not only would this increased use of domestic electricity and gas have given the landladies better resources to cater for their guests, it would also have raised the standards and expectations of the guests themselves, for whom taking a holiday and choosing accommodation was as much an act of consumption as purchasing the domestic appliances now available and with which holidaymaking would eventually, especially in the 1950s onwards, compete.

As boarding houses took over from apartment houses the demand for accommodation that was cheap enough for the increasing numbers of working-class holidaymakers with modest incomes was rising. As well as being too expensive for many working-class families, they were also not to the taste of many.

> Staying in a seaside boarding house meant sleeping in a small, clean room with a wash stand in it. A jug of hot water was brought in the morning and another at night with the proviso that the wallpaper mustn't be splashed. The lavatory was shared by everyone and there was usually no bath. Bread and jam were served for breakfast, except on Sundays, when there was something cooked. At teatime there was a hot meal, which was quickly served and eaten in silence.[39]

This gloomy picture was obviously not the unanimous experience of guests, most of whom enjoyed their holidays and frequently returned to the same resort and boarding house year after year. However, if the weather was bad, precluding outdoor and beach activities, it could be miserable for families barred from their lodgings during the day except for mealtimes. If no indoor amusements or shows were available, or were outside the holiday budget, families would huddle in the shelters on promenades or in ornamental seafront gardens, the lucky ones on seats, staring out at a rain-drenched beach, rough grey sea and

Plate 4 The Scofield family on the promenade after a freak storm at New Brighton, 1955. Guests had to be out of their boarding houses whatever the weather. *Reproduced by courtesy of Mrs Jean Miller*

leaden sky, hoping for a glint of sunshine on the blurred horizon. Parents would be under stress from the strain of trying to keep children with frustrated ambitions of sandcastle building and paddling amused whilst the youngsters themselves grizzled or were fighting the temptation to sneak outside to jump in puddles. If the house rules permitted guests to stay in, it could be equally unpleasant trying to keep bored children quiet so as not to disturb other guests or cause damage.

As the numbers enjoying a week away from home grew, in the form of paid or unpaid holidays, not just more but alternative types of accommodation were needed to meet the demands of a wider working-class market. The apartment and boarding houses did not meet the needs of the lower-paid, who needed cheaper facilities than they were offered, or those with only a fixed amount to spend who needed to know the exact cost of the holiday, including entertainment, before setting off. They also failed to meet the needs of those who desired more freedom from routine or the restrictions imposed by boarding-house life.

Alternatives to the passivity of a boarding-house holiday in a resort with attractions devised to exploit working-class culture had been sought ever since workers began going to the seaside in large numbers, not only from religious and temperance organisations but from within the socialist and labour movement itself. The commercialisation of leisure and its frivolous diversions from the progress of the working class, in terms of self-improvement or class struggle, were denounced by socialists and those concerned with the independent advance of workers.[40] As the nineteenth century progressed, and with it the number of workers taking holidays involving a stay away from home, alternatives to commercial provision were also developed. These alternative social and cultural provisions, like many of the Great Exhibition's travel clubs, were rooted in the movements for rational recreation. Alternative holiday provision tried to build on and develop the collective aspects of working-class culture and was the product of idealistically or philanthropically motivated organisations.

A loose federation of clubs and associations grew up around the *Clarion* newspaper, started in 1891 by Robert Blatchford. This was a paper with a mass circulation within the working class whose influence spread into the leisure time of its readers, who became involved in a range of social activities such as choirs and cycling clubs. These clubs also had a political focus. Members on cycling trips would dismount to distribute socialist literature and hold impromptu meetings, disturbing the Sabbath in remote country villages.[41] The emphasis of the Clarion Fellowship was not on competition or commercialism but on comradeship and companionship. This wasn't unique within the socialist movement; John Trevor's Labour Church Movement had also provided an alternative to the increasingly alienating cultural norms of capitalism.[42] Although nominally a church the organisation concentrated more on fellowship than religion. The Labour Church 'extended the hand of ethical fellowship to all classes and creeds in a gospel of social amelioration, celebrated in music and texts, religious, democratic and socialist'.[43] There were fifty-four Labour Churches by 1895, but thereafter they declined, those seeking fellowship preferring the more social atmosphere of the Clarion Clubs. The co-operative movement too had similar principles, not just confining activities to retailing and production but extending to education and social fellowship. This type of organisation was not uniquely British, either. In late nineteenth-century Germany worker supporters of the Social Democratic Party (SPD) joined in similar social and cultural activities; in a climate more hostile to the labour movement, these often became important forms of political organisation, allowing likeminded individuals to meet in a country where openly political meetings were forbidden.[44] Particularly popular in Germany were gymnastics clubs and, in common with Britain, choirs, cycling and hiking groups.

In Britain the desire to promote comradeship meant that organisations like these made an important contribution to the development of holidays. In his 1997 work *A claim on the countryside* Harvey Taylor asserts that it was the National Home Reading Union (NHRU) that was the real progenitor of the concept of rational and improving holidays at prices working people could afford.[45] The

NHRU was an organisation, according to Taylor, which exerted considerable influence on the development of provision for holidays spent in keeping with the tenets of rational recreation.[46] The NHRU held its first assembly in Oxford in 1887. Further assemblies took place in the summers of 1889 and 1890 at Blackpool. These events were based on instruction courses, which promoted the pleasurable pursuit of enlightenment of the intellect and soul, as well as encouraging attention to physical health. The NHRU decided at its Blackpool assembly in 1890 to open centres for educational and outdoor activities in a number of localities. Forgetting that those who chose to go to Blackpool were looking for relaxation to suit their own tastes and to renew their physical and mental energies after a year of numbing factory work, the NHRU hoped to rescue workers from the hideousness of the place where, according to Katherine St John Conway, writing in the *Workman's Times* in 1893 and cited by Taylor:

> In long rows stood the Cheap Jack stalls, a nightmare of stripes and stars. On the grey sea wall were grouped the sunshades and frocks of the lasses, who learn to shriek instead of laugh, to chatter instead of talk, and to parade instead of stroll in the dull blankness of brick walls and in the close confinement of the factory prison.[47]

The Co-operative Holiday Association (CHA), which originated in 1891 although not formally constituted and named until 1897, and its later offshoot of 1913, the Holiday Fellowship, aimed to provide, at a reasonable cost, holidays away from the commercialised resorts in more unspoilt areas, with the emphasis on enjoyment, not through wasteful consumption but through fellowship and communal living. The stated objects of the CHA were to provide recreation and educational holidays by purchasing or renting and furnishing houses and rooms in selected areas, catering in such houses for parties of members and guests and securing helpers who would promote the intellectual and social interests of the party with which they were associated.[48]

The CHA had been created through the inspiration of a Congregationalist minister, T. A. Leonard, a member of the NHRU. Under its influence Leonard had organised holidays for his young congregation from Colne, in Lancashire, which became annual events from 1891. Leonard resigned his pastorship and became the CHA's permanent secretary, having his office in leased holiday accommodation at Abbey House, Whitby. Leonard had hoped to provide simple holidays that poor people could afford, promoting a more edifying experience.

We offer them the healthful ways of an out-of-door life among the hills instead of the rowdy pleasures of popular resorts. We provide a homely life in our guest houses, and whilst discouraging extravagance in both food and dress, help people to find joy in music, literature, nature study, and that best of all exercises, walking, with all that it brings to mind and body. And, most important of all, during those holiday weeks we establish the unwritten law of unselfishness, and find pleasure in serving each other's needs.[49]

In the first decade of the twentieth century the CHA opened its first two Continental guest houses, at Dinan in Brittany and at Eiffel in Germany.[50] As the CHA grew to 14,000 members in 1911 and possessed thirteen holiday centres in 1913, Leonard grew concerned about its unwieldiness and what he perceived to be its growing conservatism.[51] The committee of the CHA thought its future lay in providing good-quality accommodation, whereas Leonard wanted to create new types of centres such as youth camps and mountain huts and other venues where arrangements could be kept as simple as possible. He hoped that this would bring holidays within the reach of poorer people. He also wanted to make contacts to promote international harmony and goodwill, just like the future Workers' Travel Association.

Many committee members felt that Leonard's ideals were threatening the stability of the organisation when he insisted on these changes. In 1913 he resigned as secretary of the CHA and, with a few friends, formed the first committee of the Holiday Fellowship. The Holiday Fellowship developed three camps for children at Staithes, Conway and the Isle of Sheppey but later opened camps for families as well.[52] In common with the CHA, it included vacations abroad as integral to its work.[53] The CHA and Holiday Fellowship were pioneers not just of holidays in the open air but also of the idea that people need for their full enjoyment not only natural beauty but the imponderable things of the human spirit – 'laughter and the love of friends'.[54]

The Clarion Clubs also gave mostly young people, during the late nineteenth and early twentieth centuries, the chance to experience a holiday in the open air on cycling and camping trips in a comradely atmosphere. Although these clubs offered socialist recreational activity, for every individual who engaged in political work there were large numbers of Clarion Club members who did not.[55] The club's instigator, Robert Blatchford, claimed that he desired a 'sociable socialism', that he wanted 'a family gathering, a brotherly – and sisterly, if you like – jollification, not a political conference'.[56] It was difficult to strike the correct balance between entertainment and political work. The socialist activist Tom Maguire commented on this problem of reconciling the cultural activities of the converted with the necessary work of political organising. He complained of the social side of the movement that 'political progress is not made after the fashion of a Corydon–Phyllis dance, jigging along . . . through pleasant places with the sun shining over us'.[57]

In common with other organisations aiming to promote uplifting and intellectually satisfying leisure opportunities for working people, the Holiday Fellowship faced the problem of appealing not to workers but to lower middle-class people, as the Mechanics' Institutes had done. A partial reason for this could have been, as Richard Holt argues, that most young workers before the First World War were unable or unwilling to use the trains or the bicycle 'to get away from it all' as middle-class youth did, although shorter cycling excursions became more common.[58] 'Apprentices preferred a few days at the seaside in the company of their mates, drinking and chasing the girls, to invigorating walks over mountains,'[59] a barrier to the Holiday Fellowship fulfilling its objectives. Oral evidence from Leicestershire hosiery workers, though, a long way from the sea, suggests that quite a lot of young workers did cycle to the seaside.[60]

Up to the outbreak of the First World War the Workmen's Travel Club, an offshoot of the mainly middle-class student-patronised Toynbee Travellers' Club which flourished from 1889, organised an annual visit of three or four days to a Continental city at a cost of about £2 each, a price within the means of most skilled workers in those days.[61] These clubs were based at Toynbee Hall, whose warden in the 1920s, J. J. Mallon, was to become a founding committee member of the Workers' Travel Association. Another WTA founder, its inspiration and first secretary, Cecil Rogerson, was involved in running the club.

Another means of providing alternatives to the rigidity of apartment and boarding-house accommodation, giving more opportunities for relaxation to women holidaymakers while also meeting the need for an all-inclusive price for those on restricted budgets was holiday camps. The labour movement played a leading and active role in their initiation, development and promotion. That a 'key element in the development of pioneer holiday camps was the contribution of workers' organisations' was acknowledged by Colin Ward and Dennis Hardy in *Goodnight, campers*.[62] It was a member of the Clarion Cycling Club and the Independent Labour Party, John Fletcher Dodds, who opened the Socialist Holiday Camp at Caister in 1906. After a camping holiday near Caister with his two sons, Dodds determined to set up a camping ground there for socialists. In 1906, with ten friends, he camped on the seafront. The camp was such a success that soon a thousand people were staying there each summer and by about 1911 canvas was being replaced by huts and chalets. On the early

Plate 5 The Socialist Camp, Caister, shortly after its opening in 1906. Note the ILP sign and tents in the background and the horse-drawn transport

camp site the tent dwellers, in the spirit of comradeship, sang songs around the camp fire while the camp committee, many of whom were trade unionists, organised socials, dances, debates and lectures.[63] Although the holidaymakers lived communally, sharing the camp-site chores, it was far from a socialist utopia, maintaining a gender division of labour. Cooking was done by the women and men picked the vegetables in the camp garden. This, though, kept the costs down to a price affordable by an increasing number of workers.

Although the camp hoped to respond to the needs of working-class people wanting a holiday at an affordable price, a large proportion of the guests, especially after a change of name to simply the 'Caister Camp' and the predominance of chalets over tents, were white-collar workers seeking freedom from the regimentation of the boarding houses of the time. A Manchester woman recalled how her parents met at the camp while they were students in the 1920s on holiday with their own parents.[64] The couple later followed white-collar occupations in the Inland Revenue. Tents were not entirely replaced with huts and in 1939, when a week's stay at the camp cost £2 5s, the back-to-basics-style camp offered a choice of accommodation in wooden huts or bell tents set out in neat rows. Evening entertainment was still self-initiated. Someone usually produced an accordion and led group sing-alongs of the popular hits of the day.[65]

Although not the first holiday camp, Cunningham's Young Men's Camp on the Isle of Man in 1894 owns this accolade; Dodds's was one of the first

Plate 6 Caister Camp in the 1930s: tents still predominate but note the wooden chalets in the background and the motor bike and sidecar

aimed at families rather than young men or children only and was neither religious nor philanthropic. By 1939 it was competing with commercial camps like Billy Butlin's three-year-old one at Skegness and his newly completed facility at Clacton. Faced with this competition, Dodds's maintained its clientele, part of an ever-expanding market, thanks to the growth of paid holidays. The camp was still family-run. J. Fletcher Dodds and his wife lived in an imposing bungalow on the site and, though he chatted with residents, by then he seemed to take little part in the day-to-day running of the enter-prise.[66] By 1949 every taste was catered for, the camp had a resident band and weekly cinema shows, just like the larger commercial sites. Its advertising slogan, in response to criticism of the supposed regimentation at Butlin's, boasted 'everything is provided, from the energetic round of sport to a quiet cosy armchair and a favourite book. You can do just as you please. There is no regimentation at Caister.'[67]

Not all the early camps were run on an ideological basis. In the years after the First World War, especially, other privately owned holiday camps inspired by the Caister Camp appeared, such as Potter's at Hemsby, opened in 1920.[68] For them the objective was unashamedly for their guests to have fun. The section of the coast between Yarmouth and Lowestoft, in 1934, was styled 'Holiday Camp Village' by a porter at Hopton on Sea station in 1934.[69] Around

Hopton were five of these self-contained resorts with accommodation for 1,100 visitors. In order of size there was the Constitutional Holiday Camp and Beach Club, with accommodation for 450 guests, which advertised itself as the most luxurious camp on the east coast. The Golden Sands Camp and Club was set in twenty acres of grounds that contained a luxurious clubhouse and could house 250 visitors. Potter's new Cliff Camp, 'every hut with a sea view', could take 175 guests, while the original Potter's Camp catered for 125. The smaller White Hart Camp could welcome eighty-five guests.[70] The LNER's Suffolk Camp Express carried holiday travellers to the area.[71] The Socialist Camp had an influence far wider than just within socialist circles.

Even on the journey the exuberance of seaside campers showed itself in the prevailing holiday spirit, as they travelled on the Norfolk Camp Express, a special train service to Caister and Hemsby inaugurated by the LNER in 1934 to match the popularity and demand for holiday camps.[72] 'In addition to the usual holiday equipment many of the holidaymakers provided themselves with ukuleles and other "musical" instruments; before trains left Liverpool Street concerts were in full swing which vied in volume if not in musical precision with some of the best of the BBC jazz band broadcasts.'[73]

Continuing labour and working-class organisational involvement in these developments, both the co-operative movement and the trade union movement were active in the creation of holiday camps. The claim to having 'quite by chance set going what is now a very big and flourishing industry' was made not by Billy Butlin but by W. J. Brown, the general secretary of the biggest clerical union, the Civil Service Clerical Association.[74] When a parent of young children he had experienced the 'purgatory' of a seaside boarding-house holiday in wet weather and at the same time he had memories of a holiday as a young man at Caister Camp in the discomfort of a bell tent. There was no water close at hand and candlelight was the only means of lighting. The food was poor and the countryside bleak.[75] In the early 1920s he had the following idea:

> Suppose that instead of a bleak field we could have wooden chalets, with running water and electric light. Suppose we could have a recreation hall for dancing, concerts and the rest. Suppose we could have a place where, wet or fine, the children could make all the noise they liked, in circumstances where they wouldn't upset the adults who wanted quiet? Surely this would be a vast improvement on the seaside boarding house?[76]

Brown's inspiration led to the opening in 1924 of the Corton Camp, owned by his own company, the Civil Servants' Camp Association. With the approval of the CSCA executive committee, he had found an ideal site of landscaped wooded gardens owned by Jeremiah Colman, of mustard fame. Brown's ambition was for the proposed holiday camp to be a co-operative venture run by his union on non-profit-making lines. The union, however, felt the enterprise to be too risky.

Not to be thwarted in his ambition, Brown got together with some friends to raise a few hundred pounds between them. Association members were then asked to take up £1 shares at 5 per cent, which managed to raise only another £240. Having failed to raise the funds through his association, Brown was forced to approach the chiefs of the employing government departments, who lent £50 each. Enough money was raised to justify the erection of the camp, which gave the security to allow borrowing the balance from the bank. The camp, costing thousands of pounds, was built at great personal risk to Brown and his friends rather than as the purely co-operative effort he had intended. He was still advertising shares for sale to members in the association's magazine *Red Tape* only a month before the camp opened.[77]

Despite difficulty selling shares, there was no trouble selling the holidays. Bookings, at two guineas a week and half-price for children, came in quickly for the summer of 1924. By the following season holidaymakers were being turned away and Brown began to look for a second site. One was found at Orchard Leas Estate on Hayling Island which opened in 1930. The new camp was built to an even higher standard than at Corton, with detached huts instead of ones arranged in contiguous rows. *Red Tape* magazine declared that the camp had 'secured the maximum of comfort for everyone consistent with not destroying the essential feeling that one is a camper and not a mere resident in a hotel or boarding house'.[78] During the 1930s the original camp was improved and enlarged to take 200 guests at prices hardly above their 1920s level. When the CSCA held its annual conferences at Corton, Brown was completely vindicated and reminded delegates of how they had been sceptical about the idea of the camp when he had first suggested it. These holiday camps, styled 'luxury' by Brown, originated over a decade before Billy Butlin opened his first camp at Skegness, so Brown can be justified in his claim that his camps were the precursors of the modern holiday camp industry.

Another public sector union which opened its own holiday camps was the National Association of Local Government Officers (NALGO). In occupations not famous for their trade union militancy it was recognised that services provided by the union could attract members. Holiday centres were not NALGO's first venture into holiday provision. The union already possessed a holiday cottage in Wales and in 1912 hired out a whole hotel in Montreux for two months, sub-letting rooms to members at less than commercial rates.[79] This involvement in leisure beyond workplace issues was a legacy from the Liverpool Municipal Officers' Guild, founded in 1896, a forerunner and constituent member of the national union formed in 1907. The guild had a holidays and excursion section which became a large travel agency. Every year it chartered steamers to take up to 2,000 members and friends to Llandudno. One year the guild organised an eight-day trip to Paris and another it organised a cruise of twenty-three days' duration to Portugal and the Canary Islands at an all-in charge of £10 each.[80]

At NALGO's 1930 conference a resolution from the Manchester branch, perhaps inspired by the CSCA, was passed calling for the union to build a holiday camp for the benefit of its members. A committee chaired by a sanitary inspector from St Pancras, W. G. Auger, found a newly built commercial camp in a beautiful location at Croyde Bay in Devon. Auger negotiated its purchase from the owners for £12,000 (£1,000 less than the asking price) plus £428 for stock. With ninety-five asbestos huts, a recreation room, dining hall, tennis court, putting green, garage, electricity plant and even its own artesian well, the camp was opened to members on 2 April 1931 under its original management team who came along with the undertaking's transfer.[81]

The venture was so successful for NALGO that the following year Conference resolved, in a motion passed by the National Executive Committee, to fund a second camp in the North. Within two months, after inspecting ten sites, the committee purchased land at Cayton Bay near Scarborough. Building began before the end of the year on a camp to NALGO's own specification. At a cost of £25,000 it had 124 wooden bungalows, accommodating 252 visitors, a dining hall, recreation room, billiard room, card room, bowling green, children's playground and a beach bungalow.[82] The new camp opened in July 1933. The Croyde accommodation was upgraded to brick bungalows with hot and cold running water in 1937 and a concert hall with stage and dance floor added. It was several years ahead of any other camp in the country, according to NALGO's national executive committee. A particular innovation of NALGO was that it was the first to use the title 'Holiday Centre' rather than 'Camp'.[83] The Croyde Bay Centre was extremely popular and by the 1950s profit from there was subsidising the camp at Cayton. After years of deliberation the Cayton camp was sold to another camp operator for £100,000 in 1976.[84]

The two examples of trade union involvement in the holiday camp business above were by white-collar public sector workers' organisations. This sector of the labour market enjoyed holidays with pay by custom and practice at a time when this was a provision offered only to a minority of workers. For local government employees, holiday entitlement, agreed through the national Whitley Council for the civil service by 1920, was twenty-four working days for the lowest grades and up to forty-eight for the highest.[85] This may have been a factor in the decision to go into the schemes and certainly contributed to the success of the ventures.

An example of trade union involvement in holiday provision by a manual union is that of the Derbyshire Miners' Association (DMA), which built its own camp near Skegness. Thanks to the success of the scheme to provide payment during holidays, the camp, inspired by Hicken, a DMA leader who negotiated the holidays with pay agreement, was built thanks to a £40,000 grant from the Miners' Welfare Fund and some contributions from the coal owners. It was opened on 20 May 1939 by Sir Frederick Sykes, the Miners' Welfare Central Committee chairman, who in his speech said, 'I do not think there is any other non-profit-making camp of its kind in the country. It is a pioneer venture which is being watched with close interest.'[86] The centre housed almost 1,000 visitors in chalets for families and cubicles for single visitors, with meals taken in a large communal dining hall. There were concerts and dances every night. The cost of this holiday was £1 13s a week for a couple and 8s 6d for a child over four years of age. In its first year 15,000 miners and their families took part in this pioneering venture specifically for industrial workers, assisted by a special arrangement with the railway companies for reduced fares from Derbyshire to Skegness. For most of those mining families using the newly opened camp it would have been the first time they had been able to enjoy a week's holiday by the sea in their lives.

Other unions and organisations of the working class have been active in the provision of holiday facilities for their members. Many own or owned seaside properties used as convalescent homes for members in need of rest after illness or injury. In the 1920s and 1930s Ernest Bevin, Herbert Elvin and many other trade union officers and activists had been leading supporters of the Workers' Travel Association. There was some discussion in the trade union movement as to whether or not unions should run their own hotels for members. Scarborough and District Trades Council wrote to the TUC in July 1938, drawing attention to a resolution carried at a recent meeting:

> In view of the increasing number of workers enjoying holidays with pay, this Council calls upon the Trades Union Congress to consider proposals for the affiliated unions to own hotels in the various seaside health resorts. This Council realises

that the workers are dependent upon the anti-labour boarding house and hotel keeper, and that only by the trade union movement owning and controlling the means of accommodation can the workers' needs be satisfactorily met.[87]

The sentiment behind this policy and the efforts of workers' organisations to provide holiday accommodation of various kinds was entirely in keeping with the recommendations of the IFTU Taylerle resolution of 1929, discussed in the preceding chapter, which emphasised that trade unions should establish holiday homes with the aid of state and public bodies.[88] The pseudo-Marxian phraseology of the resolution is interesting, as it refers to the 'ownership of the means of accommodation', although this probably says more about the political composition of Scarborough Trades Council than the views of the working class in general. The phrase also echoes the words in the Labour Party constitution calling for the facilitation of 'a great development of the means of recreation'.[89] The secretary of the TUC's organisation department wrote in response to the letter from Scarborough Trades Council, stating the position of Congress. The TUC's view was that at that moment the holidays with pay movement had 'not resulted in an influx to the seaside and other residential places and that the capital expenditure that would be required would be out of all proportion to the number of members who could be accommodated at such a hotel'.[90] The letter to Scarborough Trades Council goes on to describe how in the previous year, 1937, at the request of the General Council, the Workers' Travel Association (WTA) had placed six centres at its disposal for young trade unionists at prices which were £1 a week lower than advertised. The secretary explained how they circulated all unions and trades councils on the matter but were unable to secure enough applications to fill one centre, much less six, and in the end the WTA had had to absorb them into its own programme. In view of this failure any suggestion of hotels run by trade unions themselves would appear to be premature.[91] In 1937, the year of the experiment, the Holidays with Pay Act was a year away from becoming law, although it would be longer before it was fully implemented. At the time the TUC secretary's letter was written the benefits of the Act had not yet been felt. Optimism about the future expansion of workers' holidays remained high, though, as in 1939 the TUC's Joint Council had proposed a venture to provide holiday camps and boarding houses for union members in conjunction with the WTA.[92] This initiative, according to Francis Williams, the historian of the WTA, was curtailed owing to the start of the Second World War. When peace returned, trade unions carried on their involvement in providing seaside accommodation. The Transport and General Workers'

Union had centres that were used for holidays and conferences at Eastbourne, Conway and Ayr in the 1970s, demonstrating the continuity of this involvement through the years.

The first co-operative movement holiday camp was the Roseland Summer Camp overlooking Rothesay bay in Scotland, which took in its first guests, sleeping in bell tents, in 1911.[93] This camp was an inspiration to co-operative societies south of the border. Influences from other camps were instrumental again here. The president of the Renfrewshire Co-operative Conference Association, John Dewar, was keen on camping because of his experience of the Volunteers' camps and he was supported by fellow Renfrew co-operator and Cunningham's Camp visitor, John Paton, in his campaign for a co-operative camp. The Refrewshire and the United Co-operative Baking Society had initially leased a farm at Roseland for six months. Camp-style holidays were not new to the Co-op Baking Society members: they had had a holiday club since 1899, and in 1908 had sent twenty-five young people to the YMCA camp at Ardgoil.[94] The Roseland camp was such a success in its first season that the farm was bought for £600 and improvements in the water supply and communal accommodation were made with the aid of a £1,000 loan. When the camp reopened in 1913 the marquee housing the dining and communal area had been replaced by a permanent structure catering for several hundred campers. In the interests of efficiency the Baking Society took sole ownership and charge of the camp. After being requisitioned during the First World War the camp was again improved and chalets catering for up to 400 were built. The camp was popular for decades among Scottish co-operators but, following mergers between the Baking Society and the Scottish Co-operative Wholesale Society and again with the Co-operative Wholesale Society in 1973, finally closed in 1974.

Another successful early co-operative movement camp, belonging to the Coventry Co-operative Society, was at Voryd (or Foryd), near Rhyl. The original 1930 camp consisted of six sleeping huts, an old railway coach, an ex-army hut, two dozen square tents and some old bell tents.[95] Although a new venture for the society, the camp was not its first delve into camping holidays. The year before a small group of its members had camped in the Peak District over the Whitsun holiday. Following this experience one of the campers, Tom Snowdon, urged the society's education secretary to find a permanent site for annual camps. This provided the impetus for finding and renting the seaside site at Voryd. The initiative was an immediate success and by July it was announced that there was no accommodation available for the last week in July or the first two weeks in August. As it was a sound proposition, the education committee persuaded the management committee to purchase the field and to build about sixty chalets there as well as leaving space for people to pitch their own tents.[96] In the true spirit of co-operation, the camp was run on a non-profit basis from the education committee's share of the trading surpluses in Coventry and its grant from the CWS. Campers cooked their own meals, with the camp supplying Primus stoves, pans and crockery. The site had a shop operated by the Rhyl Co-operative Society, which donated the dividend to the sports and entertainment fund. To help society members to pay for their holidays at the camp, the Coventry Co-op sold savings stamps in its stores and some members used their 'divi' towards the cost.[97] The site fulfilled all its original objectives of providing cheap holidays for workers, although it was later to suffer from its non-profit-making ethos, as not enough income was generated to carry out repairs and the redevelopment needed to bring it up to modern standards. The site was eventually closed and cleared in the 1970s.

During the 1930s the CWS embarked on a new project in partnership with the Workers' Travel Association. The two organisations had many connections; at one time three CWS directors had sat as members of the WTA's management committee. The partners formed Travco Camps Ltd and in 1938 the purpose-designed and built Rogerson Hall Holiday Centre was opened at Corton in Norfok. The centre was named in honour of Cecil Rogerson, the founder and first secretary of the WTA. The Travco camp incorporated modern design features typical of the 1930s. Great thought was put into the design, and it was limited in size to catering for 500 guests, the maximum it was believed would ensure that the camp remained friendly and intimate without losing a sense of community or becoming regimented, as many of the larger camps were judged to be.[98]

For the WTA it was important to provide holidays in beautiful surroundings whether they were natural or man-made. With this in mind it sponsored an architectural competition for holiday centre designs. The design for Rogerson Hall had a central block with a lounge, dining hall, dance floor, a library and a shop. The bedroom block had single, double and family rooms. The grounds contained tennis courts, swimming pool, paddling pool, bowling and putting greens. The building costs of this triumph of functional art-deco design were very high, so no more centres of the type could be afforded. In its first season Rogerson Hall was so successful that 4,870 visitors were received and more than 1,000 turned away.[99] Travco went on to build on this success by opening a second camp at Westward Ho! in Devon. They had also planned a further collaborative development with the proposed name of Travco Hotels.[100]

Speaking on the subject of holiday camps in November 1938, Mr Smith of the London Co-operative Society said: 'There is a great need for organised holidays. The people now for the first time getting holidays with pay are used to a routine job, and their recreation is of the mass-organised kind. More camps are necessary where amusements are provided all the time.'[101] Camps enabled families of moderate means, including married women, to enjoy the seaside without domestic burdens, and brought entertainment to the holidaymaker without him or her having to go out and look for it and then pay extra to get it. Unlike that of the middle-class holidaymakers, child care was communal or shared, not privatised and individual with each family having the exclusive attention of a nanny. This type of holiday offered no opportunity for elitism or individuality, unlike those typically preferred by the middle class. Everyone was expected to join in. Unfortunately, those camps under commercial management were too expensive for the mass of the people, even though their inclusive charges covered a great deal of 'free' entertainment and the use of many facilities, thereby saving on spending money. The total number who went to them was small in comparison with those who stayed in apartments or boarding houses.[102] Even in 1965 only 5 per cent of holidaymakers stayed in camps, compared with 27 per cent who lodged in boarding or guest houses and unlicensed hotels.[103]

Although the war of 1939–45 put any further development of holiday centres on hold, in the financial year 1946–47 the WTA opened five new holiday centres, including Trebovir Court in London and Dunraven Castle in South Wales, leased from the Earl of Dunraven and Killerton in north Devon.[104] Like the years after the First World War, this post-war period saw a change in land use and much property changed hands as the great country houses and estates became a relic of an earlier age, often because inheritors were unable to meet death duty taxation and as the economic function of such estates changed.[105] In 1947 the WTA opened Rustington Lido on the south coast and renamed it Mallon Dene after J. J. Mallon, a long-serving and original committee member of the WTA. Travco Hotels, the partnership of the WTA and the CWS, was formed in 1945, although the Travco partnership did not last. At the annual conference of the Co-operative Union, the CWS resolved that it ought to operate a complete travel service of its own on the same lines as the WTA, thus posing a conflict of interests as well as outlook.[106] In the circumstances, the ending of the partnership meant that the WTA gave up its interest in Travco Hotels and the Westward Ho! camps but became solely responsible for Rogerson Hall and Mallon Dene.

Providing holidays in Britain was a move in a new direction for the WTA. Its original object was to contribute to internationalism and peace by enabling ordinary workers to visit other countries. As part of this aim the intention had been to make travel possible for people for whom the ordinary tourist agencies did not cater. The WTA, according to a former manager of Leicester Co-op Travel, was the first to offer all-in holidays abroad.[107] Using its labour movement connections, it organised many trips abroad at lower prices than any other organisation. It was not entirely inconsistent with its objectives for the WTA to embark on the provision of cheap family holidays in Britain for groups that could not otherwise afford even the most modest of boarding houses. Nevertheless these people had, by the WTA's standard of social values, the right to expect something better than was offered by the cheaper commercial and sometimes excessively large and regimented holiday camps. These were in any case too expensive for many working-class families.[108]

The WTA had its origins in the inspired idealism of Cecil Rogerson, who in 1921 was a minor official in the League of Nations Organisation in London. His idealism was not matched by practicality and the organisation decided that it could no longer employ him, but as a gesture of goodwill sent him to Geneva to look after a British group visiting the International Labour Office. Sitting beside the lake, with representatives of workers' organisations from many countries, Rogerson was possessed 'of a vision of the ordinary workers of many lands visiting each other, coming to know each other, forging out of their understanding for each other's lives such bonds of peace as should never again be broken'.[109]

This idealism was entirely consistent with the feelings of many people in those early days after the Great War had ended. The establishment of the League of Nations and its popular support typified this sentiment. In her autobiographical work *Testament of youth*, about her experience of the war and its aftermath, Vera Brittain described the League as 'that international experiment in the maintenance of peace and security which I felt, in common with many other students of modern history, to be the one element of hope and progress contained in the peace treaties'.[110]

Back in his hotel room, Rogerson composed a draft convention for a Labour Travel Association. Its objectives were to promote foreign travel by workers and to facilitate social intercourse among them and with other nations; to support the real ideals of the League of Nations and the ILO and to strengthen the Labour Party by additional ties of co-operative effort and friendship. Other members of the party in Geneva were impressed by this draft. They included a number of influential figures in the labour movement, such as Harry Gosling, who was to become the first president of the WTA, Duncan Carmichael, who was secretary of the London Trades Council, and some union leaders such as J. W. Bowen, General Secretary of the Post Office Workers' Union. The WTA always had close links with the labour movement although the name Labour Travel Association was shunned in order to represent the organisation as non-politically affiliated. Despite its non-political stance, the WTA's founders and committee members were all well known in the trade union movement. A letter signed by a number of union leaders as well as Gosling of the (newly formed through mergers) Transport and General Workers' Union was drawn up. Signatories included John Turner of the Shop Assistants, Herbert H. Elvin of the National Union of Clerks and Administrative Workers, A. S. Walkden of the Railway Clerks' Association and J. J. Mallon of Toynbee Hall. The letter opened with the words 'After the great tragedy of the war, it would seem a favourable time for meeting and making friends with other nations. Co-operative effort, added to the advantages of the exchange rates, makes the cost of foreign travel more possible.' It went on to suggest the formation of a travel association through which workers of Britain and other countries could obtain cheap and interesting holidays, knowledge of Continental people, scenery and conditions and broadened horizons.[111]

This letter was sent to more than seventy organisations, inviting their representatives to a conference at Toynbee Hall to discuss the possible formation of a Workers' Travel Association. Among more than fifty letters of support came ones from Ernest Bevin, Margaret Bondfield, the future Minister of Labour, Arthur Pugh and John Baker of the Iron and Steel Trades Confederation, W. A. Hutchinson of the Amalgamated Engineering Union, Bill Bowen of the Post Office Workers and T. A. Leonard of the Holiday Fellowship. Despite this support only a few of those invited were able to attend. Fortunately the few who did were enthusiastic and became the national committee of the new association. In summing up the conference Rogerson, the chairman, said that the feeling of the meeting was that properly organised travel among workers of the various countries could by co-operative effort be brought within the reach of all, and that such friendly visits would augment greatly needed comradeship among nations.[112]

Early in 1922 Rogerson produced the first circular announcing the WTA's ambitious initial programme of trips. This publicised programme

was extremely over-ambitious. Easter tours to Belgium and the battlefields and
summer tours to Belgium, France, Switzerland, Germany, Austria, Italy and
Sweden were promised at prices ranging from £5 to £8 a week.[113] In reality
the only trip actually organised was a Whitsun visit to a château in Normandy
which promised the sharing with guests of beautiful things and friendly
hospitality from the lady owner. The extremely low charges, even by 1922
standards, of £5 for one week or £8 for two, covered return fares from
London, accommodation, meals and excursions. Even these modest prices were
too high for most of the workers the WTA wished to introduce to foreign travel.
In this first party were a bus driver and one or two skilled industrial workers
but the majority were clerks and a few trade union officials and teachers. It
was their first trip abroad for all of them, which in itself was a success for the
WTA, although it had hoped to attract more industrial workers. The trip to
Normandy did not turn out as planned. Rogerson was supposed to travel
with the party as its guide but owing to pressure of work due to the amount
of bookings coming in he could not spare the time. Meals promised on the
journey to the château did not materialise and when the travellers arrived, tired
and hungry, in the small Normandy town where they were supposed to be met
by their hosts, nobody came for them. They had to find their own way to the
château on foot, seeking directions from locals. Accommodation, which had
been promised in comfortable dormitories in the luxurious surroundings of
the château, turned out to be in a dormitory rigged up in the stable block and
private rooms no more than cubicles formed with wooden partitions. They
slept on camp beds with straw mattresses. Exquisite French cooking turned
out to be frugal, mostly black bread and bean soup.[114]

During this first season the WTA received many knocks as holidays did not
match up to publicised expectations or the aspirations of the travellers. A party
visiting Brittany complained that their hotel was derelict, dirty, and instead of
the promised sea view all they could see was the town gaol. Two days before
the departure of the first party to Paris it was discovered that Rogerson had
completely forgotten to book accommodation of any kind. There were lots of
difficulties, many due to Rogerson's unpractical nature and the need to impro-
vise as bookings flooded in. Complaints were received regarding lost luggage,
overcrowding in the student hostels and third-rate hotels in Berlin and
Vienna, bad food, poor beds and general inefficiency. A letter from Edward
Knight, appointed by the committee to help in the administration of the WTA,
to Arthur Creech-Jones began: 'Dear Comrade, I have had an unpleasant experience during my short time while on the job, which I would on no account

have accepted, even though I am economically down at the moment, if I had known such treatment would be my lot.'[115] He accused Rogerson of being insulting to staff and failing to do adequate bookkeeping. Knight went on describing the problems with Rogerson's style of management and complained he had a complete lack of interpersonal and organisational skills. Something had to be done to save the organisation, he divulged.[116] Poor Rogerson seems to have taken on more than he could cope with and, because he seemed to find it impossible to work with others, he was asked to leave. Rogerson was understandably upset and wrote to Gosling that:

> Mallon told me while I was away in Vienna, you, he and Carmichael and a few others met and decided that the WTA must be run better and practically told me that this meeting had decided to turn me out. I feel disappointed as you will remember I drafted plans at Geneva when you and Carmichael promised to back me. I leave it to them (the committee) to decide a) if they want to get rid of me entirely, b) appoint a good enough man for me to wish to work under, c) that I remain on the Committee and help them with my experience and service.[117]

Rogerson left the association and formed Friendship Holidays after some argument with the committee over mailing WTA clients promoting his new organisation using WTA facilities while he was still employed by the association.

The WTA's tourists, though, enjoyed their holidays, which had been secured at the cheapest possible cost, despite the disappointments. The number of bookings continued to increase. The organisation had discovered a genuine demand from those of limited income for travel abroad on inclusive tours. It had taken the first faltering steps in a social revolution in holidaymaking that was to take thousands of ordinary people abroad and show that, even for those with very little money and no knowledge of foreign ways or languages, the world need not end at the cliffs of Dover. The WTA was established primarily to promote personal contact between workers of all countries on a reciprocal basis of holiday travel as an aid to peace.[118] In its first year the WTA handled 700 holiday bookings and 1,996 in its second. By 1925 the Association had over 6,000 bookings and its turnover was more than £45,000. By 1939 the turnover had reached a phenomenal £595,000, dropping suddenly owing to the war to only just over £94,000 in 1940.[119] But economic success was not the main concern of the organisation, whose priority was not only with making foreign travel available to those for whom earlier agencies had not catered but with widening political and social horizons in order to increase international understanding.

The co-operative movement helped to build the WTA through the patronage of its members and promotion through its travel agencies, to the point where it was feared by Thomas Cook & Son as a serious rival.[120] The organisation had local fellowship and rambling groups that helped generate repeat business and gain customer loyalty. It also had annual reunion events in London where it promoted travel and organised exhibitions and entertainment. The WTA continued to grow right up to the outbreak of the Second World War, by which time it was the largest agency and the only one catering specifically for working-class travellers. There was a grand total in 1938–39 of 62,579 bookings.[121] In July 1939, just weeks before war broke out, 21,998 Continental bookings were received, 3.5 per cent up on the preceding year, and in August, with war only hours away, the WTA had already passed the highest figures of previous years in Continental departures.[122] This was partly due to the increase in paid holidays and the passing of the Holidays with Pay Act the previous year. The Act itself was passed thanks to the support of the TUC, with evidence presented by, among other union representatives, Ernest Bevin, a staunch supporter of the WTA who later became its president.

In the post-war years the WTA continued its expansion after the wartime hiatus, when its skill and expertise in organising transport and familiarity with foreign travel enabled it to play a part in the rescue of many refugees from occupied Europe. The association was also represented on committees preparing government reports, such as the Catering Wages Commission.[123] As well as its overseas trips the Association continued to expand its provision of holiday facilities in Britain, not only developing its own guest houses but making booking arrangements with privately owned hotels and boarding houses. It also acquired an interest in a coach company and initiated a wide programme of activity holidays. All this additional activity was made possible by the almost universal application of holidays with pay. However as the self-image of the working class evolved with the coming of a mass consumer society, the name Workers' Travel Association lost its appeal and some tourists even felt stigmatised by the name. Travellers didn't like luggage labels bearing the brand name. Due to this 'terrible snobbery', according to a manager at Leicester Co-op Travel, the organisation lost business because of its name. For that reason the association changed its name to Galleon Travel, after the picture on its logo. The WTA chairman told the meeting of shareholders in April 1966 that for some years everyone had been aware 'that widespread social changes which had taken place since 1939 had caused many people to regard the name "worker" as something not quite in keeping with their social status'. This not only applied to people's thinking in connection with their employment, but seemed to extend to their social activities. To go on a 'Workers' Travel' holiday, many thought, implied that one was of the working class or that the holiday would not be of the standard desired. According to the chairman's speech 'the idea of class, whether working, middle or upper, was a narrow and out-dated one. As prosperity grew and spread the old demarcation lines between so-called classes became increasingly blurred. In this atmosphere people were more and more inclined to avoid – perhaps quite unconsciously – identifying themselves with the outmoded idea of a class barrier by booking a holiday with the Workers' Travel Association.'[124] Galleon Travel survived until 1984, when it was taken over by Kennedy Brookes and was no longer owned by the WTA Trust, which maintained a small shareholding. This was bought out in 1988 when Kennedy Brookes was taken over by Trusthouse Forte.[125]

The main achievement of the WTA, apart from introducing foreign travel and later providing reasonable-cost British-based holidays for working people, was the offering of a low inclusive price for an all-in foreign holiday, an over-seas package tour that was later copied by many other travel organisations. This innovation of the package tour really did make the world seem safer and eas-ier to move around in to many people who would not otherwise have dared or been able to afford to venture beyond their own shores. The WTA set out to break down insularity and widen understanding of other peoples. It sought to overcome not just the economic barriers to travel but also the psycholo-gical ones, such as fear of the unknown, prejudice against foreigners, suspicion of strange food, fear of being made a fool of, or even a victim, in a strange land with a strange language. The groups led by leaders or tour guides who could cope with the language and unforeseen problems made the Continent less intimidating; travellers could feel safe and secure in what, to most of them, was a very new and potentially dangerous adventure. The all-in price satisfied the need of those of moderate means to know exactly what their holiday would cost so that they could fit it into a tight budget, with the aid of the WTA's own savings schemes, begun in 1931, if necessary.[126]

Popular and fully subscribed as these alternative holidays were, they were only ever available to a small minority of workers. Although the purpose of these organisations was to enable more of the working class to benefit from a holiday combined with enriching experiences and comradeship at low prices, they were not completely successful in this objective. Bookings came mostly from lower middle-class and better-paid clerical workers who were attracted by value-for-money prices and perhaps the more intellectual environment compared with commercial holidays. This prevented working people on low incomes from benefiting from them because the holidays were all snapped up early by better-off people, with deposits at the ready, who were already accustomed to taking holidays and who may have been able to afford to pay more.[127] Even so, travel agent Albert Lynn said the WTA was well patronised by working-class people, as well as trade union activists, because it offered such good value for money.[128] The majority of clients were single people or older couples. Families with children under fourteen made up no more than 10 per cent of the total and fourteen to eighteen-year-olds comprised only 5–10 per cent.[129] But this was not unusual. Mass-Observation had noticed similar statistics in Blackpool because of the low level of participation in holidaymaking by families with dependent children who contributed nothing to household income.[130]

The apartment, boarding house or holiday camp vacation did not suit all workers' tastes or pockets. Increasing numbers of people sought independence and a break from organised routine on holiday, preferring their own or a rented self-catering holiday home. Most people lacked the means to purchase or rent their own holiday home in a desirable location. For some the desire overcame the lack of financial resources. They achieved their ambition by building their own, sometimes by erecting a hut or placing caravans, old railway carriages or buses on plots of marginal land by the sea or in the countryside that was either squatted or purchased cheap. This was in response to the lack of other accommodation that members of the lower classes could afford.[131] All along the coast developments of huts, 'chalets' and later caravans appeared, providing a second home for those with little financial means that could also be rented out to neighbours, friends or relatives who could not afford boarding houses or holiday camps. Springing up mostly between 1919 and 1939, by the 1930s the rural idylls of their owners had become a great worry to those concerned with the preservation of the coastline, public health and planning. Conflicts arose regarding access to the beach where development blocked pathways or occupied large areas of the sands or dunes.[132] Many of these 'holiday homes' were on wheels, although they did not move for years, in order to avoid rates. Whole fields were packed with them in insanitary conditions. Moreton in the Wirral's bungalow town was described by the Medical Officer of Health in 1926 as 'beggaring description'.[133] It contained 150 bungalows in every stage of disrepair, bounded on one side by a foul-smelling stream and on another by a ditch of stagnant water that was almost pure sewage. In many places these holiday homes were described as ugly and misplaced shacks, almost worse than the industrial areas from which their inhabitants came. A settlement at Flamborough Head was described as one of the worst by J. A. Steers of the Geography Society in his coastal survey of 1944. There he claimed a 'whole town of hutments had completely ruined the scenery of that fine chalk headland'.[134] In North Wales there was an unsightly spread of shacks between Point of Ayr and Prestatyn. Miles of the Lincolnshire and Norfolk coasts were 'disfigured' by long lines of jerry-built wooden erections. Other 'eyesores' were noticed along the Holderness, Essex and South-east coasts. Canvey Island and Jaywick Sands were holiday estates, with some permanent residents.[135] These were created by private enterprise, by an individual buying an area of land that was subdivided and resold in small plots to other individuals on which to construct their own habitations. These makeshift dwellings, despite being looked down on by middle-class and government observers, were obviously desirable to their inhabitants, who were proud of them and decorated them to the best of their ability.

The construction of a holiday home was not confined to the seaside. The countryside around the major cities was also a popular location for innovative self-builders. For instance, since 1920 many Leicester people have had the pleasure of a second home next to Swithland Woods in the Charnwood Forest area. A Leicester resident, Leslie Sherwood, recalled that in its early days the camp site enjoyed by her family had a small group of bell tents and bivouacs.

> Our tent had its superior points. The floorboards were raised so that no rats could nest underneath. Other people were not so wise, our fox terrier was much in demand when floorboards were lifted. He could despatch ten rats in as many minutes as they ran out. We also boasted that our food was kept cool in a zinc container buried in the ground. But pride goeth before a fall! One day the pigs came, removed the cover and ate the lot. Water was carried from the farm across a field – of course, we had a yoke.

It was an important day when the campers were allowed to build wooden bungalows. Paraffin stoves and chemical toilets were coveted improvements. Leslie Sherwood's family bungalow was built by her mother. In the dark evenings in September they kept the fire burning with pine cones and wood collected from the spinneys. Many bungalows were built, until five fields were occupied. A sports day and 'end of season supper' were organised by the camp committee.[136] The bungalows, or wooden huts, built by the pioneers in the 1920s were still in use eighty years later.

These plotland developments, as they were dubbed, were characterised by the lack of any overall planning or services as well as their location on land marginal to normal economic activity because of its poor quality for agricultural purposes or liablity to flood. The sand dunes and other coastal strips fall into this category. Falling land prices due to a decline in agricultural profitability in the inter-war years led to a rush to sell land and there were few buyers for farms.[137] Ward and Hardy, in their 1984 study of these plotland developments, *Arcadia for all*, described the sites as 'offering a place in the sun for the enterprising if not rich; a landscape put together on the cheap, a manifestation by the poor people of the fashionable trend for a place in the country. Plots of land were bought cheaply and sometimes, through squatting, acquired at no cost at all.'[138] Land offered for purchase was subdivided into small plots that were the quickest and easiest to sell. Although they were sold cheap, the aggregated cost of a field divided into plots was usually much more than it was worth as a whole.

Coincidental with and facilitating this pattern of demand for building holiday and weekend homes was the availability of cheap materials to enable their development either for individuals or as camps with accommodation for letting out. During the inter-war years railway companies were shedding out-of-date rolling stock. The sturdy Victorian carriages were ideal for conversion to holiday properties. A railway coach could be delivered to a site for as little as £15, a ready-made 'chalet' which could be built upon and improved over the years.[139] Army huts from the First World War were another popular source of ready-made accommodation. A valuable form of temporary accommodation for use while the potential occupant was building a hut were bell tents, also military surplus. In the days before Green Belt restrictions and the Town and Country Planning Acts there was very little to restrict the growing abundance of such ramshackle, unplanned sites, which came to an abrupt end with the introduction of effective planning legislation in 1947, although, obviously, the expediencies of wartime, and invasion fears, between 1939 and 1945 had curtailed and often caused the removal of existing coastal plotlands.

This kind of holiday development of individual huts and caravans appealed to a growing number of working-class families trying to break through the limitations of income to acquire their own form of holiday cottage. It appealed to the independently minded, to whom a communal way of life did not appeal.[140] This individuality was echoed in the way these makeshift developments actually spoiled the seaside experience for others who were deprived of the use of sections of beach because one family monopolised the space or blocked the path to it. This lack of collective spirit seems to be the opposite of the ideal holiday offered by the workers' organisations that tried to incorporate communal activities and the idea of sharing in the philosophy behind them. However, many plotland developments had committees and had to campaign for amenities and sometimes even the right to remain, forcing a collective organisational experience. The plotland experience does seem to have had something in common with earlier movements. Ward and Hardy identified these as 'pastoralism' that looked back to an age of lost rural bliss and to an affinity with Nature, the other 'agrarianism' which idealised peasant proprietorship and reclaiming land which had been wrongly appropriated in times past.[141] These two outlooks coalesced in the plotland developments, which were symptomatic of an anti-urbanism. This 'back to nature' interest was idealised and strengthened by such writers and political theorists as William Morris, Peter Kropotkin and Feargus O'Connor with his land campaign in the 1840s. It was not entirely a symptom of individuality with its bourgeois overtones; many socialist leisure activities also focused on the enjoyment of nature, such as the rambling and cycling groups and campers under canvas who wished to enjoy the natural environment and open air. However, they did not attempt to claim ownership of the countryside and coast or deprive others of its use. The socialists' desire to share it was a sign of their being against private property that deprived the majority of the right to share in the beauty of the world. Even so, inhabitants of holiday huts did not monopolise nearly as much land as aristocratic, military or commercial owners who deprived others of access to far greater areas of beauty.

The Lincolnshire coast, with its sandy beaches and dunes, was particularly vulnerable to unplanned development. Until the 1920s most holidaymakers travelled by rail to the resorts, as the area was well served by trains. The sandhills between Mablethorpe and Skegness on the east coast were very popular.[142] At Mablethorpe the owners of land adjacent to the coast claimed they automatically owned the sandhills and beach above the high-water mark. Some parts of it they let out to the Urban District Council, which sub-let it to amusement caterers at rents that increased as the trippers came in. In 1912 the owners took the initiative to let it directly to the caterers themselves. This alarmed the council, which had lost a source of income, and in 1914 it obtained an Act of Parliament by which it acquired ownership of the sandhills. In one of the ensuing disputes over title before the Court of Appeal in 1918 it was judged that the owners of adjacent land did not have an automatic right of ownership of the sandhills but that title might be acquired as a result of having exercised acts of ownership over a period of at least twelve years.[143] The effect of this was to encourage 'inlanders' elsewhere to enclose and build on the dunes by erecting fences and bungalows in order to acquire title as quickly as possible, in effect by squatting. Bungalows, shacks, caravans, old bus bodies and railway carriages appeared wherever a track gave access to the sandhills and the seashore.

That large profits could be made from hiring out holiday homes and camping sites to working-class families was soon realised by the owners, and this conferred value on the sandhills. Chapel St Leonards was transformed from three farms and an inn to a flourishing seaside-oriented centre within five years. At Anderby Creek houses were built on top of the dunes and bungalows were erected at Soldiers' Hole, giving a unique view of the sea. 'Artistic brick bungalows and homes are being erected from £250 upwards,' declared an advertisement on the back of a pamphlet promoting Anderby Creek to visitors.[144] The advertisement, dating from around 1930, went on to proclaim that 'a limited number can be let furnished'. Some holiday homes were built behind the dunes, too. A photograph of Anderby's shop and café dating from the 1920s shows a poster announcing 'For sale. Choice sites for bungalows'.[145] Dorothy Walton of Leicester recalls happy days spent there in the 1930s when after work on Saturday morning she 'zoomed out of the factory gates, straight along the Melton Road towards Six Hills to Newark, Lincoln, Spilsby crossroads and on to a dear little place called Anderby Creek'. From Easter to October weekends and holidays were spent there. The thing to wear in the daytime, Mrs Walton recalls, was a 'snazzy' pair of beach pyjamas (the very latest fashion)!

> We joined in the midnight bathing parties every Saturday night; imagine it being warm enough on the east coast to bathe at midnight. The very thought fills me with horror now, but at the time we thought it was grand. There were supper parties round the fires on the beach. (Primus stoves – but who cared?) The sausage and hot dogs never tasted better, especially washed down with Tizer. Ukeleles and mouth organs provided most of the music and we sang and danced – well, we tried: imagine doing the Charleston on sand. (Think about it.) It was all such innocent fun then.[146]

One regular family of visitors to Ingoldmells in the inter-war years used to call the shore there 'our beach' and any strangers were unwelcome intruders. 'Mother rang a bell on the sea bank to call the family in for meals'.[147] Camps appeared at Ingoldmells and by 1921 at Bohemia, near Sutton on Sea. The Trusville Holiday Camp of caravans at Trusthorpe also dates from this time. In a newspaper of 1932 happy holidays were advertised in seafront farm bungalows with every convenience for long and short periods at Trusville. The advertisement was placed in the name of a private individual called Henshaw who gave the site as his address. At nearby Mablethorpe, Bourneleigh building estate offered separate chalets, a lounge and free tennis and the use of beach hut.[148]

Not all developments involved the occupation of sandhills or the beach. These latter two advertisements were for sites on the land immediately behind the beach and there seems to have been some attempt to create a less ambitious holiday camp at Bourneleigh with the addition of some leisure facilities. Such was not always the case. Bohemia was a development of circular corrugated iron huts built on the dunes, 15 ft in diameter, with a living room and bedroom. These 'Osocosy' huts for two people were double-lined for insulation and had a stained wooden floor. They were let furnished with electric light, running water, oil stoves, linen, crockery and cutlery. Prices, in the 1920s, ranged from 15s a week from October to March up to £2 12s 6d in August. There was no sanitation or drainage, however, and the earth closets of Bohemia and other such developments were regarded as a health hazard by the county Medical Officer of Health.[149]

An intervention into the ownership rights of the sandhills was triggered in 1927 by the case of a hotel car park on unenclosed land at Sutton on Sea. This and the other developments which were restricting traditional rights of access to the beach through the sandhills for the public in general led, in 1930, to the promotion of a parliamentary Bill by Lindsey County Council for powers to preserve all the sandhills and beaches between Donna Nook and Gibraltar Point as open space and to regulate future development. Enclosing parts of the sandhills deprived the public of access and enjoyment. Many buildings and structures erected upon the sandhills were described as unsightly or otherwise of an undesirable character and many of those used for human habitation had no proper water supply or sanitary conveniences.[150] Increased use of private individual road transport – cars, motor bikes and even bicycles – allowed people to travel to places away from the railway stations, making these remote holiday homes a practical destination.[151]

As a result of this 'Sandhills Act', passed in 1932, by 1937 seventeen areas had been designated, forty-eight new huts were on the controlled sandhills at Mablethorpe and Sutton and about thirty at Anderby Creek, Chapel St Leonards and Ingoldmells. About 500 acres of land were purchased from around 130 owners for over £35,000; the camp sites at Huttoft and Ingoldmells were acquired and the caravans evicted.

This Act of Parliament was a unique piece of planning legislation in the coastal zone. It introduced a system of licences in the Lindsey coastal area covering some 40 km in length and up to 500 m in width, representing the longest such area in a natural state in Britain. In spite of the demand for holiday development that led to the erection of all manner of shacks and huts, the council was able to designate controlled areas where it could prohibit or remove buildings and enclosures through a licensing system. It could also zone areas for different land uses and acquire land by compulsory purchase for five years after the Act came into force. Under the direction of its clerk, Eric Scorer, the council, although at first reluctant, bought as much land as possible before the power of compulsory purchase ceased in 1937.[152] At Bohemia holiday camp the eastern part was incorporated into a controlled area and some of the rusty 'pork pie' huts were demolished at a cost to the council of £4,750 in compensation payment for the disturbance. 'Ernest du Soleil Tipper, owner of Bohemia, was to remove ten huts by 1 November 1932 and was paid compensation to allow passage over his land to the sandhills and shore.'[153] The rest of the camp was allowed to remain, as the owner had invested heavily in it over the preceding decade.[154]

The call for clearance of the holiday huts indicates another example of elitism regarding accommodation and a clash of class cultures and values. Although to the middle-class observers these settlements were an 'eyesore' which 'beggared description', they were perfectly acceptable to their working-class owners, who took pride in the properties that often they had made themselves. The accusation that they barred access to the beach by others was true but upper and middle-class property owners prevented or restricted access to far greater areas of land along the coastline and in the countryside.

The council's Sandhills Sub-committee prioritised the more vulnerable parts of the coast around Mablethorpe and Skegness with the aim of regulating the most popular areas for holidaymaking. After evicting the caravans from Huttoft Point and Ingoldmells Point the county architect was employed to design new camp layouts. Unfortunately the outbreak of war before much progress was made led to the sites being requisitioned for military use.[155] The Sandhills Act did not put an end to all development; huts and caravans, providing low-priced holidays, would still be encouraged on most of the dunes, as a hut near the beach was part of the charm of a Lincolnshire seaside holiday.[156] Indeed, the Act itself offered protection from competition to some existing entrepreneurs. No tea or refreshment rooms other than Sun Castle were allowed within 400 yards of the designated zone.[157] George Beasley or any successor of his at Theddlethorpe St Helens was explicitly protected from council acquisition provided he did not use his property for anything other than a dwelling or boarding house or hotel and did not interfere with passage on an adjacent footpath.[158] The result was that although the Lincolnshire coastline remained covered with caravans and chalet parks in the fields immediately behind the dunes, the sandhills themselves are free from development apart from pathways to the beach.

The 1932 Sandhills Act enabled the County Council to control the growth of caravan and camping facilities between the main resorts in the years after the Second World War. The Town and Country Planning Act of 1947 curtailed ramshackle development of holiday huts throughout the country but left a loophole that could be exploited by owners of sites for immobile caravans. The fact that a caravan has wheels left it exempt from many of the controls applying to similar structures without them, for example holiday huts and shanties.[159] It wasn't until the Caravan Sites Control of Development Act, 1960, that a licensing system was brought into force to control the location of sites.[160] The number of static caravans between Cleethorpes and Skegness rose from 4,200 in 1950 to 11,000 in 1959, 18,600 in 1969, peaking at 21,000 in 1974, when 8 per cent of the United Kingdom's caravans were sited on that part of the coast, over a third of them at Ingoldmells. There were 2,500 chalets at Humberston, Mablethorpe and Sutton on Sea, 3,000 including 1,700 for self-catering at Butlin's and 500 at the Derbyshire Miners' Camp.[161] These figures, all for self-catering holiday accommodation, are illustrative of the demand for cheap holidays by the working class when the Holidays with Pay Act came into real effect after the war. Later many of the traditional boarding houses would be converted into self-catering holiday flats.

All the different types of accommodation discussed here provided for the working-class market. Although differing widely in the content of the product offered they had one thing in common: the price was kept to a minimum, which for working-class holidaymakers was a primary consideration when deciding where to go, if at all. While the middle classes went farther afield, escaping the growing crowds of workers on holiday, they were quickly replaced in many resorts by the people they sought to evade. For working-class families, moving up one step to accommodation they could not previously afford was a sign of increasing affluence and the declining exclusivity of the holiday. The numbers taking holidays grew continuously between the wars. Between July 1922 and July 1934 the number of advertisements for holiday accommodation placed in one newspaper, the *Leicester Mercury*, increased more than a dozen times, from only eleven entries in the column in 1922 to 135 in the equivalent date edition of 1934.[162] In one year alone, the number of small advertisements for holiday accommodation more than doubled, from sixty-three in 1932 to 130 in 1933.[163]

Plate 7 The Miller family outside the beach hut they rented every year on the promenade at Mablethorpe. They always stayed at the same boarding house and used the same hut. *Reproduced by courtesy of Mrs Jean Miller*

For most people a week away in even the most modest accommodation was out of the question before the 1950s. The holiday for them was a day trip by train or charabanc to the seaside or to a local place of interest. For Nottingham families, in the 1920s and 1930s, this might have been a trip to the 'Bridges', a day out by the river Trent, including a boat trip to or from Clifton.[164] The poorest families relied on charitable efforts to provide a holiday treat for themselves or for just their children.

The intervention of working-class organisations in the provision of accommodation had a double innovatory effect. First of all it enabled more people, especially families, to enjoy a holiday away from home at a moderate price. Secondly it set standards and expectations of the facilities provided in accommodation. As the wealthier tourists began to take holidays abroad or, with increased ownership of private cars, drove farther afield to more remote locations away from the crowds to either hotels or privately owned villas by the sea, the working-class holidaymaker's leisure facilities owed little to individual private ownership, except in the case of the huts or caravans by the coast, which were so despised by the middle class for their squalor and impact on the landscape. Travel for working people was normally by public transport and accommodation was rented. Where organisations of the working class became involved in the provision of holidays the relationship changed, from one of entrepreneur and consumer to mutuality, as facilities were collectively owned or shared. This was the 'ownership and control of the means of accommodation' as Scarborough Trades Council had described it,[165] or the means of production in the tourism industry.

By 1940 the minimum cost of a week's holiday for a family with two children was about £10, including home rent: still too high for many to contemplate. By the end of the 1930s only a third of those who earned less than £4 a week took a week's holiday.[166] The National Council of Social Service's 1945 report put the cost of a holiday at £1 15s a week for an adult, with reduced charges for children. For a family with three children it was estimated that a holiday could be obtained for £6 to £7 a week, that is, about £10 or £11 a week including fares, rent and home charges.[167] The inclusive charges at commercial holiday camps ranged from about £2 10s a week. The charges at the hostels run by voluntary associations such as the WTA and Holiday Fellowship at the time were about £2 a week, except at especially cheap centres, where the price was about £1 15s weekly. The average family could therefore achieve its holiday, at minimum prices, if it saved about 3s a week throughout the year.[168] Sadly there wasn't enough cheap accommodation to allow all those who might have wanted a holiday to take one.

Commercial holiday camps were usually too expensive for most people, even those receiving paid holidays, although they solved the problem of what to do with the children during bad weather, inherent in an apartment or boarding house holiday. Buying food, cooking on a self-catering or apartment holiday and child care were all problems ensuring that for working-class women even a week away from home was not entirely a holiday. Because of the huge rise in demand, the growing attempts by the trade union, co-operative and workers' movements to provide a real holiday at an all-in affordable price was not an available option for most families because of the small scale of these ventures and the fact that many people who could afford to pay more booked up all the places before the poorer aspiring holidaymaker could get the money together. In 1945 the National Council of Social Service could report in its study of holidays that 'three things seem in the past to have prevented working-class families from going away for a holiday: lack of means, lack of accommodation other than seaside apartments, and lack of ideas, or natural conservatism.'[169] It now remains to be shown how these restricting factors were overcome.

Notes

1 Four million workers received payment for holidays in 1937, according to *Holidays: a study by the National Council of Social Service*, London, 1945, p. 3.

2 Political and Economic Planning (PEP), *Planning for holidays*, Planning No. 194, 13 October 1942, p. 5.

3 Donald Chapman, *Holidays and the state*, Fabian Society, London, 1949, p. 8.

4 Harold Perkin, 'The "social tone" of Victorian seaside resorts', in *The Structured Crowd*, Hassocks, 1981, pp. 70–85, p. 71; John K. Walton, *The English seaside resort: a social history, 1750–1914*, Leicester, 1983, pp. 22–5.

5 See the chapter on the music hall in Peter Bailey, *Leisure and class in Victorian England: rational recreation and the contest for control*, London, 1978.

6 Perkin, 'The "social tone" of Victorian seaside resorts', p. 72.

7 *Ibid.*, pp. 74–5.

8 *Ibid.*, see also Walton, *The English seaside resort*, pp. 22–5.

9 Gary Cross (editor), *Worktowners at Blackpool: Mass-Observation and popular leisure in the 1930s*, London, 1990, pp. 41–2.

10 Margaret Hewitt, *Wives and mothers in Victorian industry*, London, 1958, p. 55.

11 Richard Ayton, *Voyage around Britain*, 1813, cited by Morris Brooke Smith, 'The growth and development of popular entertainment and pastimes in the Lancashire cotton towns, 1830–1870', M.Litt. dissertation, University of Lancaster, 1970, p. 131.

12 C. Aspin, *Lancashire: the first industrial society*, 1969, cited by Brooke Smith, 'The growth and development of popular entertainment', p. 131.

13 Manchester Reference Library, M6/3/10/58, Circular of the London Central Register Office of houses and accommodation for visitors to the Exhibition of the Works of All Nations, London, 1851.

14 Eric Hobsbawm, *The Age of Capital, 1848–1875*, London, 1962, 1995 edn, p. 203.

15 J. Christopher Holloway, *The business of tourism*, 3rd edn, London, 1989, p. 51.

16 Oral reminiscences of Winifred Feltwell, 1908–84, and Joan Beer, b. 1924.

17 Thea Thompson, *Edwardian childhoods*, London, 1981, p. 137.

18 Christopher Hibbert, *The English: a social history, 1066–1945*, London, 1987, p. 636.

19 *Preston Chronicle*, 20 July 1850.

20 Barrie Newman, 'Holidays and social class', in Michael A. Smith, Stanley Parker and Cyril S. Smith (eds), *Leisure and society in Britain*, London, 1974, p. 235.

21 Joseph Gutteridge, 'Autobiography', in William Anderson and Joseph Gutteridge, *Artisan and master in Victorian England*, London, 1969, pp. 211–18.

22 Arthur Sketchley, *Mrs Brown at the seaside*, London, n.d. (*c.* 1860), p. 22.

23 *Ibid.*, pp. 24–5.

24 Leicester Oral History Archive, a Leicester man's reminiscences, 'Holidays: making the most of time off', in *I remember Leicester*, audio-cassette, 1985.

25 John K. Walton, *The Blackpool landlady*, Manchester, 1979, p. 105.

26 *Ibid.*, p. 3.

27 Leicester Oral History Archive, a Leicester man's reminiscence, 'Holidays: making the most of time off'.

28 *Ibid.*

29 Gutteridge, 'Autobiography', p. 216.

30 In the 1930s 86 per cent of tourists found lodgings through recommendation, 12 per cent through advertisements and 2 per cent through a travel bureau (figures cited by James Walvin, *Beside the seaside*, London, 1978, p. 117).

31 Walton, *The Blackpool landlady*, p. 4.

32 John K. Walton, 'The Blackpool landlady revisited', *Manchester Region History Review*, 1994, pp. 23–31, p. 23.

33 Walton, *The Blackpool landlady*, p. 105.

34 Claire Langhamer, *Women's leisure in England, 1920–1960*, Manchester, 2000, p. 37; Cross, *Worktowners in Blackpool*, p. 42.

35 Elizabeth Brunner, *Holidaymaking and the holiday trades*, Oxford, 1945, p. 10.

36 Walton, *The Blackpool landlady*, p. 4.

37 Catherine Horwood, 'Housewives' choice: women as consumers between the wars', *History Today* 47:3, 1997, p. 25.

38 *Ibid.*

39 Sue Read, *Hello campers! The story of Butlin's*, London, 1986, p. 18.

40 Chris Waters, *British socialists and the politics of popular culture*, Manchester, 1990, p. 27 and pp. 40–2.

41 John Belchem, *Industrialisation and the working class: the English experience, 1750–1900*, Aldershot, 1991, p. 228.

42 Mark Bevir, 'Labour churches and ethical socialism', *History Today* 47:3, 1997, pp. 50–5.

43 *Ibid.*

44 Vernon L. Lidtke, *The alternative culture: socialist labour in imperial Germany*, Oxford, 1985.

45 Harvey Taylor, *A claim on the countryside: a history of the British outdoor movement*, Keele, 1997, p. 195.

46 *Ibid.*, p. 195.

47 *Ibid.*, p. 194.

48 J. A. R. Pimlott, *The Englishman's holiday*, London, 1947, repr. Hassocks, 1967, p. 168.

49 *Ibid.*, p. 195.

50 National Council of Social Service, *Holidays*, p. 66.

51 Philippa Bassett, Introduction, 'A list of the historical records of the Holiday Fellowship, compiled as part of a research project funded by the Social Science Research Council, Centre for Urban and Regional Studies, University of Birmingham, and the Institute of Agricultural History, University of Reading, 1980.

52 Colin Ward and Dennis Hardy, *Goodnight, campers*, London, 1986, p. 31.

53 National Council of Social Service, *Holidays*, p. 66.

54 *Ibid.*, p. 29.
55 Waters, *British socialists and the politics of popular culture*, pp. 170–1.
56 *Ibid.*, p. 171.
57 Tom Maguire, cited by Waters, *British socialists and the politics of popular culture*, p. 171.
58 Richard Holt, *Sport and the British: a modern history*, Oxford, 1989, p. 196.
59 *Ibid.*
60 North Warwickshire and Hinckley College, ERDF, Arqueotex Textile Heritage Project, reminiscence of Neville Evans of Hinckley, 10 September 1997, recorded by Rhianydd Murray.
61 Francis Williams, *Journey into adventure*, London, 1960, p. 18.
62 Ward and Hardy, *Goodnight, campers*, p. 35.
63 *Ibid.*, p. 16.
64 Reminiscence of Judy Paskell of Manchester, 1997, noted by the author.
65 Mr Eddie Doughty, *Leicester Mercury*, 27 June 1996, p. 10.
66 *Ibid.*, 27 June 1996.
67 Ward and Hardy, *Goodnight, campers*, p. 16.
68 *Ibid.*, p. 28.
69 J. H. Reeve, 'Holiday camps', *London & North Eastern Railway Magazine* 24:6, June 1934, p. 334.
70 *LNER Magazine* 24:7, July 1934, p. 384.
71 *Ibid.*
72 *Ibid.*
73 *Ibid.*
74 Ward and Hardy, *Goodnight, campers*, p. 43.
75 *Ibid.*
76 W. J. Brown, *So far*, London, 1943, cited in *ibid.*
77 *Red Tape*, February 1930.
78 *Ibid.*
79 Alec Spoor, *White-collar union: sixty years of NALGO*, London, 1967, p. 101.
80 *Ibid.*, p. 15.
81 *Ibid.*, p. 108.
82 *Ibid.*, p. 108.
83 *Ibid.*, p. 109.
84 Ward and Hardy, *Goodnight, campers*, pp. 45–7.
85 Civil and Public Servants' Association, Annual Report 1919–20; Spoor, *White-collar union*, p. 84.
86 J. E. Williams, *The Derbyshire miners*, London, 1962, p. 629.
87 Modern Records Centre, University of Warwick (MRC), MSS 292 114/3, letter from R. E. Hardy, Secretary, Scarborough and District Trades Council, 10 July 1938.
88 MRC, MSS 292 114/1, Taylerle resolution, Draft resolution on holidays for workers and salaried employees, for the TUC Executive meeting of 22 May 1929.
89 Waters, *British socialists and the politics of popular culture*, pp. 154–5.

90 MRC, MSS 292 114/3, letter to R. E. Hardy, Secretary, Scarborough and District Trades Council, from the Secretary of the Organisation Department of the TUC, 16 August 1938.

91 *Ibid.*

92 Williams, *Journey into adventure*, p. 138; Ward and Hardy, *Goodnight, campers*, pp. 41–2.

93 Ward and Hardy, *Goodnight, campers*, p. 36.

94 *Ibid.*, p. 36.

95 G. C. Martin, 'Working-class holidaymaking down to 1947', M.A. thesis, University of Leicester, 1968, p. 77.

96 Ward and Hardy, *Goodnight, campers*, p. 37.

97 Martin, 'Working-class holidaymaking', p. 77; *The Wheatsheaf*, Coventry, August 1930.

98 Williams, *Journey into adventure*, p. 137.

99 *Ibid.*

100 National Council of Social Service, *Holidays*, p. 60.

101 Brunner, *Holidaymaking and the holiday trades*, p. 16.

102 National Council of Social Service, *Holidays*, p. 12; PEP, *Planning for holidays*, p. 12.

103 Centre for Kentish Studies (CKS), U2 543/Z5/14, British Travel Association Survey of 1965, Workers' Travel Association Annual Meeting of Shareholders' Report for year ended 31 October 1965, *Travel Log*, WTA magazine, June 1966, p. 6.

104 Williams, *Journey into adventure*, pp. 144–6.

105 PEP, *Planning for holidays*, p. 12.

106 Williams, *Journey into adventure*, pp. 144–6.

107 Leicester Oral History Archive, Mr Albert Lynn, former manager of Co-op Travel, Leicester, started work 1929, C32 'The travel agent', in *I Remember Leicester*, 1985.

108 Williams, *Journey into adventure*, p. 137.

109 *Ibid.*, p. 15.

110 Vera Brittain, *Testament of youth*, 1933, repr. London 1978, p. 538.

111 CKS, U2 543/C1, letter to trade unions about the formation of the WTA from Cecil Rogerson and others, 12 November 1921.

112 CKS, U2 543/C1, Report of a conference held at Toynbee Hall on Friday 25 November, to discuss the formation of the Workers' Travel Association.

113 Williams, *Journey into adventure*, p. 35.

114 *Ibid.*, p. 38.

115 CKS, U2 543/C1, letter to Arthur Creech-Jones from Edward Knight, 24 July 1922.

116 *Ibid.*

117 CKS, U2 543/C1, letter to Harry Gosling from Cecil Rogerson, 22 November 1922.

118 National Council of Social Service, *Holidays*, p. 29.

119 Williams, *Journey into adventure*, p. 141.
120 Leicester Oral History Archive, Mr Albert Lynn, in *I remember Leicester*.
121 Brunner, *Holidaymaking and the holiday trades*, p. 14.
122 Williams, *Journey into adventure*, p. 128.
123 Report of the Post-war Holidays Group to the Catering Wages Commission, September 1944; National Council of Social Service, *Holidays*.
124 CKS, U2/543/Z5/14, Report of the forty-third annual meeting of shareholders, 22 April 1966, *Travel Log*, June 1966.
125 Colin Doyle, project manager, Employment and corporate affairs, CWS Ltd, Manchester (employee of Galleon Travel, 1981–87), letter to Su Barton, 16 May 1990.
126 CKS, U2543/Z4, WTA 'Saving for summer holidays' leaflet, 1931.
127 Brunner, *Holidaymaking and the holiday trades*, p. 20.
128 Leicester Oral History Archive, Mr Albert Lynn, in *I remember Leicester*.
129 National Council of Social Service, *Holidays*, p. 30.
130 Cross, *Worktowners in Blackpool*, p. 158.
131 Philip Wren, 'Holiday shanties in Britain: a history and analysis', dissertation, University of Hull, School of Architecture, 1981, p. 5.
132 David N. Robinson, 'The changing coastline', in Dennis R. Mills (ed.), *Twentieth-century Lincolnshire*, Lincoln, 1989, pp. 155–80, p. 161.
133 Colin Ward and Dennis Hardy, *Arcadia for all*, London, 1984, p. 36.
134 J. A. Steers, 'Coastal preservation and planning', *Geography Journal* 104, 1944, pp. 7–37, p. 11.
135 Ward and Hardy, *Arcadia for all*, p. 86.
136 Leslie Sherwood, 'A second home in Charnwood Forest', *Living History: the news-letter of the Living History Unit*, No. 20, Leicester, spring 1998.
137 Ward and Hardy, *Arcadia for all*, p. 21.
138 *Ibid.*, p. 2.
139 *Ibid.*, p. 3.
140 National Council of Social Service, *Holidays*, p. 24.
141 Ward and Hardy, *Arcadia for all*, p. 24.
142 John D. Sheail, 'The impact of recreation on the coast: the Lindsey County Council (Sandhills) Act, 1932', *Landscape Planning* 4, 1977, pp. 53–77, p. 55.
143 Robinson, 'The changing coastline', p. 160.
144 Anderby Creek visitors' guide, dating from around 1930.
145 Photograph estimated to date from the late 1920s, displayed in Anderby Creek Tea Rooms and Bar, 2001.
146 Dorothy K. Walton, *Queenie Musson: memories of a Leicester life*, Leicester, 2002.
147 Rev. Wilfred F.-H. Curtis, Rector of Ingoldmells 1960–67, *Ingoldmells: a short history of the village in the county by the sea, and of its ancient parish church*, Ramsgate, 1965.
148 *Leicester Mercury*, 3 May 1932.
149 Robinson, 'The changing coastline', p. 160.

150 'An Act to provide for regulating certain lands in the parts of Lindsey, Lincolnshire, known as the Sandhills; to confer power upon the County Council over the said parts of Lindsey with reference thereto; and for other purposes', royal assent 12 July 1932, 22–3 George V, session 1931–32, pp. 1 and 2.

151 Walton, *The British seaside*, pp. 81–1.

152 Sally Scott, 'The early days of planning', in Dennis Mills (ed.), *Twentieth-century Lincolnshire*, Lincoln, 1989, pp. 181–211, p. 200.

153 Sandhills Act, p. 56.

154 Sheail, 'The impact of recreation on the coast', p. 63.

155 *Ibid.*, p. 66.

156 *Ibid.*, p. 63.

157 Sandhills Act, p. 47.

158 *Ibid.*, p. 56.

159 Wren, 'Holiday shanties in Britain', p. 15.

160 Philippa Bassett, 'A list of the historical records of the Caravan Club of Great Britain and Ireland', compiled as part of a research project funded by the Social Science Research Council, Centre for Urban and Regional Studies, University of Birmingham and the Institute of Agricultural History, University of Reading, 1980, p. vi.

161 Robinson, 'The changing coastline', p. 175.

162 The sample was taken from Saturday editions of the *Leicester Mercury* for early July over a fifteen-year period. The figures in brackets refer to the number of advertisements offering accommodation in the 'Seaside apartments, lodgings and other holiday accommodation' column. 8 July (seven) and 15 July (eleven) 1922; 4 July 1925 (twenty-eight); 2 July 1927 (twenty-one); 6 July 1929 (twenty-three); 5 July 1930 (thirty-five); 4 July 1931 (fifty-nine); 2 July 1932 (sixty-three); 1 July 1933 (130); 7 July 1934 (135); 6 July 1935 (102); 4 July 1936 (seventy-two, comprising forty-one boarding houses, sixteen apartments and fifteen hotels), 3 July 1937 (seventy-six, comprising twenty hotels and fifty-six general accommodation).

163 *Leicester Mercury*, 2 July 1932, 1 July 1933.

164 Pauline McClelland, oral reminiscence, Leicester, 1999.

165 MRC, 292/114/3, letter to TUC from R. E. Hardy, Scarborough and District Trades Council, 10 July 1938.

166 Ward and Hardy, *Arcadia for all*, p. 24.

167 National Council of Social Service, *Holidays*, p. 11.

168 PEP, *Planning for holidays*, p. 13.

169 National Council of Social Service, *Holidays*, p. 20.

7

Holidays and the state: planning for workers' needs after the Holidays with Pay Act

Despite the passing of the Holidays with Pay Act, the outbreak of the Second World War delayed its full implementation until the arrival once more of peace. When the Act became law in July 1938, wage-regulating authorities were permitted to provide for holidays and paid leave and at the same time the Minister of Labour was enabled to assist voluntary schemes, arrived at through collective agreements. After an interval to allow the extension of paid holidays by negotiation, legislation was to have been passed in 1940 or 1941 making them compulsory throughout industry.[1] As discussed in the last chapter, existing accommodation could not meet the demand for cheaply priced vacations by the lower income groups, receiving paid holidays for the first time.

During the war years there was unprecedented involvement by the government in economic and social life. The state regulated production and also consumption through rationing. Employment was directed to meet the needs of wartime. There was state provision of services normally performed by women in the home, such as communal canteens and nurseries to release them from some of the obligations of domestic labour, in order to make them available for work in wartime industry. Rationing, Utility clothing, uniforms and the practical needs of work even dictated how people dressed. Requisitioning of property, the building of hostels, billeting of evacuees, military personnel and civilian workers all affected traditional property rights and domestic arrangements. With most of the coastline out of bounds to civilians and families separated by military service, directed labour and evacuation, the normal routine of summer holidaymaking was obviously going to be disrupted. At the same time the phenomena of evacuation, industrial transfers and the innumerable postings of those in the services made the habit of travelling more widespread among people who had rarely gone away from home.[2]

Loss of long fought-for paid leave was not something the labour movement would accept quietly, and employers and government realised how important breaks from work had become, both as a motivator and as a means of maintaining health and preventing absenteeism. The prospect of disruption or sacrifice of the holiday period had led Tynemouth District and Whitley Bay Trades Council to discuss the matter at its meeting in April 1940.[3] A letter from its secretary, George Steele, to the TUC described the 'apparent uneasiness and apprehension as to the possibility of interference either by the Government or employers to in some way nullify the advantages workers have derived from the many agreements in various industries'. The trades council felt that the wartime emergency might be used as an excuse for curtailing holidays with pay or perhaps postponing such holidays until after the war.[4]

Steele requested the TUC General Council to watch the matter carefully and asked it to take whatever steps were necessary to counteract any move in the direction feared by some members in Tynemouth and Whitley Bay. The secretary of the TUC's research and economics department, George Woodcock, wrote in reply to Steele:

> I think you may rest assured that the fears expressed in your letter are not well founded, since there is much evidence that the Government and the employers are fully aware of the increasing need for holidays during the war period. As one piece of evidence, may I say that the representatives of the British Employers' Confederation upon the National Joint Advisory Council joined with the TUC representatives on that body in advising the Government that it was more than ever necessary to maintain paid holidays during the war period.[5]

Opinion polls and Mass-Observation provided data for government and quasi-official reports on the morale of the population and emphasised the need for planning for social reconstruction once peace returned. The recent precedent of state involvement in almost all aspects of life encouraged social researchers to anticipate that such involvement would continue in peacetime. Officially commissioned reports into the future use of natural resources, leisure needs and holidays all indicated that this would be imperative.

On the basis of a number of reports, the government feared that the demand for holidays would double while only 75 per cent of pre-war accommodation would be available.[6] Different interventionist policies were advocated to spread the demand through the season and to make low-priced accommodation available to prevent overcrowding and overpricing during the August peak period. If most of the population went away, and there was no more staggering of holiday dates than there had been in 1937, it was calculated, the maximum number seeking accommodation at any one time would be in the region of 5 million.[7] This was in comparison with a pre-war peak of around 1.25 million. Planners estimated that the 5 million could be reduced to between 2 million and 4 million or perhaps even halved by spreading holidays between May and October. Staggering could be assisted by cheaper rates being offered outside August which would help spread the load and also reduce peak prices by 10–20 per cent. In the first year of peace, 1946, a campaign for staggered holidays was conducted by the Ministry of Information to distribute the demand over a longer season. Another way of spreading the load was through diversifying holiday venues. Country holidays could provide an alternative to the highly popular seaside for some people. The Ministry of Agriculture encouraged the young and active to take working holidays on farms to help with the fruit, cereal and potato harvests. In the years immediately following the war, agricultural camps attracted 200,000 city workers a year and this kind of minority holiday remained popular throughout the 1950s.[8] The Workers' Travel Association made great efforts to provide as full a holiday programme as possible in the first post-war years. Because of the shortage of holiday centres and accommodation, it offered temporary centres in boarding schools to attempt to meet the high demand. The Woodlands School at Deganwy Bay and West Cornwall School in Penzance were leased for the school summer holidays as moderately priced holiday centres.[9]

As holidays with pay became a reality for the majority of workers during the war the government began to grow worried about the effects of millions of them converging on the resorts at the same time when the war ended. The government therefore began to look at ways of encouraging the staggering of different towns' holidays[10] on similar lines to the Lancashire wakes, where communities celebrated during different weeks of the summer. The Great Western Railway was advocating June, with its long sunny days, as a desirable month for taking holidays in the 1930s.[11] This was to spread demand on train services over a longer period. Even earlier, in 1925, the *Leicester Mercury* editorial had raised the question of congestion and hence the discomfort and stress suffered by travellers.[12]

Official publications during the Second World War, such as those of the Political and Economic Planning Unit and the report *Holidaymaking and the holiday trades*, discussed this issue and also concern about the potential lack of accommodation.[13] The answer seemed to lie in government and municipal intervention and regulation of the business of tourism, a process that had already started in the 1930s. Some local authorities had become involved in the provision of low-priced accommodation in holiday camps. At a national level the Select Committee on Holidays with Pay investigated the desirability of legislation to enforce the granting of paid holidays in most fields of employment before it became law. In the resorts themselves, local councils had been involved in tourism provision from around the late nineteenth and early twentieth centuries, building amenities to attract visitors such as promenades, swimming pools, tramways and street lighting as well as infrastructure like enlarged sewage systems to cope with the increased population. These investments benefiting the whole town were financed communally by the towns' high numbers of business rate payers. To warrant this level of official concern the number of potential tourists had to be high enough to justify the expense, and so local authorities needed to become involved in marketing their attractions and amenities to prospective visitors.[14]

At national government level the Scott Committee recommended the setting up of a central planning authority to control the use of land and to preserve amenities in rural areas. Ease of access to the countryside without disrupting agriculture would be promoted. In England and Wales a National Parks Authority would control areas of natural beauty that would be classified as national recreation zones. In the expectation of a huge increase in demand for holiday accommodation, the committee assumed that camp sites would be provided in the National Parks. The Hobhouse Report on National Parks discussed holiday facilities and arrangements within them.[15] The report of the Committee on Land Utilisation in Rural Areas recommended that the whole of the coastline should be administered by the National Parks Authority, an idea never put into effect despite threats to the shoreline in many places.

Provided they would all come under the appropriate planning controls, the Committee on Land Utilisation in Rural Areas was in favour of an increase in the number of youth hostels, camp sites, commercial holiday camps and holiday villages. This was with reference to the provisions of the Camps Act of 1939 facilitating the construction, maintenance and management of camps of a permanent character.[16] War began while the National Camps Corporation set up under the Act was still in its early days. After consultation, the location of camps on suitable sites relative to population centres was ensured.[17] These purpose-built camps became used in an attempt to solve the problems of finding enough places to stay for those displaced through the exigencies of wartime. The Parliamentary Labour Party, on the opposition benches, welcomed the camps as a step towards national planning which in peacetime could enable everyone, even the unemployed and low-paid, to enjoy a holiday away from home.[18] It was believed the camps would make ideal family holiday accommodation when the war was over but in the meantime the National Camps Corporation was required to give priority to education authorities who would use them for schools. This raised the prospect of a holiday in the country being available to every schoolchild for the first time. In 1944 Sir Edward Howarth, managing director of the National Camps Association, gave evidence before the Rehabilitation Sub-committee of the Catering Wages Commission. Sir Edward opined that it had never been seriously contemplated that the camps should be used for adults. They were structurally unsuited to the purpose in that the sleeping accommodation was in dormitories and the common rooms were inadequate. The corporation might be prepared to extend its facilities if given the necessary powers and resources. It had at least the benefit of its experience in the management and running of the camps, and the types of domestic staff required for a school or adult holiday camp would be similar. Sir Edward had no particular views on the sort of authority that could most appropriately control the development of holiday camps.[19] The camps became the responsibility of the Ministry of Education as during the war they were used for accommodating evacuated schools.

The government's interest in camps, which resulted in the formation of the National Camps Corporation, came about because of the Ministry of Health's concern over evacuating 4 million women and children from vulnerable cities to home billets. By mid-1940, out of a planned fifty camps, thirty-one with dormitories, classrooms, kitchens, dining and assembly halls and accommodation for staff had been built in England and Wales, with a further five in Scotland. The camps in England and Wales, administered by the National Camps Corporation, were let to local education authorities and used by secondary or post-secondary schools, many of which were escaping city bombing. This use of camps by secondary and post-secondary schools caused political accusations of elitism when accommodation was reserved for secondary pupils at a time when the poorer sections of the working class could not afford to keep their children on at school after the minimum leaving age. For this reason the Scottish camps under the auspices of the Scottish Special Housing Association were used by elementary pupils, hard to billet elsewhere.[20]

Camps were used not just by evacuees: internees, military personnel and relocated workers all needed to be housed. Building and running camps and catering for large numbers of people were not tasks in which the government had a lot of experience and so some of the holiday camp proprietors were enlisted to advise and oversee proceedings. Almost all the existing holiday camps were requisitioned, many of them for use by the armed forces. Not enough places were provided, though, to satisfy the need to accommodate those displaced as part of the war effort or for reasons of civil defence.

The government did a deal with the most flamboyant of all the holiday camp entrepreneurs, Billy Butlin, who was in the process of building a new camp at Filey when the war began. Butlin had refused to believe the rumours that were circulating about war being imminent although the Tannoy systems at Clacton and Skegness were continually interrupting entertainment broadcasts with the names of men who had to report back to their home town for call-up.[21] Reservists, schoolteachers and air raid wardens were all told to cancel their holidays. The War Minister, Hore-Belisha, negotiated with Butlin to complete the unfinished Filey camp for use by the RAF at a price of £175 per occupant, considerably cheaper than the army's own cost of £250 per person.[22] Where Butlin did well out of this deal was in stipulating that he would have the right to buy the camp back at the end of the war. This would mean that the canny Butlin would have a new, ready-made camp just when there was a huge demand for holidays as peace returned. He had even devised a sunken parade ground that could later be used as a boating lake. The government had also got itself a good deal, as after the previous war it had cost more to dismantle camps and restore the land than it had to build them.[23] Butlin developed two further camps with the same buy-back agreement as at Filey. The 'stone frigate' HMS *Glendower* was built at Pwllheli in North Wales and another, HMS *Scotia*, was built near Ayr in Scotland.

Butlin had another wartime role: raising the morale of those in existing government camps. The Minister of Supply asked him to report on the reasons for the low morale in hostels for female ordnance factory workers. He recommended exchanging their internment-camp atmosphere for a bit of a holiday feeling when the women weren't working. He encouraged dancing, whist drives, amateur theatricals, variety shows and bright paint, all features of his holiday camps. Butlin was then asked, in 1943, to assist towns to organise holiday weeks to encourage people to take 'holidays at home'. This was an important acknowledgement by the government that even in wartime workers needed holidays. Butlin purchased the main travelling fairs that toured from town to town during their respective holiday weeks. His next venture was to organise leave centres for the services in Belgium.[24] The arrival of peace found Butlin in a powerful position to take advantage of the massive market for holidays now that the war was over.

Butlin was not the only proprietor of holiday camps who gained practical experience running wartime hostels. Fred Pontin was manager of a hostel for steel and sugar-beet workers. When he took over he found his predecessor in hospital with his ribs kicked in by workers protesting over food grievances.[25] In response, Pontin acquired an alsatian guard dog and a bodyguard, then set to work improving conditions. After the war, financed by a syndicate in which he had a controlling 50 per cent interest thanks to a bank loan, raised £25,000 to buy a former military camp at Bream in Somerset, successfully anticipating the urge of newly demobbed servicemen and women to spend their demob gratuities on a holiday. He bought more camps, personally running each until it was established, then sold them to the syndicate he still controlled. The Pontin's company was formed in July 1946, with 400,000 shares all placed in one day, a feat never before accomplished.

As part of the process of planning future holiday accommodation, a working group made a proposal for a national holiday centre corporation. There were hopes that this would be able to meet some of the problems of post-war demand through the conversion of some of the government's wartime sites such as industrial and Royal Ordnance hostels and services' camps. A semi-public body, similar in form to the National Camps Corporation and National Service Hostels Corporation, was suggested to manage these centres: a National Holiday Centre Corporation which would be responsible for maintaining good standards of holiday provision at minimum prices. An obvious difficulty envisaged in the state provision of holiday hostels was the fear that those who might use them would feel 'pauperised', at a disadvantage to their neighbours who went to boarding houses or commercial centres for their holidays.[26] For the government to assume direct control of holidays in a thoroughly planned Britain was a rather premature thought, according to the National Council of Social Service. It was not even clear which Ministry ought to be responsible for holidays, as aspects affecting them fell within the remit of various Ministries, such as Labour, Health, Education, Supply, Public Building and Works and Town and Country Planning. The government agency responsible for holiday matters at the time was the Catering Wages Commission. This commission, set up under the Catering Act, had the primary function of rehabilitating the catering industry but also had the duty of planning for post-war holidays in general. It was officially responsible to the government through the Minister of Labour and National Service.

The Post-war Holidays Group was a working party instigated by the Catering Wages Commission. It comprised members from groups representing workers and their needs in the areas of leisure and health, such as the Co-operative Holidays Association, the Holiday Fellowship, the Industrial Welfare Society, the Workers' Travel Association and the Miners' Welfare Association as well as the YMCA, the Camping Club of Great Britain and the Royal Institute of British Architects.[27] In its report back to the Catering Wages Commission the group recommended the formation of an *ad hoc* body rather than direct governmental responsibility and control. This body would 'hold and manage government hostel accommodation, grant financial aid to local authorities and voluntary organisations to help with the capital cost of new holiday provision that lack of funds prevented them from doing at the rate required'.[28] This proposed central authority would include representatives of the voluntary sector, and its administrators would have civil service status. The authority was to have responsibility for the conversion, at government expense, of existing government hostels selected as suitable for holidays. The hostels would be leased during the summer holiday months to local authorities and voluntary organisations. The charges for accommodation would be fixed, at 30s for example, and voluntary organisations would act as managing agents on a 'no profit, no loss' basis, as the Royal Ordnance Factory hostels had been during the war. Alternatively the hostels could be rented at nominal rates to cover normal depreciation of property and be free of capital costs, the tenants to make their own arrangements regarding charges. Outside the holiday season the premises could be put to other uses as conference centres, for rallies, adult education or rest homes.[29] It had not been envisaged that the new central authority should necessarily be a permanent body. If its hostels and camps were successful the authority could continue indefinitely. If public support declined after the first few seasons, then it should be seen as only a temporary expedient. These ideas did not come to fruition, as the Ministry of Works retained many of the best places for other government departments or demanded commercial prices for them. In most places the premises were too costly to adapt.[30]

Another report, this time by the British Tourist and Holidays Board, looked at the demand for accommodation to assist the preparation of development plans under the Town and Country Planning Act. In 1948 the board concluded that 'most people were much better off and better educated than in the past'.[31] They therefore expected a higher standard of holiday provision than previously. They would not be satisfied with crowded accommodation, indifferent service and gloomy conditions. This was identified as the reason for the slackening of demand for low-grade apartments and boarding houses. The demand for holiday camps was increasing and most camps were practically booked to capacity over a year in advance, it was noted.[32] Bringing requisitioned accommodation and camps into public use as quickly as possible was vital. By the autumn of 1946 over 1,000 camps in England and Wales had been squatted by nearly 40,000 homeless families.[33] On some sites chalets were occupied by people bombed out of nearby towns, many of whom were not rehoused by local authorities until the 1960s.[34] The huts and chalets around the coast were now squatted from necessity, not to achieve a holiday home for leisure use.

The government was anxious to dispose of its camps that were now a liability and welcomed their sale back to the former site owners, as this avoided demolition costs. The site owners were now holiday camp proprietors who had to continue the wartime ethic of 'make do and mend' while preparing their camps to receive guests. Building materials were strictly rationed but there were plenty of army surplus beds, tables, chairs, blankets and catering equipment to be acquired cheap at auction. As capital became available many were completely redeveloped. Pontin's, discussed above, was one of the commercial firms that established themselves by offering cut-price holidays in patched-up military bases and pre-war camps from 1946 onwards.

The post-war years saw the pioneer camps of voluntary associations such as the co-operative movement and trade unions, as well as smaller private operators, starved of the necessary funds for improvements to bring their camps up to the standards now expected by working people. This led to some, like the civil service camp at Corton, being bought out by commercial chains such as Harry Warner's, Holimarine and Hoseason's.[35] As a consequence of the need for major capital investment to provide the facilities demanded by the rising expectations of the working class, the era of the socialist, co-operative and trade union camps came to an end. This was due not to unpopularity but to a paucity of financial resources at a critical time when both expansion and refurbishment were required. Nevertheless, these early, unashamedly ideological providers of cheap holidays to working-class activists, trade unionists and their followers had demonstrated that there was a demand for that type of accommodation.[36] Their pioneering example was followed by commercial camp proprietors, who continued and developed the holiday-camp or holiday-centre style of vacation.

Not forgetting that the Holidays with Pay Act covered only industries that were under the auspices of trade boards, the TUC continued its campaign for paid leave for all workers when it established a Committee on the Forty-eight-hour Week and Holidays with Pay in 1946.[37] This group co-ordinated the campaign for reduced working hours and the extension of the 1938 Act to all employees, either through legislation or agreement through collective bargaining.

Wartime state regulation set a precedent for the reformist policies of the post-war Labour government. Nationalisation by that government of many essential services was the fulfilment of years of campaigning within the labour movement. All the nationalised industries and services were essential to economic recovery and reconstruction. It is surprising, therefore, that among the services taken into public ownership were the operations of two travel agencies, Thomas Cook & Son and Dean & Dawson. A holiday camp venture at Prestatyn by Cook's in partnership with the London Midland & Scottish Railway offering a complete holiday package for up to 2,000 guests at a time had been opened in 1938. This was in anticipation of the additional 8 million expected to be entitled to a holiday with pay following the Act, but the war years were tough on travel companies. Cook's share capital in 1942 was vested in Hay's Wharf Cartage Company, owned by the four main-line railway companies, which paid off some of the travel agency's losses, which amounted to around £500,000 by 1945. After the war Cook's remained part of the railway companies. It was kept busy repatriating refugees who were given travel vouchers by the UN Relief and Rehabilitation Agency that could be exchanged only at Cook's offices. Dean & Dawson, another great Victorian and pre-war travel agency, with thirty-one branches, had been taken over by the London & North Eastern Railway. Following an initial boom in demand for holidays in 1946, which took place despite currency restrictions, a ban on foreign tourism followed in 1947, lasting for about a year.[38] This was an attempt to remedy an acute shortage of foreign exchange. On 1 January 1948 the Labour government nationalised the railways and as subsidiaries Thomas Cook and Dean & Dawson were nationalised along with them.

Government involvement in policies affecting tourism had become an established fact. The post-war Labour government founded the British Tourist and Holidays Board, with its executive functions carried out by four divisions: tourism, home holidays, hotels and catering. The Home Holidays Committee, which included representatives of the industry and 'consumers', was created at the board's first meeting, in 1947. Its duties were based on the 1945 report of the Catering Wages Commission and included the compilation of an authoritative and comprehensive list of all holiday establishments, the provision of suitable guidebooks, co-operation with the National Parks authority, co-operation in the provision of new types of holiday facilities and helping to effect the staggering of holidays. It was pledged to pay particular attention to the holiday accommodation of low-income groups.[39] Sadly, the committee had no powers and no funds, so its work was mainly confined to surveys of existing holiday provision and building up knowledge to produce a holidays policy.

It is significant that one of the original functions, which was later dropped, was 'to pay particular attention to the holiday accommodation of lower-income groups'. Without money and responsibilities it would, of course, have been unable to do much in this respect. The findings of the committee, though, would provide a basis upon which a plan for cheap holidays could be based.

The government did not allow the Tourist Board to hold any properties of its own to lease out, or even to have first call on large houses and estates handed over in payment of death duties. The Home Holidays Committee did, however, supervise the Olympic Games of 1947 and so had a little experience in the area of managing accommodation.[40]

Policies to extend holidays to poorer social groups were not entirely given up by the Labour Party during its term of office. The previously abandoned principle of the British Tourist and Holidays Board, 'to pay particular attention to holiday accommodation for lower-income groupings', was reinstated in party policy. 'More family holidays' was the heading of a section of Labour's draft election programme for 1950, issued by its National Executive.[41] The policy statement proposed that there should be a Holidays Council, set up with government support, to begin providing centres where families could have reasonably priced holidays. These centres would be leased to non-profit-seeking holiday organisations, relieving them of excessive capital costs. Some of the stately homes that were envisaged coming into public ownership in lieu of death duties could have become some of the first properties used for this purpose.

A series of pamphlets with the theme 'the Challenge of 1950' was published by the Fabian Society as an aid to debate and discussion within the labour movement. One of these pamphlets was entitled *Holidays and the state* and gave a full-length description of the issues behind the statement 'More family holidays' from the draft election programme: 'The development of social services during Labour's first five years has inevitably and rightly been confined mainly to such basic needs as social security, education and health services – measures to protect against misfortune and to secure for everyone a higher minimum standard in the basic needs of life.'[42] Even so, funds had been found to foster the arts and other creative recreations. If Labour were re-elected, it was recognised, any further advance in social services would be limited because of the lack of resources. Priority would be given to the consolidation of the measures of the previous term of office. Holiday provision was practically the only new service proposed. The policy would have been to co-ordinate and to make the benefit of a holiday more widely available by supporting voluntary agencies in extending their facilities to provide more accommodation afford-able to the lower-paid. 'Labour policy has often been for the State to intervene in order to co-ordinate and then make more widely available benefits which have been developing piecemeal or through voluntary agencies – to build on or to extend facilities which, up to now, have not reached most working homes.'[43] Holidays, though, were beyond the limit of what it was thought ought to be taken away from personal initiative and be provided free by the state. The Labour Party recognised the impossibility and undesirability of free facilities that would be interpreted by some members of the electorate as 'bribes for all'. As a form of recreation influenced by personal taste and so easily ruined by regimentation, any schemes for state holiday camps and the like would have been unpalatable. The discussion pamphlet issued by the Fabian Society suggested using the voluntary sector, for instance the Co-operative Holidays Association, the Holiday Fellowship and the Workers' Travel Association, as managing agents in joint initiatives.

Securing the supply of enough accommodation to meet demand was seen as imperative. By 1947 some 12 million workers had paid holidays, plus another 5 million with voluntary agreements. Of this 17 million, 74 per cent proposed to go away, two-thirds of them to the seaside. Including children, this would mean accommodation was required for 30 million visitor weeks. The difference in pre-war demand was for working-class families with children, who had not hitherto been in a position to have a holiday, planning to go away. The problem was not only in providing cheap places to stay but ones where the wife could have a respite from household duties and the care of young children. It also had to provide popular forms of recreation and amusement for adults. The seaside landlady was not in a position to satisfy these demands. The success of the commercial camp and the experience of the voluntary holiday organisations demonstrated the advantages of larger units of accom-modation, run at full capacity over a season of up to twenty weeks and pro-viding food, recreation and care of children on rationalised lines.

There was a very large and unsatisfied demand for holiday camps. This was the conclusion of a report compiled by Dr Daniel for the British Tourist and Holidays Board. If it were left to the private sector he feared that new provision would take the form of development of virgin coast sites and would compete with and prejudice the prosperity of many existing resorts.[44] Lack of adequate accommodation was perceived as such a problem that the British Tourist and Holidays Board promoted the proposal that a new coastal town dedicated to tourism should be developed under the New Towns Act. Commissioned by the board to report on the issue, Dr Daniel recommended the stretch of coast between Kidwelly and Prestatyn as the most suitable for future development. He did add the proviso that the only justification for building a new holiday resort was if expansion of the holiday industries themselves was thought to be more important to the national interest than the allocation of national resources for other purposes. Investing in this and not in productive industries could also increase the difficulty of balancing the country's international trade accounts and raising national income. There was also the danger that people might not like the new town. Shortages of labour and materials could prejudice the prospects of a new holiday town because of the great importance of well designed and constructed buildings, with expensive parks and promenades. The report concluded that the development of holiday industries should be deferred and that it would be best to extend and improve existing resorts.

This did not satisfy the Tourist and Holidays Board or the Ministry of Town and Country Planning. In 1949 it was proposed that a new town might reverse the trend of more people leaving the country for holidays abroad than came in as visitors from overseas. A really attractive seaside town might help earn more dollars.[45] Lewis Silkin wrote from the Ministry of Town and Country Planning to Harold Wilson, President of the Board of Trade, urging him to consider a holiday new town. Wilson replied, addressing the letter to 'My Dear Lewis':

> While I appreciate that holiday habits have undergone marked changes in recent years and that holidays with pay have created a considerable demand for cheap family accommodation in holiday centres, I am not convinced that the situation is so bad that we have seriously to contemplate providing a New Town on the coast for this purpose. I do not think it to be advisable to divert attention from the more urgent tasks to consider one which, I take it from your letter, cannot be regarded as a practical proposition for some years to come.[46]

In these circumstances Wilson preferred to leave the question of examining the case for a special seaside new town until it became more practical. He concluded his letter with the handwritten comment, 'I take it, in any case, that nothing will interfere with consideration of what I feel is, on industrial grounds, New Town Priority No. 1, Ellesmere Port'. Labour failed to get re-elected and so its proposed schemes regarding tourism never materialised. Holidays, though, became more widely available to lower-income groups throughout the 1950s, not because of state intervention but because of rising real incomes across society generally.

Meanwhile demand for holidays continued to rise and the need to stagger them to spread the pattern of demand over a longer period became obvious. It was an issue that was to concern various bodies for another decade and beyond. Soon after the end of the war the National Joint Advisory Council of the Ministry of Labour and National Service had held discussions on the possibility of changing the date of the August bank holiday from the beginning to the end of the month, or possibly delaying it until early September. In a document marked 'strictly confidential', it was reported within the TUC that the committee considered that a substantial reason why there was so very pronounced a peak holiday period at the end of July and the beginning of August was that, while there were many persons who would be on holiday at this favourite period of the summer, there were also many others whose holiday dates took into consideration that a week's holiday at that time, plus the bank holiday weekend, meant, in effect, a ten-day break. It was felt that if the first Monday in August ceased to be a bank holiday, and a similar incentive was provided earlier or later in the holiday season, a substantial contribution would be made to staggering.[47]

The question of demand for holidays throughout the summer season was also addressed by the government through the Ministry of Labour and National Service, which set up a body to look into the matter. The resulting Standing Committee on the Staggering of Holidays in England and Wales had agreed at its meeting on 20 October 1948 that immediate consideration should be given to two proposals. The first one was to substitute for Whit Monday a fixed bank holiday on the second Monday in June. The second was to substitute for the August bank holiday, a bank holiday on the first Monday in September.[48] Regarding the first proposal, the committee was of the opinion that, if August bank holiday were postponed to September, the bank holiday immediately preceding it should not be earlier than mid-June, to avoid an excessively long gap between the two which were of most interest from the point of view of those wishing to go away for holidays. Such a date was likely to be more attractive than the variable Whit Monday to people who were prepared to consider taking their annual holiday earlier in the year than in the past, but who wished to combine their annual holiday with a bank holiday because of the extra days they could then take at a single stretch. If there were a fixed holiday in mid-June it would seem likely that it would inaugurate the holiday season. This would have encouraged taking holidays earlier in the season, it was argued. The committee also had no hesitation in accepting that the August bank holiday should be postponed to a later date. If a day was fixed on the last Monday in August, it was feared that it would lead to a new peak period at the end rather than the beginning of the month. If it were delayed until the second Monday in September, it might not be attractive enough to potential holidaymakers owing to the shorter evenings and colder weather. The committee concluded that the first Monday in September would be the most suitable date for a revised bank holiday.[49] These proposals were submitted to the TUC and the British Employers' Confederation for discussion before any legislative change was promoted.

No immediate change was made and discussion about the length of the holiday season and the timing of the bank holidays continued until 1960, when the issue was again discussed in Parliament. The Workers' Travel Association discussed the matter at its annual meeting of shareholders in April 1960 and, noting the recent debates in both Houses of Parliament, adopted a resolution calling for a change in bank holiday dates. The decision to establish a 'committee of officials to review the problem and report on whether there were any further steps which might profitably be pursued by the Government to extend the holiday period' was welcomed. The WTA urged the need for speedy action by Local Education Authorities in regard to the alteration in the existing pattern of school holidays and calls for a change in the date of August bank holiday from the first to the last Monday in the month. It also noted with pleasure the action of trade unionists in the Midlands suggesting that holiday dates in that important industrial area should be staggered.[50] The WTA also called for an additional bank holiday during the year.

The previous year the WTA had called for another change that would help stagger the demand for summer holidays, the extension of statutory summer time. There was much discussion in the TUC and in Parliament around this too and in 1961 the government decided to extend summer time in both the spring and autumn periods. In a written reply to questions from Members of Parliament, the Home Secretary proclaimed that the weight of opinion was clearly in favour of the extension and in consequence it was proposed that in 1961 summer time should run from 26 March to 29 October. In 1960 summer had run from 10 April until 2 October. The WTA was 'glad to have been associated with the efforts to obtain the benefits of an additional evening hour of daylight for periods in the spring and autumn'.[51]

In June 1960 a conference on the extension of the holiday season was organised by the British Travel and Holidays Association, attended by around eighty representatives of the hotel, travel and transport trades, as well as industrial and educational organisations. The Parliamentary Secretary of the Board of Trade addressed the conference, which considered the effect of bank holidays upon the general pattern of holidays, the difficulties of families with children at school, fixed factory holiday dates and the extension of summer time.[52] The conference considered these matters in the light of a report that between 1951 and 1959 the number of holidaymakers in the British Isles had risen from about 23 million to 27.5 million, with 9.5 million on holiday during August 1959, compared with 7.25 million on holiday at that time in 1951. The conference decided to recommend that government should move the August bank holiday to the end of the month and fix the date of the spring bank holiday, which did not necessarily need to be tied to a religious feast. More controversially, it recommended that all school examinations should be concluded by mid-May and school holidays should be staggered on a regional basis. It also called for summer time to be extended even further, from Easter to the end of October. Other recommendations were made to the holiday industry itself, for greater price differentials to make off-peak travel more desirable.

During 1959 and 1960 workers and trade union officials were asked by the Ministry of Labour for their views on the staggering of summer holidays. The idea of a four-term school year was discussed, with holidays in June and September. This would give a longer summer holiday period to enable more staggering of school, works and town holidays in accordance with a national plan. In consequence of all this pressure-group activity by the unions, the Workers' Travel Association and the tourism industry, yet another committee was established by the Board of Trade to look at proposed changes in bank holidays.[53] The idea of an extra bank holiday in September was rejected but the bank holidays in August and spring were moved to the last Monday in August and the end of May respectively.

Staggering the timing of holidays through lengthening the season was intended to alleviate the high demand and accommodation shortages during July and especially August at seaside resorts. Holidays in seaside towns were beginning to be supplemented by trips abroad from the 1950s onwards. Before the Second World War the WTA had provided holidays for travellers of modest means in many overseas locations. Despite the barbarism of that war the WTA had not departed from its primary purpose of creating international friendship and by 1946, when exit permits were no longer required, was proposing to attempt to arrange Continental holidays again, owing to popular demand from potential tourists. Soon after V-J Day the WTA's postbag seemed to indicate that many people had not realised what had happened to the machinery by which the careful planning, operation and maintenance of their peaceful and pleasant pre-war journeys had been possible.

> Maybe it was a determination to restore as soon as they could their personal contacts – broken by the war. Maybe it was just curiosity to see what had happened on the Continent. Maybe it was ignorance of the real extent of the damage and desolation, the breakdown of ordinary relationships, the shortage of food and other essentials, but whatever it was we were amazed, disturbed and yet relieved at the volume of inquiries as to when this and that pre-war traveller could go away again with the WTA.[54]

By 1947 holidays were planned to Switzerland, Belgium, Denmark and Holland. Of holidays in Germany, Italy and Austria, it said, 'we must not talk yet and probably for some time to come'.[55] It was not just the demand for domestic holidays that could not be met.

Notes

1 Political and Economic Planning (PEP), *Planning for holidays*, *Planning* No. 194, 13 October 1942, pp. 2–3.
2 *Holidays: a study by the National Council of Social Service*, London, 1945, p. 68.
3 Modern Records Centre, University of Warwick (MRC), MSS 292/114/3, letter to Sir Walter Citrine, General Secretary, TUC, 4 April 1940, from George Steele, Secretary, Tynemouth and District and Whitley Bay Trades Council, 4 April 1940.
4 *Ibid.*
5 MRC, MSS 292/114/3, letter to Tynemouth and Whitley Bay Trades Council from Secretary, Research and Economic Department, TUC, 8 April 1940.
6 PEP, *Planning for holidays*, p. 4.
7 *Ibid.*, p. 5.
8 Colin Ward and Dennis Hardy, *Goodnight, campers*, London, 1986, p. 75.
9 Centre for Kentish Studies (CKS), U2543/22/5, Workers' Travel Association holiday programme, 1946.
10 National Council of Social Service, *Holidays*, pp. 4–7.
11 *Great Western Railway Magazine* 49:4, April 1937, p. 175, and 50:4, April 1938, p. 147.
12 *Leicester Mercury*, 1 August 1925.
13 Elizabeth Brunner, *Holidaymaking and the holiday trades*, Oxford, 1945; PEP, *Planning for holidays*, p. 5.

14 For a detailed account of resort marketing see Nigel J. Morgan and Annette Pritchard, *Power and politics at the seaside: the development of Devon's resorts in the twentieth century*, Exeter, 1999.

15 Donald Chapman, *Holidays and the state*, Fabian Society, London, 1949, p. 16.

16 *Report of the Committee on Land Utilisation in Rural Areas*, presented by the Minister of Works to Parliament, 1942 (National Archives HLG 80), paras 178–80.

17 *Report of the Royal Commission on the Distribution of the Industrial Population*, 1940 (National Archives HLG 27).

18 Ward and Hardy, *Goodnight campers*, p. 49.

19 Public Record Office (PRO), LAB 30/240, Workers' holiday camps; National Camps Corporation Ltd and the Camps Act, 1939, Evidence of National Camps Association before the Rehabilitation Sub-committee of the Catering Wages Commission, 6 January 1944.

20 Ward and Hardy, *Goodnight campers*, p. 73.

21 *Ibid.*, p. 73.

22 *Ibid.*, p. 70.

23 *Ibid.*, p. 70.

24 *Ibid.*, p. 72.

25 Dennis Barker, Sir Fred Pontin, obituaries, *Guardian*, 4 October 2000, p. 24.

26 National Council of Social Service, *Holidays*, p. 54.

27 *Report of the Post-war Holidays Group to the Catering Wages Commission*, 1944 (National Archives LAB 11/2055).

28 *Ibid.*

29 *Ibid.*, paras 133–41.

30 Chapman, *Holidays and the state*, p. 17.

31 *Ibid.*, pp. 6–7.

32 Ward and Hardy, *Goodnight, campers*, pp. 75–6; Chapman, *Holidays and the state*, p. 7.

33 Ward and Hardy, *Goodnight, campers*, p. 79.

34 *Ibid.*, p. 79.

35 *Ibid.*, p. 80.

36 Chapman, *Holidays and the state*, pp. 9–10; PEP, *Planning*, p. 8.

37 MRC, MSS 292 114/3, TUC policy document, 1946.

38 Piers Brendon, *Thomas Cook: 150 years of popular tourism*, London, 1996, pp. 281–2.

39 Chapman, *Holidays and the state*, p. 18.

40 *Ibid.*, p. 17.

41 *Ibid.*, p. 3.

42 *Ibid.*, p. 3.

43 *Ibid.*, p. 4.

44 PRO, HLG 90/140, British Tourist and Holidays Board, report on the demand for holidays and the accommodation required to meet that demand, 1946–47.

45 PRO, HLG 90/140, minute to the Departmental Secretary, Ministry of Town and Country Planning, from Lewis Silkin, MP, 27 July 1949.

46 PRO, HLG 90/140, Harold Wilson, MP, President of the Board of Trade, letter to Lewis Silkin, MP, Ministry of Town and Country Planning, 25 August 1949.

47 MRC, MSS 292/114/3, Ministry of Labour and National Service, National Joint Advisory Council, 'Staggering of holidays, dates of bank holidays', NJC 47, 18 January 1949.

48 *Ibid.*

49 *Ibid.*

50 CKS, U2 543/25/8, report of the annual meeting of shareholders of the Workers' Travel Association, 30 April 1960.

51 *Ibid.*

52 CKS, U2543/25/8, *Travel Log*, WTA magazine, September 1960, p. 19.

53 *Ibid.*

54 CKS, U2543/25/3, 'Continental holidays 1946. Where? When?' *Travel Log*, 1946.

55 *Ibid.*

8

Brits abroad

Holidays with pay enabled more lower and moderate-income families with young children to have a stay at the seaside in a boarding house, self-catering accommodation, caravan or holiday camp. Young adults, too, continued to enjoy seaside holidays with family or friends but new locations overseas were beginning to offer a more exciting alternative. Social changes beginning in the 1950s meant that young adults had more independence both financially and socially. As a consequence the demand grew not just for family holidays but for ones for single people travelling with friends and for childless couples.

The urge to travel after the war led, in 1950, to about a million Britons going abroad. The trade unionist clients of the Workers' Travel Association began writing in with enquiries about holidays abroad as soon as the war was over but 'conditions had changed since the organisation had offered a series of some hundreds of WTA Holidays abroad in every country in Europe'.[1] Even so there were still people who were willing to venture overseas, even at higher prices. In 1946 'only about half the countries featured in the 1939 programme were available for holiday travel' and to meet some of the demand by workers for trips abroad an exchange scheme was initiated enabling overseas guests to holiday in Britain despite currency restrictions imposed by their country of origin. These holidays did not necessarily involve staying in someone else's home. Travel companies akin to the WTA acted as host, booking guests into hotels and camps of their own. Reciprocal arrangements allowed their own customers to holiday in Britain while spending money only in their own country, omitting the need to spend anything abroad. By the following year 'transportation facilities of every kind were rapidly increasing' and in 1947 many more travellers than in 1946 were able to 'go abroad in reasonable comfort on the new ships and trains that were available for service by the early summer months'. Due to high demand the WTA included 'an extensive Continental section in its programme with arrangements covering almost every European country that was a practicable proposition from the holidaymakers' point of view at that time'. An all-in price was still promoted as an important feature of WTA holidays, as were companionship, comradeship and international understanding.

> Though the term all-in has been widely borrowed, the technique is not easily reproduced, for it depends on the loyal co-operation of a large number of knowledgeable people at home and abroad with a definite flair for leadership work and with no personal axe to grind. From its early days the WTA has been fortunate in getting the right kind of people, with a sound knowledge of some particular country, and social qualities that soon weld a group of individuals into a party of friends.
> Coupled with this unique leadership service is the policy of including the most worthwhile excursions in the all-in terms. This tends to inflate the initial cost, or shop-window price, but pays the traveller a handsome dividend in the long run.[2]

Hotels, restaurants and motor coaches used by the WTA on the Continent were chosen for maximum comfort and value within the spending power of the average trade unionist. 'All things being equal' the organisation 'attached more importance to a place that conveys the atmosphere of the country visited to one which does not'. The WTA included holidays to Majorca in its 1949 programme. This was Majorca's first post-war appearance in the programme; the island had first been offered to WTA travellers in the early 1930s. Travellers were lured with the promise that 'upon the beaches of this "Island of Charm" under shady pine groves, even during the hottest day, there are strong fresh sea breezes. The island offers a rare combination of natural beauties of variety and colouring.'[3] Holidays in mainland Spain were also available but not to the *costas* of later popularity.

> A holiday in Spain will be chosen by those who desire warmth and sunshine, and San Sebastian offers these with the additional advantages of good sea bathing and a variety of amusements. Madrid, the capital, will attract those who ask for an insight into Spanish social and industrial life. Andalusia, with its mild climate and semi-tropical flowers, is typified by Seville while on the Mediterranean coasts Barcelona is the most important commercial town and whence the Balearic Isles may be conveniently visited.[4]

The Spanish Civil War soon put an end to these inter-war Spanish holidays. On these early holidays to Spain transport was by sea and rail, using the mail boat from Barcelona to reach the island of Majorca. In 1949 the option of flying between Barcelona and Palma was offered by the WTA for an extra £4 1s on top of the holiday cost of between £34 10s and £39 3s 6d, prices considerably higher than they would be twenty years later.[5] One of the highlights of this holiday was a 'folk-dancing display by the villagers'. Farther away from the sun-warmed beaches of Palma were 'the wild scenery and quaint little ports of the North West coast, reached easily, cheaply and adventurously by public conveyance or more luxuriously by motor coach'.

During the war aircraft technology had improved dramatically, making flying both safer and faster than before. The Berlin Airlift of 1948–49 created spare aviation capacity in its aftermath that enabled working people to take part in overseas holidays by air for the first time. There were considerable numbers of aircraft available for charter; supply far outstripped demand at that time.[6] The hire of a thirty-two-seat Dakota cost just *2s 6d* a mile, offering the possibility of relatively cheap package holidays to the Continent. The National Union of Students, a members-only 'closed group', had organised charter flights for its members in 1949, although Thomas Cook had run a charter flight in the United States even earlier, in 1927, to take boxing fans from New York to Chicago to watch the heavyweight title fight between Dempsey and Tunney.[7] The earliest company specialising in charter flights as the major transport component of a package holiday was Horizon Holidays, which began when journalist Vladimir Raitz chartered a plane and organised a package tour to Corsica for two weeks, although the WTA had offered flights between Barcelona and Majorca in 1949 as part of a package whose main transport element was overland. Included for £32 10s with the cost of the flights was accommodation in ex-US Army tents. The price was not cheap by 1950 standards but nevertheless was the beginning of commercial mass tourism abroad by air.

Restrictions imposed by the Civil Aviation Act of 1947 to protect flag-carrying scheduled airlines from competition meant that the licence for Horizon's charter planes allowed them to carry only teachers and students, a so-called 'closed group', and not the public in general, even though no BEA flights went to Corsica. There wasn't even an airport: a runway built by US forces in 1943 for the invasion of North Africa had to be used.[8] Horizon carried 300 holidaymakers to Corsica in its first season of operation, falling short of its break-even target of 350. The following season showed an improvement, the teachers and students-only clause of the licence was dropped, and by 1953 Horizon was offering holidays to Majorca with hotel accommodation as well as to Corsica. The newly created Air Transport Advisory Council granted charter flight licences to Palma despite protests from BEA, even though the airline flew no nearer to Majorca than Barcelona.[9]

All the features of Horizon Holidays had already been developed and would have been familiar to many working-class tourists. The chartering of vehicles for transport was first undertaken in the early days of the railways, most notably by Mechanics' Institutes and Friendly Societies from the late 1830s. Holidays inclusive of travel and accommodation, the services of a guide, excursions and some entertainment had been developed by the Great Exhibition travel clubs in 1851. Package holidays made overseas travel less intimidating by helping travellers overcome the three fears identified by Holloway and Plant and discussed in Chapter 3.[10] The psychological barriers to overseas travel were fear of flying, foreign food and foreigners themselves. These fears had been overcome for rail travellers to the Great Exhibition by the travel clubs' trips there and to subsequent French exhibitions. Overseas travel for workers had been pioneered by worker excursionists to exhibitions in Paris in the 1850s and 1860s. In the twentieth century the WTA had played a similar role for thousands of new overseas tourists. Labour movement contacts in other countries helped the WTA to further develop workers' expeditions abroad. None of the package holiday features of Horizon Holidays or those of other commercial tour operators was an entirely new concept. It was the method of transport, flight, which was different. By chartering aircraft for a series of flights to holiday destinations abroad it was possible to provide air travel at rates much lower than scheduled fares. Although coach tours to European destinations had been popular throughout the 1950s and earlier, and continued to be so, it was the affordable flight that transformed not just working-class holiday expectations but the destination resorts as well. Spain became the most popular destination for British workers travelling abroad to the sun on holiday, although coach tours to the Alps and north European cultural destinations continued to attract custom. Spanish resorts had long been accessible to wealthy tourists with the time to undertake the lengthy overland journey by road and enough money to afford the cost of luxury hotels. Charter flights or block booking on scheduled airlines and low-priced hotels, sold at an inclusive price, brought holidays abroad within the reach of more modest income groups. Flying cut the time of the journey from several days by road or rail to a few hours, making Spanish or other Continental holidays practical for people constrained by work to just one or two weeks' away. At the same time as these technological changes were taking place, General Franco's regime was prioritising tourism, hoping it would become not only a valuable economic sector but a means of legitimising the Spanish economic model and demonstrating its acceptance and legitimacy in the eyes of other countries.[11] Entry visas were abolished in 1959, reducing the formalities involved in a visit to Spain, and by 1960 arrivals had increased by 500 per cent.[12]

Another early package holiday company that made use of ex-military planes was Flair Holidays, run by Polish former wartime airmen. A passenger travelling with this company to Majorca recalled a terrible journey.[13] He and his new wife did not understand Continental twenty-four-hour clocks. They missed their flight when they turned up in the afternoon for the 0200 departure. After rescheduling they were flown from London Airport to Perpignon in southern France, from where they were to be taken by bus to Barcelona and then on another plane to Majorca. Perpignon was the usual arrival point of tourists travelling to Majorca and the Costa Brava before airport facilities in Spain improved. They set off on the first part of this voyage on an old Dakota with uncomfortable tubular steel seats. It dripped oil and couldn't go above 5,000 ft, as the cabin was not pressurised. This was low enough for the passengers to be visibly reminded of their peril as they could clearly see the wreckage of another plane that had crashed in the Pyrenees. Perpignon had only a grass runway, and no smoking was allowed there in case it was set alight. The tourists were locked in a hangar to prevent them escaping into France while they waited for the customs officers to arrive by taxi. They then caught their coach to Gerona, where they were due to get the plane for the next leg of the journey to Majorca. Unfortunately the coach crashed into a ditch beside the road. They had to continue to Barcelona by taxi. After a night in a hotel they continued their journey next day. Boarding the plane, our adventurous traveller fell over the crouching body of a woman who had bent down to cross herself before getting on board. They eventually arrived in Palma amid clouds of dust from the hard, dry earth runway. Other tourists of those times speak of the terror and noise of flying in unpressurised cabins and the horrors of turbulence, not unlike the alarm felt by early rail travellers discussed earlier and which had to be overcome by the civilising process in which the shock of a new experience was soon replaced by familiarity.[14]

Another tour operator selling a holiday product aimed at moderate income groups was Universal Sky Tours, which began trading in 1953. Better known as simply Sky Tours, the company operated back-to-back charter flights just as Horizon did. 'Back-to-back' meant that a plane carried passengers outwards to the destination airport and returned carrying people coming home from their holiday. This kept costs low by cutting down on empty flights. The only empty legs were when the first party of the season travelled out and there was no group already there waiting to come home, and at the end of the season when the plane flew out without passengers to pick up the last party returning. The proprietor of Sky Tours, Ted Langton, was not new to the travel business. He had owned a company providing coach holidays called Blue Cars in the inter-war years, which from 1933 was offering tours abroad to Ostend and Paris.[15] His coach holidays had also been run on the back-to-back principle. Sky Tours was able to lower prices further by taking beds in a hotel for an entire season, guaranteeing the hotelier income in return for a discount on room prices. It is alleged that he then put pressure on the hotel owner to reduce prices even further for Sky Tours, threatening to withdraw his business if the hotelier refused.[16] According to hotel owners of the 1950s in Benidorm, the man from Sky Tours came round and offered villagers involved in other trades money to build a hotel on their land with the promise of providing guaranteed numbers of guests if they agreed.[17] Sky Tours even loaned money to pay for the develop-ment work in return for a room discount of 35 per cent. The owner of the Hotel Bristol recalled that his father ran a bicycle repair shop until he was approached by Sky Tours and decided to open a hotel. Many people living near the Benidorm seafront sold their plot of land for hotel building and built new homes with the proceeds. Tourists were arriving weekly before the hotels were even finished. Hotels seemed to be built anywhere there was space. A guest in a Lloret de Mar hotel, on the Costa Brava, in the 1960s remembered how he was sitting in the bar with his wife and another couple they had met there when it began to rain. Luckily they were indoors enjoying themselves but the barman seemed to look worried. As the rain got heavier the barman got more and more agitated until suddenly he stripped off his clothes down to a pair of swimming trunks. He dashed downstairs to the basement room of the couple they had met in the bar. The room was flooded and things were floating about, including a pair of fluffy mules. The hotel had been built in a dried-up river bed where rainwater drained. The barman began bailing out the water with the help of the guests. By next day the room was restored to its former clean, dry condition and no trace of the flood remained.[18]

Many Spanish residents were grateful for the opportunities offered by tourism, as poverty caused by agricultural and industrial dislocation due to Franco's economic policies had meant that prior to these developments many people were leaving the area, some of them going overseas. There were people who were concerned about the dramatic change of lifestyle and environ-ment that tourism development entailed. However, under the dictatorship of Franco they had no opportunity for open protest. The impact of tourism, as Pi-Sunyer notes, was 'sudden, disturbing and far-reaching' but in a repressive political environment a great deal of dissent would be muted and coded, seldom accessible to the casual visitor.[19]

The Workers' Travel Association went into the air package market with charter flights to Spain in 1955 at a time when many other commercial tour operators were beginning to offer inclusive holidays abroad. Attractive prices were offered to holidaymakers but tour operators faced a heavy financial risk. Prices were based on a predicted number of passengers on each flight but whether or not that figure was reached the full cost of the charter had to be paid. Heavy losses could be incurred if the number of passengers did not come up to expectations. As more operators came into the field competition became keen and dangerously high load factors were used to keep prices down.[20] The market was competitive, but, because there were still relatively few of them, all tour operators managed to secure a fair share of business. As the market became more competitive, companies began to introduce special holiday brochures to publicise their products. In 1959 in one of its earliest separate Continental Tours brochures, the WTA attracted potential visitors to Majorca thus: 'Each day brings a variety of unforgettable experiences and when the day's activities are over there is dancing and gaiety in the spontaneous fashion of the island and perhaps a display of flamenco, the haunting, traditional simple art of the gypsies, to round off the day.'[21] At this time Torremolinos could still be described in brochures as 'the ideal place for a quiet holiday' while a visitor to Benidorm in 1961 remembers there seemed to be only two or three hotels.[22] There was a market there and holidaymakers could take excursions to a basket maker and a fishing village. Visitors to Mediterranean resorts were impressed by the welcome accorded by Spanish people. 'The Spanish people were so nice. They all seemed really pleased to see us. The waiters were friendly. They were glad to get the work, I suppose,' reminisced an Englishwoman, now retired and living in Spain, of a holiday she took there in 1962. She related how she and her companions went to a café but a hotel was being built on the site, creating a lot of dust. The woman owning the café invited the party to eat in her house because the restaurant was so dusty from the building work.[23]

Political decisions affecting package holidays and charter flights remained contentious throughout the 1950s and 1960s when they began to be challenged by tour operators acting together as a campaigning body, the Tour Operators' Study Group, with Tom Gullick, the owner of Clarkson's, as its spokesman. Currency controls restricted the amount of money that individuals could spend outside the United Kingdom. The Air Traffic Act regulations were reiterated in the Civil Aviation Act of 1960 that created the Air Traffic Licensing Board (ATLB) and were reaffirmed in 1964 in the Civil Aviation (Licensing) Regulations. The ATLB was under the control of the Board of Trade and was

responsible for granting licences to charter-flight operators. To protect publicly funded BOAC and BEA no package holiday using a charter flight was
allowed to cost less than the normal scheduled air fare. Closed groups, like
Horizon's first tour group of students and teachers, were exempt from this
specification, so clubs or interest groups such as trade unions and football clubs
could travel at any price with no lower limit. Whitehall Travel specialised in
closed group holidays for unions and transported members of the National Union
of Bank Employees, the National Association of Local Government Officers
and the Association of Civil Servants.[24] British European Airways claimed in
a report of 1958–59 that almost as many travelled to Europe in closed groups
as on approved inclusive tour services but a good deal of that traffic was far
from genuine.[25] Some operators evaded licensing by ferrying passengers to
Continental airports across the Channel where no British approval was
needed. Another method of evasion or fallback if a licence was refused was to
use a foreign airline which did not need a UK licence from a British airport.
Milbanke Tours were offering flights from London in 1959 without Air
Transport Advisory Council approval, using Spanish Aviaco planes with
clearance authorised by the Minister of Transport, in a different Ministry.
According to Board of Trade information, more operators were planning to
use foreign carriers in 1960.[26]

The creation of the Air Traffic Licensing Board in 1960 did little to
improve relations between travel companies and government. BEA and BOAC
complained that if a package holiday was priced lower than the scheduled fare
their potential passengers might buy the holiday but not check in at the hotel,
just to get the cheaper flight. In 1967, to counter these claims, Clarkson's
put a new condition on their booking form: 'the special low price has been
approved by the Air Transport Licensing Board only for the use of persons
with a *bona fide* intention of booking the inclusive holiday arrangements
advertised by Clarkson's. If anyone does not make use of the inclusive arrangements the right to the return flight will be forfeited.'[27]

Tour operators could be refused a licence on the grounds of too low a price.
A director of the tour operator Martin Rook wrote to the Board of Trade in
January 1968 following official complaints that the company's winter holiday
to the Costa Brava was too cheap. The selling price of an eight-day full-board
holiday in a hotel was £17 10s. The licence was approved on the condition
imposed by the ATLB that the price must be raised to twenty-two guineas.
Martin Rook included three excursions, wine and champagne, a night-club visit
and entertainment at no extra charge as compensation to clients for the £5 12s

price increase. BEA lodged and won an appeal against this licence, raising the price yet again to £28 4s, but it was impossible for any more extras to be included.[28] Martin Rook conducted a survey of its clients and found that, out of 148 consulted, 134, or 91 per cent, averred that they would not have booked the holiday if they had known that the eventual price would be £28 4s. 'It was obvious that the great majority of clients had a relatively tight domestic budget and it was the low inclusive charge which had decided them to enjoy a winter Continental holiday by air, a luxury previously only available to the wealthier section of the community.'[29] Although BEA claimed unfair competition, Gerona airport, the flight destination, was not even open in the winter months and no other charter or scheduled service flew there.

The *Sun* newspaper took up the cause of the package tour holidaymakers among its working-class readership against the Labour government. In an editorial of December 1967 'The *Sun* says':

> An unpleasant surprise awaits thousands of people who have booked an eight-day holiday in Majorca and Spain for about £26. To the dismay of the tour organisers, the holidaymakers will each have to pay another £6 – by order of the Board of Trade. This is at the very moment when the Board appeals for prices to be kept down . . . The result is farcical. Compelled to accept additional money they don't want, the tour organisers propose to give it back to the passengers in the form of holiday extras. Apparently free drinks, free cigars and free excursions are all right. But if you just want a cheaper holiday you can't have it, say the Board of Trade . . . Why shouldn't the public have a right to benefit from all the cheap facilities that holiday firms are willing to give them? It is nonsense to suggest that holidaymakers travelling on package tours take business from the regular airlines. They are people who would not otherwise fly at all.[30]

Even at these artificially inflated prices, a holiday to Spain in 1967 cost much less than in the 1940s and 1950s. An unwitting consequence of companies compensating travellers for higher prices with free extras, affecting mostly working-class tourists, contributed to the creation of the stereotypical package holidaymaker. On outings organised by the holiday company drinks were free. Participants understandably eagerly drank the free wine and champagne but they were not used to it and became drunk and sometimes rowdy. A resort 'rep' in Benidorm during the 1960s told how the British treated wine like beer and drank large glassfuls. Tourists were taken to barbecue evenings where drinks were free and partaken of in copious amounts. The rep got so fed up having to clean up vomit in the coaches afterwards that he distributed plastic bags at the start of the journey. As an incentive to use the bag he introduced a

£2 cleaning deposit, forfeited by anyone who soiled the coach.[31] The rowdy popular image, though much publicised by the press, applied only to a minority of working-class tourists. In the early 1960s visitors were smartly dressed and well behaved. They dressed for dinner but their humble origins were given away by their footwear. They were 'ladies and gentlemen in plastic shoes', to the amusement of hotel staff.[32] Women wore long dresses and men suits in the evenings. It has been claimed that it was only later, in the 1970s, as holidays became even cheaper and attracted less respectable types of people, that drunkenness became a problem.[33]

Advances in aeronautical technology created the possibility of cheaper flights for holiday traffic but also led to conflict between charter companies and the licensing body. The government was faced with the dichotomy of protecting flag-carrying state-owned airlines while at the same time encouraging trade growth in the aviation industry and the economy generally. By the late 1950s jet aircraft had become safer and larger in passenger capacity. To stimulate demand for sales of new jet planes a buoyant market for second-hand aircraft was vital. At a meeting at the Board of Trade in November 1959 the Minister of Aviation emphasised the need to encourage 'second line' use of older planes to promote a thriving market for new transport aircraft.[34] The only way a second-hand market for aeroplanes was likely to develop was encouraging independent airlines providing charter flights to increase their traffic using British planes. The system of licensing, where applications for many routes were turned down, did nothing to stimulate the high level of investment needed by independent airlines and tour operators to increase the traffic. Inclusive tour operators did not know until October each year whether or not they would be licensed to carry out a particular programme with British aircraft, leaving little time for brochures to be printed before bookings started for the next summer. The economics of flying larger and more expensive planes meant that aircraft needed to be practically in constant operation and full almost to capacity. Not being able to plan ahead with confidence inhibited not only growth in traffic but also investment in second-hand aircraft, slowing down state airlines' purchase of new ones. It also meant the cost of flying remained higher than it might otherwise have been.

Since the war there had been restrictions on how much money individuals could take abroad. In 1946 the limit was £75 and by 1955 the foreign exchange limit was set at £100, an amount which was increased to £250 in the following few years. Few working-class holidaymakers in those days were likely to spend that much on holiday, and so it had very little impact on package holiday traffic. When Harold Wilson's Labour government was elected in 1964 it faced a sterling crisis due to currency speculation on the stock market. In that year £197 million was spent by British travellers abroad, 80 per cent of it in Western Europe, three-quarters of it on holidays. In the same year £131 million was spent by overseas visitors to Britain, leaving a net debit on the balance of payments of £66 million. Price rises in Europe would have increased this spending further.[35] The Labour government felt it imperative to restrict expenditure on travel. Discussions held at the Treasury about a proposal to tax those who went abroad on holiday were recorded in a dossier marked 'Top secret'. A flat rate of tax of £5 was proposed, with exemptions for those travelling on business or for educational reasons. In a memorandum marked 'Secret' the Chancellor, the future Prime Minister James Callaghan, wrote, 'let us keep this up our sleeves. At £5 a head it would raise £20 million in revenue.'[36] Debate within the Treasury focused on how this tax could be collected. A certificate or stamp purchased at post offices or banks and then fixed to passports was one suggestion. Immigration officers would have to check them on departure and cancel them on the return. The Intelligence branch of HM Customs and Excise recommended exit permits, some taxed, others free. A flat-rate tax would penalise working-class and lower-income holidaymakers most heavily: £5 might be a week's wages for some low-paid and women workers. It would not have been a popular tax and the idea was dropped in favour of other measures. A tax on currency exchange would not have been acceptable to the International Monetary Fund and so as, an alternative, stringent currency restrictions were resorted to. A limit of £100 on expenditure abroad might have saved £20 million, while a £75 limit could have saved £25 million on the estimated holiday spending figure for 1966, giving a forecast of £210 million against a projection of £238 million if no controls were imposed.[37]

Commercial travel companies were able to benefit from the rising wages and paid holidays achieved by the efforts of the trade union movement. By 1965 package holidays had come down in price as more operators came into the trade and existing ones expanded their programmes. The industry was now operating against a fiercely competitive background. Keen as ever to protect the interests of its working-class customers and supporters, the WTA made cautionary remarks regarding the rapid increase in the number of travel agents promoting inclusive tours abroad that had brought about a situation where the additional holiday capacity on offer far outstripped the increase in demand for holidays abroad. Thus a buyers' market was created, with the inevitable result that prices had to be reduced in an effort to attract more bookings.

The lowering of prices was commendable if kept within sound economic limits but when brought about by the over-capacity of holidays being offered, it causes prices to be forced down below a reasonably satisfactory level from the tour operator's point of view [warned the WTA]. With the heavy financial risk involved in chartering aircraft and coaches, the profitability of tours depends to a large extent on achieving high load factors on all departures but this proved difficult in 1965 for many tour operators because of excess capacity over demand.[38]

In 1965 the first major collapse of a tour operator, Fiesta, left many holiday-makers stranded abroad to be rescued by other companies or losing their money and getting no holiday. The WTA's cautionary remarks had been correct.

To counteract the inflationary tendency, in July 1966 the government imposed a £50 limit on the amount of foreign currency holidaymakers were able to buy. This £50 had to include the cost of hotels and meals, as they were paid for in local currency. To allow customers to calculate how much spending money they could take on holiday with them, a document called a V form had to be completed at the time of booking. The V form showed the amount of the holiday price actually spent in the destination country on the holiday-maker's behalf by the tour operator. This was then deducted from the £50 currency limit, showing how much remained for spending money. This policy affected the lower-income tourists least, as they were likely to stay at the cheaper hotels, thereby leaving a greater amount of the allowance for spending money. Callaghan, however, was taking an enormous risk of alienating Labour's traditional supporters, the skilled working-class trade unionists. These were precisely the group of workers most likely to be taking, or aspiring to take, a package holiday abroad. However, holidaymakers who went abroad during the years of the currency controls in the latter half of the 1960s and the early 1970s do not remember the controls on spending and don't believe the restrictions affected them, as they did not take that much spending money with them.[39] For most working-class travellers the restrictions were of little significance, unless they wanted to take more than one holiday abroad in a year, when an annual allowance of £50 would have been difficult to stretch over two trips.

The following year, war in the Middle East and rising oil prices had another major impact on Britain's balance of payments and as a consequence the government was forced to devalue the pound, making the amount of foreign currency travellers could exchange for their £50 allowance even less. As the Spanish were soon forced to devalue the peseta, Spain became relatively more attractive to holidaymakers from Britain. Whether or not it was a psychological effect of the limit on spending money or not, Spanish hotel workers of

Plate 8 A British tourist attempts to drink wine from a *bota*, Benidorm, c. 1965

the 1960s have commented that British guests seemed determined to spend every last penny of the money they took with them. By Spanish standards they spent a lot of money in bars, as the drinks were so cheap compared with British prices, and they were very generous tippers, adding to their popularity with waiters and bar staff.[40] Popular drinks with young people of both sexes were Cuba Libre (rum and Coke) and gin and tonic, almost luxuries at home. Older people seemed to enjoy Benedictine and Tia Maria. Bottled beer was brought in from England, as there was no draught beer on tap.[41]

The £50 limit on foreign expenditure remained in force throughout the rest of the decade, as did the system of licensing charter flights. The Labour government did not seem to realise that overseas holidays were no longer a prerogative of the wealthy. Restrictions keeping package holiday prices high were affecting its own supporters among the working class. As well as inflation, Selective Employment Tax and the prices and incomes policy were resented by the working class and industrial unrest among the unionised sections of the work force became more and more common. Declining real wages and loss of confidence led to a drop in the number of working people taking package holidays; the WTA even pulled out of that market at the end of the 1968 season and two privately owned airlines closed down.[42] A committee of inquiry into civil air transport was initiated in 1969, chaired by Sir Ronald Edwards. The Edwards Committee, as it became known, produced a report with the title *British air transport in the seventies*. Following the recommendations of the report the outcome of the ensuing Civil Aviation Act of 1971 was the merger of BEA and BOAC to form publicly owned British Airways, with British Caledonian as the new second-force airline in the private sector on Atlantic routes. The Air Transport Licensing Board was abolished and responsibility for granting licences to charter flights was removed from the Board of Trade. This job was now the task of the newly formed Civil Aviation Authority, which also acted as a watchdog for air transport passengers.[43] The Act also brought liberalisation of the licensing system for smaller private airlines, allowing lower prices to be charged on many routes and flights to more destinations. This, coupled with the abolition of currency restrictions, gave another boost to the package holiday market, which was to have its confidence temporarily shattered by the collapse of Clarkson's in 1974 and high prices caused by another oil crisis due to conflict in the Middle East. In the meantime, however, the working class had stamped its cultural preferences on resorts overseas. Hotels under contract to British tour operators had to adapt their facilities to British tastes by introducing large communal lounge areas, 'international' cuisine and flamenco dancers, perceived to be what was authentically Spanish even in Majorca and on the Catalan Costa Brava, where no such tradition had existed previously. This suited the Franco regime, as its tourism policy was designed to offer the visiting foreigner images and representations of a 'Spain' that was unitary, authoritarian, monocultural and monolingual. As Pi-Sunyer emphasises with regard especially to Catalonia that contained the Costa Brava, this went beyond a process of thematic homogenisation and simplification: tourism functioned as a vehicle for denying the history and identity of a people.[44] Accusations that these resorts are not the 'real' Spain are to be challenged, however, as they reflect aspects of the growing multiculturalism of Europe in general. Benidorm is as typically Spanish as Brighton and Blackpool are English or Llandudno is Welsh.

When British workers went on holiday abroad on package holidays they did not go to a completely alien world, as their tastes and expectations were known to the tour operators catering for a working-class clientele. Through experience of the holidaymakers' likes and dislikes, package tours were soon tailored to meet their requirements. All the travel arrangements were made for them so they did not have to enter into negotiations with businesses overseas. English-speakers were employed as tour guides, resort representatives and hotel staff, protecting tourists from having to communicate in a foreign language. Hotel restaurants adapted their menus to British tastes, cooking in butter or lard in response to the dislike of olive oil. A revulsion at eating squid among many visitors in the 1960s meant that British people would not eat anything they didn't recognise, fearing it might be squid or octopus.[45] At one hotel in Benidorm the chef prepared *coca estofada*, tomatoes, peppers and tuna in a pastry case. All the British guests returned it untouched, as they could not identify the contents: perhaps it contained squid. At another hotel all the British guests complained that the fish in batter they were served was bad. Waiters were surprised, as fish wasn't even on the menu that day, but the British continued to complain: they knew they had been given bad fish because of its colour and texture. What they had been eating was aubergines in batter but they would not believe it until a number of them had been taken to the kitchens to see for themselves.[46] Hotels had to change mealtimes, as the British ate much earlier than was the custom in Spain. As seaside landladies had already found, even on holiday the British liked lunch at 1.00 p.m. and the evening meal had to be started by 7.00 p.m. Water shortages in Spain meant the authorities advised hotels to provide en-suite showers and bidets as an alternative to baths.[47] The British preferred baths, but showers quickly became accepted and were soon expected in boarding houses at home. Bidets were a strange feature to the British. Spanish hotel workers report bidets being used to store and cool beer, for washing feet, as a sink for washing clothes and even as a fruit bowl. Someone is even reported as having complained that the baby's bath was too small.[48]

Above all, the British on holiday were determined to enjoy themselves and would spend every last penny of their holiday money to do so, asserting their own cultural preferences on the resorts at the same time, just as they had done a century earlier in Blackpool and soon after in other British resorts. By the 1970s critics were beginning to berate resorts like Benidorm and Torremolinos as being rowdy and of a low character. All fish and chips, British bars, garish and loutish, they averred, or simply Blackpool on the Med.[49] What these middle-class critics seemed to forget was that working-class people chose to go to these resorts because they liked what was on offer, just as previous generations had enjoyed (and still continued to enjoy) Blackpool, Southend and Skegness. These resorts had been the subject of similar criticism because they provided what their working-class visitors wanted, which was not necessarily what middle-class commentators thought they should want. Many preferred the inherent garrulousness of a busy resort with other people there of their own class and nationality whom they could meet up with in the bars and night clubs. They also preferred the promise of warm sunshine to the likelihood of rain and dull skies in British resorts. Recognising that the above descriptions are generalisations, it is important to avoid the stereotypes of 'mass tourism'; the holiday was an individual experience to tourists who used the package formula as the cheapest means to an end and pursued their own itinerary once in a resort. They moved beyond the boundaries of the package and used it as a springboard to independent activity, using local public transport rather than the excursions provided by the tour operators.[50] The characteristic English seaside holiday did not decline during the 1960s but remained high in popularity and was replicated abroad to attract workers as customers on package holidays. As nineteenth-century critics of commercialised leisure predicted, entertainment, even in different countries, had become more standardised. As Victorian advocates of rational recreation feared a century earlier, standardisation and the development of a national and later an international market in the drive to maximise profit threatened to overwhelm regional diversity in culture and recreational life.[51] The reliability of sunshine in the Mediterranean resorts, not just of Spain but of Italy, Greece and Yugoslavia, coupled with relatively low-cost package holidays created a steady flow of holidaymakers from the affluent countries of northern Europe to the less economically developed south of the continent which had the potential for low-cost development of a tourism infrastructure. By the end of the 1960s each year about 2.5 million people from Britain were taking package holidays abroad.[52]

Notes

1 Centre for Kentish Studies (CKS), U2 543/22/5 Workers' Travel Association (WTA) holiday programme booklet, 1947, p. 61.
2 *Ibid.*
3 CKS, U2 543/Z4, *The Independent Traveller*, WTA publicity, *c.* 1930–33.
4 *Ibid.*
5 CKS, U2 543/22/5, WTA programme of continental tours, 1949.
6 Roger Bray and Vladimir Raitz, *Flight to the sun: the story of the holiday revolution*, London and New York, 2001, p. 16.
7 J. Christopher Holloway, *The business of tourism*, 5th edn, Harlow, 1998, p. 32.
8 Bray and Raitz, *Flight to the sun*, pp. 4 and 8.
9 *Ibid.*, p. 17.
10 J. C. Holloway and R. V. Plant, *Marketing for tourism*, London, 1988, p. 6.
11 Manuel Valenzuela, 'Spain: from the phenomenon of mass tourism to the search for a more diversified model', in Allan M. Williams and Gareth Shaw (eds), *Tourism and economic development: European experiences*, 3rd edn, Chichester, 1998; O. Pi-Sunyer, 'Tourism in Catalonia', in M. Barke, J. Towner and M. T. Newton (eds), *Tourism in Spain: critical issues*, Wallingford, 1996, pp. 231–64, p. 236.
12 V. Bote Gomez and M. Thea Sinclair, 'Tourism demand and supply in Spain', in Barke *et al.*, *Tourism in Spain*, pp. 65–88, p. 66.
13 Mr Leslie Wilson, oral reminiscence, York, May 2003.
14 Wolfgang Schivelbusch. *The railway journey: trains and travel in the nineteenth century*, Oxford, 1980, p. 132.
15 Bray and Raitz, *Flight to the sun*, p. 34.
16 *Ibid.*, p. 36.
17 Interview with retired Benidorm hoteliers, Benidorm, July 2002.
18 Interview with Mr Trevor O'Neill, Torremolinos, 2003.
19 Pi-Sunyer, 'Tourism in Catalonia', p. 238.
20 CKS, U2 543/Z5/13, WTA annual meeting of shareholders, report for 1965, p. 7.
21 CKS, U2 543/Z5/7, WTA, 'Continental tours', brochure 1959.
22 Mr Leslie Wilson, oral reminisence, York, 2002.
23 Interview with retired Englishwoman living on the Costa del Sol, July 2002.
24 Bray and Raitz, *Flight to the sun*, p. 64.
25 Public Record Office (PRO), BT 245/82, Board of Trade, scheduled routes and services, inclusive tours policy, 1960.
26 PRO, BT 245/82, scheduled routes and services, inclusive tours policy.
27 PRO, AVIA 106/4, review of the price control policy on inclusive tours (charter).
28 PRO, AVIA 106/4, letter to Mr R. Colegate, Board of Trade, from Martin Rook & Co. Ltd, 30 January 1968.
29 PRO, AVIA 106/4, to Mr R. Colegate, Board of Trade, letter from Martin Rook & Co. Ltd, 14 February 1968.
30 *Sun*, 16 December 1967.

31 José Palanca, tour guide and former 'rep' for Lord Brothers in the 1960s and Horizon in 1970s, interviewed in Benidorm, July 2002.

32 Sr Martorell, Benidorm councillor in charge of tourism in the 1950s, interviewed in Benidorm, July 2002.

33 José Palanca, interview, July 2002.

34 PRO, BT 245/82, meeting at the Board of Trade with the Minister of Aviation, 19 November 1959.

35 PRO, BD T 295/313, paper on restriction of travel expenditure, 1965.

36 *Ibid.*, memorandum to Mr Rawlinson at HM Treasury, dated 15 February 1964, imposition of a tax on UK residents who holiday abroad.

37 *Ibid.*, paper on restriction of travel expenditure, 1965.

38 CKS, U2 543/Z5/13, forty-fourth annual report of the Workers' Travel Association, 31 October 1965.

39 Information from interviews and questionnaires completed by 1960s holiday-makers to Spain by Su Barton, 2002, as part of a British Academy-funded project.

40 Juan Agulló, former bar manager of Hotel Costa Blanca, Benidorm, interviewed in Benidorm, July 2002.

41 *Ibid.*

42 CKS, U2 543/Z9/4, *Travel Log* 25:2, November 1969.

43 Holloway, *The business of tourism*, p. 92.

44 O. Pi-Sunyer, 'Tourism in Catalonia', p. 242.

45 Juan Agulló, interview, July 2002.

46 Charles Wilson, *Benidorm: the truth*, Agència Valenciana del Turisme, Ayuntamiento de Benidorm, 1999, p. 302.

47 Antonio Fabregas, former head waiter, Lloret de Mar, interviewed in Lloret de Mar, July 2002.

48 José Palanca, interview, July 2002.

49 Wilson, *Benidorm*, p. 27.

50 Sue Wright, 'Sun, sand and self-expression: mass tourism as an individual experience', in Hartmut Berghoff, Barbara Korte, Ralf Schneider and Christopher Harvie (eds), *The making of modern tourism: the cultural history of the British experience, 1600–2000*, Basingstoke, 2002, pp. 182–202.

51 Chris Waters, 'Social reformers, socialists and the opposition to the commercialisation of leisure in late Victorian England', in Wray Vamplew (ed.), *The economic history of leisure: papers presented at the eighth International Economic History Congress*, Budapest, 1982, p. 109; see also Chris Waters, *British socialists and the politics of popular culture*, Manchester, 1990.

52 Holloway, *The business of tourism*, p. 34.

9

Conclusion

By the late twentieth century free time had become as much a feature of advanced capitalist society as work. As a component of the reward for labour, leisure is now as vital as salaries and wage rates; paid time off and limitations on hours of work are part of the conditions of service in all but casual employment. It must be realised that for most of the period under discussion tourism and holidaymaking were confined to a minority of workers in most areas of England, apart from the Lancashire cotton towns. The nearest thing to a holiday the majority were likely to experience would have been the works outing, Sunday school treat or day trip. Even the pre-war peak in 1937 of almost 15 million people taking holidays away indicates that two-thirds of the working population stayed at home.[1] At the time only between 1.5 million and 1.75 million manual workers out of the 2 million or 3 million total were receiving payment through formal agreements with their employers during their period of leave. This figure would probably double if informal arrangements are taken into account.[2]

The preceding chapters have investigated the processes by which the leisure activities of a minority of organised workers in England spread to become a near universal expectation, if not an annual reality, for the rest of the working class. The holiday industry catering for this emerging popular market had to develop according to this group's taste and culture, often to the dismay of middle-class observers and the more respectable artisans and socialists.[3] Holidays became part of an urban industrial working-class culture and were not imitations of upper and middle-class leisure and travel experiences. The working class and its organisations clearly played a major role in the innovatory stages of the development of popular tourism. Collective enforcement of holidays, savings clubs, campaigns for paid leave, holiday camps and travel organisations were all initiated by working-class, socialist or trade union activity. Early achievements were thanks to the commitment of voluntary effort and a sense of collectivity and solidarity. The travel clubs that organised the earliest package holidays to the Great Exhibition, as well as providing savings facilities, incorporated many features of modern inclusive tour operation. Holiday camps pioneered by socialists and trade unionists were imitated and developed further by commercial operators. Providing holidays, though, was not the main function of unions, and even when demand exceeded supply further camps were not opened to capitalise on market growth. As non-profit-making bodies they had no motive to extend provision and as custodians of members' subscription money no risk of over-extending resources could be taken. Providing holidays was a diversion from the real task of a workers' organisation. Organisations set up specifically to organise and provide holidays for working people were not limited by the same constraints as unions that had to contend with constitutions and articles of association restricting the types of activity in which non-profit-making bodies could be engaged as well as conference decisions that determined policy. Providers of alternative holidays based on the principles of co-operation and socialism, such as the Holiday Fellowship, the Co-operative Holiday Association and the Workers' Travel Association also influenced later commercial tour operators. By the late 1930s the WTA was the biggest provider of holidays at home and abroad devised and promoted explicitly for working people.

The biggest contribution made by workers in the growth of mass tourism was the fight for paid holidays. From their beginnings, for only a very few workers in the exceptional circumstances of the Great Exhibition, which had no real permanent impact on holidays with pay, there gradually developed a steady trickle of manual workers off on paid holidays by the sea, starting initially with those in the municipal and public service sectors. This indulgence was linked with discipline: those without good attendance and conduct might not be rewarded with a paid holiday. Municipal workers and their families were joined by those who had made their own financial provision for holidays, notably textile workers from the North-west of England. Groups of workers who were not paid during their holidays had to cope with closures as best they could; these were feared rather than looked forward to by the low-paid who could not afford to put money by.

Some groups employed on piece rates were able to earn enough to recover the money lost during holidays by working longer and harder in 'calf', 'cow' and 'bull' weeks preceding workshop or factory closures.[4] Those in steady employment, especially in areas where women's paid work created a family income as opposed to that of the male breadwinner, were able to set aside small amounts each week as savings to pay for the period when no income was generated plus an amount to fund their wakes activities or trips away. From the late 1920s onwards some employers administered savings or subsidised contributory schemes to cover the cost of holidays, the worker contributing the greater amount. Examples of this were in the boot and shoe trades, building and, in some districts, the mining industry. For some workers, being able to save for their holiday was a sign of independence. Paid leave was not an aspiration, saving was a voluntary act and savings could be used to pay for a holiday if the worker chose. However, increased mechanisation and employment in factories as opposed to small workshops meant that taking a holiday was not a matter of choice. If the workplace closed down entirely for a week, there was no choice but to use any money saved to cover the cost of the period without earnings.

During the first half of the twentieth century it became more acceptable for the state to become involved in aspects of life which formerly were left to private individual arrangements. Starting with old-age pensions in 1911, there was increasing intervention by the government in all aspects of social provision through the National Insurance scheme and other initiatives.[5] Social change, escalated by the First World War, was coupled in the immediate post-war years with a change in the balance of class forces in favour of the working class for a very short time. The idea of being paid during holiday periods began to gain acceptability as an ideal among both workers and some employers. During the first year or two of peace, deferred wages-and-conditions settlements meant that the unions in the most organised trades such as printing were able to secure holidays with pay as part of their negotiations with employers. The post-war industrial boom which in terms of paid holidays benefited those workers who were organised and in a bargaining position to take advantage of the situation was short-lived and the less fortunate majority had to wait, some until the 1930s or 1940s, for agreements to be reached or even the coming into effect of the Holidays with Pay Act after the next war. In 1925 only about 1.5 million manual workers were paid during their holidays as part of their formal conditions of employment and about another half-million were covered by informal arrangements.[6] From negligible growth through the 1920s and early 1930s, increased confidence as firms started to take on more workers at the end of the Depression in the traditional staple industries meant that workers were once more able to add paid leave to their list of demands in negotiations with employers. Numbers enjoying paid holidays increased rapidly during the latter years of the 1930s: there were up to 3 million of them in 1937, rising rapidly to around 4 million by September the following year.[7] Many of these new agreements were entered into to pre-empt any compulsion through the anticipated legislation. Although 15 million people took a holiday in that year, they constituted only about a third of the population of about 46 million. In 1938 it was estimated that there were still 11 million workers with no entitlement to paid leave. By the time of the Amulree Report from the Select Committee on Holidays with Pay in that year, it was acknowledged that the state could become involved in social and industrial matters. Industrial relations had long been subject to legislation but this had previously been confined to limitations on hours of work and industrial relations. Payment for holidays was actually an issue that overlapped both these aspects of employment. The select committee acted as a spur to further voluntary agreements between workers and employers anxious to avoid any compulsion that might arise from its recommendations. Legislation regarding payment for holidays was a new venture into arrangements that had previously been left to individual industries or workers to sort out. Even so, to avoid government interference voluntary agreements concerning paid leave were reached in most industries.[8] By the outbreak of the Second World War the total estimate was that there were 11 million workers receiving paid holidays, although the war delayed any further progress.

By the end of the Second World War it was predicted that the holidays-with-pay figure would stand at 15 million, an increase of 11 million on the mid-1930s total. Although the benefits of the limited scope of the Holidays with Pay Act were not realised until after the war, concerns of 1940s planners put holidays on the social and political planning agendas. A massive surge in pre-war figures indicating the number of people heading for the seaside was predicted, while wartime requisitions of accommodation and camps meant that there were fewer places to stay than in the previous decade. Based on the assumption that this increase would be spread across the whole employable age range from fifteen to sixty-five, they, together with their dependants, would represent 22 million people.[9] By 1945 80 per cent of all workers were entitled to a paid break, with the number still rising. However, this did not mean that they could actually afford to go away on holiday. Even assuming that only half those newly paid workers and their families would actually go away on holiday, the 15 million of 1937 would, at a conservative estimate, have increased to 26 million holidaymakers. In 1948, when there was less accommodation available than a decade previously, 20.9 million people took a holiday by the sea or in the country, while another 4 million took different kinds of holidays in towns or abroad, making a total of 24.9 million holidaymakers, about 66 per cent of the population. Another 4.9 million went on day trips but 14.7 million still had no holiday of any kind.[10] Statistics show the continuing popularity of holidays, and by 1951 the number of holidaymakers remained at nearly 25 million, about half the British population, representing a 15 per cent increase from the 35 per cent of people going away in 1937. By 1951 the total entitled to two weeks' paid leave was 66 per cent, with a minority of 28 per cent receiving just one week.[11]

The summer rush to the coast continued, as had been predicted in reports of the 1940s, boarding houses maintaining their position as the most common form of accommodation. Holiday camps grew in number and capacity; the all-inclusive type with chalet housing, entertainment and leisure facilities on site became accessible to more working families but still remained a minority provision. The British Travel Association survey revealed that 30 million British people took 35 million holidays in Britain and abroad during 1965. Of these, 29.5 million holidays were taken in Britain, just over 5 million abroad. A quarter of all holidays away from home were spent staying with friends or relatives, slightly less than the 27 per cent of holidaymakers using unlicensed hotels, boarding or guest houses. Self-catering accommodation was used by 8 per cent, compared with only 5 per cent who stayed in holiday camps. At the cheaper end of the tourism market parks for static caravans, with many vehicles individually owned as second homes but let out when not in use by owners, stretched out along the coasts between resorts, particularly in the east of England. Small agricultural villages, such as Ingoldmells and Chapel St Leonard's, became downmarket holiday centres during the summer.

The mobile working-class crowd, a source of anxiety at the beginning of the period under study, is no longer imagined to be a threat to society so much as an economic opportunity and, taking advantage of this opportunity, commercialised leisure, including tourism, has expanded into a massive industry.[12] However, tourism itself, despite the apparently respectable behaviour of the majority of holidaymakers, has generated its own moral panics as opposed to earlier perceived political anxieties. This is not to suggest that conflict between classes ceased to be an issue, just that the arena of those struggles moved from the proto-industrial community to the workplace or political party. The campaigns over holidays and paid leave became part of that workplace-based industrial and political struggle. From the middle of the twentieth century, high wages gained priority over reduced working hours and longer periods of leave. By the 1960s trade unions were campaigning to share in economic prosperity not through more and longer paid holidays but through higher wage rates, bonus pay and overtime agreements. Taking holidays became an aspect of consumption, the tourism product a commodity to be consumed in competition with other products for the workers' increasing disposable income.[13] Having achieved a two-week summer holiday with pay and perhaps a third elsewhere in the year, in addition to Christmas and bank holidays, workers were content and focused on money rather than more time off as the central employment issue before industrial decline and the right to employment and union organisation itself became paramount.

A new age of mass tourism within or from Britain, facilitated by almost universal holidays with pay for those in full-time work, began to emerge in the 1950s. Thanks to earlier workers' industrial and political campaigning, the 1950s and 1960s were the start of an era of mass tourism. It was during these decades that the British seaside holiday, boarding house, holiday camp or even caravan park, reached its peak in popularity. From relatively modest beginnings in the 1950s, during the 1960s there was the phenomenal rise of the relatively cheap package holiday to sunspots abroad, linked with the growth of a highly commercialised consumer market. Even so, despite holidays with pay, even in the mid-1960s a fifth of British adults had not had a holiday away from home in the previous five years.[14] The widespread prevalence of holidays with pay and the increases in the amount of holiday entitlement of workers in the late twentieth century have not overcome the problems of low pay, unemployment and poverty often associated with the demographic life cycle. It is still low income, despite over a century of struggle and reform, that remains the biggest barrier to working-class holidaymaking. This means that whether employees are able to make a holiday away from home or not is still a trade union and class issue.

Notes

1 Political and Economic Planning (PEP), *Planning for holidays, Planning* No. 194, 13 October 1942, p. 3.
2 Alice Russell, *The growth of occupational welfare in Britain*, Aldershot, 1991, pp. 65–72, quoted by John K. Walton, *The British seaside: holidays and resorts in the twentieth century*, Manchester, 2000, p. 59.
3 Chris Waters, *British socialists and the politics of popular culture*, Manchester, 1990; Harvey Taylor, *A claim on the countryside*, Keele, 1997.
4 Select Committee on Holidays with Pay, evidence of Sir Walter Citrine, p. 44, paras 261–7; Sidney Pollard, *The history of the labour movement in Sheffield*, Liverpool,

1957, p. 62; W. Felkin, *An account of the machine-wrought hosiery trade and the condition of the framework knitters*, 1844.

5 M. J. Daunton, 'Payment and participation: welfare and state formation in Britain, 1900–1951', *Past and Present* 150, February 1996, pp. 169–216.

6 Russell, *The growth of occupational welfare in Britain*.

7 Donald Chapman, *Holidays and the state*, Fabian Society, London, 1949, p. 6.

8 Russell, *The growth of occupational welfare in Britain*.

9 *Holidays: a study made by the National Council of Social Service*, London, 1945, p. 3.

10 Chapman, *Holidays and the state*, p. 7.

11 Alan Dunn, 'Changes in holiday accommodation in the English Riviera since the Second World War', M.A. dissertation, University of Leicester, 1986, pp. 9–10, figures from the *Employment Gazette*.

12 J. M. Golby and A. W. Purdue, *The civilisation of the crowd: popular culture in England, 1750–1900*, London, 1984, repr. Stroud, 1999, p. 194.

13 Hartmut Berghoff, 'From privilege to commodity? Modern tourism and the rise of the consumer society', in Hartmut Berghof, Barbara Korte, Ralf Schneider and Christopher Harvie (eds), *The making of modern tourism: the cultural history of the British experience, 1600–2000*, Basingstoke, 2002.

14 CKS, U2 543/Z5/13, British Travel Association Survey of 1965, WTA annual meeting of shareholders' report for year ended 31 October 1965, *Travel Log*, June 1966, p. 6.

Select bibliography

Manuscript sources

Bolton Metropolitan Libraries, Arts and Archives, Bolton Local Committee for the Great Exhibition Minute Book, FZ 39/1

Centre for Kentish Studies, Workers' Travel Association Archive, U2 543

Index to the Report on the Select Committee on the Bank Holidays Bill, House of Commons, 22 June 1868

Manchester Reference Library, documents relating to the Great Exhibition, M6/3/10/3–72

Minutes of Evidence before the Select Committee on Holidays with Pay, 1937–38

National Archive, PRO BD T 295/313; BT 245/82; records of the Board of Trade AVIA 106/4, records of the Ministry of Aviation

Report of the Post-war Holidays Group to the Catering Wages Commission, September 1944

Report of the Royal Commission on the Distribution of the Industrial Population, January 1940

Report of the Select Committee on Land Utilisation in Rural Areas, presented by the Minister of Works to Parliament, August 1942

Tyne and Wear Archives Service, Sunderland Local Committee Minute Book, 745/1

University of Warwick, Modern Records Centre, TUC archive, MSS 292/114/1–3

Oral reminiscences

Leicester Oral History Archive cassette no. C15 and C32, Leicester 1985

Arqueotex European Regional Development Fund project on the history of the knitted textile industry in Hinckley, North Warwickshire and Hinckley College, recorded 1997–98

Spanish holiday interviews recorded or transcribed by the author as part of a British Academy small research grant-funded project, 2002

Newspapers

Ashton-under-Lyne Reporter
Bolton Chronicle
Daily Worker
Derbyshire Times
Friend of the People
The Guardian
Journal of Design and Manufacture, London, 1851
Leeds Mercury
Leicester Advertiser
Leicester Chronicle
Leicester Exhibition Gazette
Leicester Journal

Printed primary sources

Age Exchange, *Our lovely hops: memories of hop-picking in Kent*, London, 1991

Andrews, William, and Gutteridge, Joseph, *Master and artisan in Victorian England*, London, 1969

Archives of the British Chemical Industry, 1750–1914: a hand list, ed. Peter J. Morris, Colin A. Russell and John Graham Smith, British Society for the History of Science Monograph 6, Faringdon, 1988

ASLEF 1880–1980, centenary pamphlet

Bagwell, Philip S., *The Railwaymen*, London, 1963

Bamford, Samuel, *Early days, 1848*, Cassell, 1967

Barker, T. C., *Pilkington Brothers and the glass industry*, London, 1960

Bassett, Philippa, *List of historical records of the Caravan Club of Great Britain and Ireland*, compiled as part of a research project funded by the Social Science Research Council, the Centre for Urban and Regional Studies, University of Birmingham, and the Institute of Agricultural History, University of Reading, 1980

Bassett, Philippa, *List of historical records of the Holiday Fellowship*, compiled as part of a research project funded by the Social Science Research Council, the Centre for Urban and Regional Studies, University of Birmingham, and the Institute or Agricultural History, University of Reading, 1980

Benson, John, *British coal miners in the nineteenth century*, Dublin, 1980

Birchall, F., and Ross, R., *A history of the potters' union*, Stoke on Trent, 1977

Booth, Charles, *Life and labour of the people of London* IV, *The trades of east London connected with poverty*, London, 1889 (1902 edn), repr. 1969

Brown, Cynthia, *Wharf Street revisited*, Leicester, 1997

Brunner, Elizabeth, *Holidaymaking and the holidaymaking trades*, Nuffield College, 1945

Chapman, Donald, *Holidays and the state*, Fabian Society, London, 1949

Civil and Public Servants' Association, annual reports, 1919, 1919–20, 1932, 1933, 1943 and 1944

Child, John, *Industrial relations in the British printing industry*, London, 1967

Class against class, the general election programme of the Communist Party of Great Britain, London, 1929

Clegg, H. A., *General union: a study of the National Union of General and Municipal Workers*, Oxford, 1954

Clunn, Harold, *The face of Paris*, London, n.d., *c.* 1950

Cook, Thomas, *Twenty years on the rails: reminiscences of excursions and tours in England, Ireland, Scotland, Wales, the Channel Islands and the Continent*, Leicester, 1860

Curtis, Rev. Wilfred F.-H., *Ingoldmells: a short history of the village in the county by the sea, and of its ancient parish church*, Ramsgate, 1965

Cuthbert, Norman, H., *Amalgamated Society of Operative Lace Makers and Auxiliary Workers*, Nottingham, 1960

Fowler, Alan, and Wyke, Terry, *The barefoot aristocrats*, Littleborough, 1987

Fox, Alan, *A history of the National Union of Boot and Shoe Operatives*, Oxford, 1958

Fyrth, H. J., and Collins, Henry, *The foundry workers*, Manchester, 1957

G. le M. M., *A history of Mander Brothers', 1773–1953*, London, 1953

Great Central Railway Journal 2:4, October 1906, and 2:10, April 1907

Great Eastern Railway Magazine 1:8, August 1911, and 9:98, February 1919

Great Western Railway Magazine 49:4, April 1937, 49:8, August 1937, and 50:4, April 1938

Grossmith, George and Weedon, *Diary of a nobody*, Wordsworth edn, 1994

Gurnham, Richard, *200 years: the hosiery unions, 1776–1976*, Leicester, 1976

Hilton, H. S., *Foes to tyranny: a history of building trade workers*, London, 1963

Hopwood, Edwin, *A history of the Lancashire cotton industry and the Amalgamated Weavers' Association*, Manchester, 1969

Lloyd, G. I. H., *The cutlery trades: an historical essay in the economics of small-scale production*, London, 1913

Iron and Steel Trades Confederation, *Men of steel, by one of them: a chronicle of eighty-eight years of trade unionism in the British iron and steel industry*, London, 1951

Municipal workers, Oxford, 1954

Musson, A. E., *The Typographical Association: origins and history up to 1949*, London, 1954

National Council for Social Service, *Holidays: a study made by the National Council for Social Service*, London, 1945

Page Arnot, R., *The miners: one union, one industry*, London, 1979

'Planning for holidays', *Planning* (a broadsheet issued by Political and Economic Planning) 154, 13 October 1942

Reader, W. J., *Metal Box: a history*, London, 1976

Rogers, Charlie, a.k.a. Tom Treddlehoyle, *Tom Treddlehoyle's trip ta Lunnan*, Rochdale and Leeds, 1851

Saturday half-holiday and the earlier payment of wages: speeches delivered at the Exeter Hall meeting, 24 April 1856

Sketchley, Arthur, *Mrs Brown at the seaside*, London, n.d. (*c.* 1860)

Staton, J. T., *Th'visit to th' greight Parris eggsibishun of Bobby Shuttle un his woife Sayroh*, Manchester, 1867

Strathclyde Regional Archives, *Archive Notes* 21, Glasgow, September 1983

Suthers, R. B., *The story of NATSOPA*, London, 1929

Thomas Cook's Guide to Leicester, Leicester, 1843

Unofficial Reform Committee, *Miners' next step*, Tonypandy, 1912

Walton, Dorothy, *Queenie Musson: memories of a Leicester life*, Leicester, 2002

Williams, J. E., *The Derbyshire miners*, London, 1962

Wilson, Ronald E., *Two hundred precious metal years: a history of the Sheffield Smelting Company, 1760–1960*, London, 1960

Working lives I, *1905–1945*, Hackney, 1975

Wright, Thomas (The Journeyman Engineer), *The great unwashed*, 1868, repr. London, 1970

Secondary sources: books

Aron, Cindy S., *Working at play: a history of vacations in the United States*, Oxford, 1999

Auerbach, Jeffrey, *The Great Exhibition of 1851: a nation on display*, New Haven CT, 1999

Bailey, Peter, *Leisure and class in Victorian England: rational recreation and the contest for control*, London, 1978

Barke, M., Towner, J., and Newton, M. (eds), *Tourism in Spain: critical issues*, Wallingford, 1996.

Belchem, John, *Industrialisation and the working class: the English experience, 1750–1900*, Aldershot, 1991

Bray, Roger, and Raitz, Vladimir, *Flight to the sun: the story of the holiday revolution*, London and New York, 2001

Brendon, Piers, *Thomas Cook: 150 years of popular tourism*, London, 1996

Brittain, Vera, *Testament of youth*, repr. London, 1978

Bushaway, Bob, *By rite: custom, ceremony and community in England, 1700–1880*, London, 1982

Cross, Gary, *Worktowners at Blackpool: Mass-Observation and popular leisure in the 1930s*, London, 1990

Cross, Gary, *Time and money: the making of consumer culture*, London and New York, 1993

Croucher, Richard, *Engineers at war, 1939–1945*, London, 1982

Davies, Andrew, *Leisure, gender and poverty: working-class culture in Salford and Manchester, 1900–1939*, Buckingham, 1992

Delgado, Alan, *The annual outing and other excursions*, London, 1977

Foster, John, *Class struggle and the industrial revolution: early industrial capitalism in three English towns*, London, 1977

Golby, J. M. and Purdue, A. W., *The civilisation of the crowd: popular culture in England, 1750–1900*, 1984, rev. edn Stroud, 1999

Graves, Robert, and Hodge, Alan, *The long weekend: a social history of Great Britain, 1918–1939*, London, 1941

Greenhalgh, Paul, *Ephemeral vistas: the Expositions Universelles, Great Exhibitions and World's Fairs, 1851–1939*, Manchester, 1988

Harrison, Brian, *Drink and the Victorians: the temperance question in England, 1815–1872*, London, 1971

Hewitt, Margaret, *Wives and mothers in Victorian industry*, London, 1958

Hinton, James, *Labour and socialism: a history of the British labour movement, 1867–1974*, Brighton, 1983

Hobsbawm, Eric, *Labouring men*, London, 1964

Holloway, J. C., and Plant, R. V., *Marketing for tourism*, London, 1988

Holloway, J. Christopher, *The business of tourism*, 5th edn, Harlow, 1998

Holt, Richard, *Sport and the British: a modern history*, Oxford, 1989

Humphries, Stephen, *Hooligans or rebels? An oral history of working-class childhood and youth, 1889–1939*, Oxford, 1981, 2nd edn 1995

Hutton, Ronald, *The rise and fall of merry England: the ritual year, 1400–1700*, Oxford, 1994

Ingle, Robert, *Thomas Cook of Leicester*, Bangor, 1991

Jones, Stephen G., *Workers at play: a social and economic history of leisure, 1918–1939*, London, 1986

Joyce, Patrick, *Visions of the people: industrial England and the question of class, 1848–1914*, Cambridge, 1991

Leapman, Michael, *The world for a shilling: how the Great Exhibition of 1851 shaped a nation*, London, 2002

Leeson, R. A., *Travelling brothers*, London, 1979

Lidtke, Vernon, *The alternative culture: socialist labour in imperial Germany*, Oxford, 1985

Mangan, J. A. (ed.), *Pleasure, profit, proselytism: British culture and sport at home and abroad, 1700–1914*, London, 1988

McKibbin, Ross, *The ideologies of class: social relations in Britain, 1880–1950*, Oxford, 1994

Mills, Dennis R., *Twentieth-century Lincolnshire*, Lincoln, 1989

Morgan, David Hoseason, *Harvesters and harvesting, 1840–1900*, London, 1982

Morgan, Nigel J., and Pritchard, Annette, *Power and politics at the seaside: the development of Devon's resorts in the twentieth century*, Exeter, 1999.

Morton, A. L., and Tate, George, *The British labour movement*, London, 1956

O'Neill, Gilda, *Pull no more bines: hop picking memories of a vanished way of life*, London, 1990

O'Reilly, Karen, *The British on the Costa del Sol: transnational identities and local community*, London, 2000

Orwell, George, *The collected essays, journalism and letters of George Orwell* I, *An age like this, 1920–1940*, London, 1968

Paterson, A. Temple, *Radical Leicester: a history of Leicester, 1750–1850*, Leicester, 1954

Pearson, Geoffrey, *Hooligan: a history of respectable fears*, London, 1983

Pemble, John, *The Mediterranean passion*, Oxford, 1987

Perkin, Harold, *The structured crowd*, Brighton, 1981

Phelps Brown, E. H., with Browne, Margaret, *A century of pay*, London, 1968

Pimlott, J. A. R., *The Englishman's holiday*, 1947, repr. Hassocks, 1967

Pollard, Sidney, *The history of the labour movement in Sheffield*, Liverpool, 1957

Pudney, J., *The Thomas Cook story*, London, 1953

Purbrick, Louise (ed.), *The Great Exhibition of 1851*, Manchester, 2001

Rae, William Fraser, *The business of travel: a fifty years' record of progress*, London, 1891

Read, Sue, *Hello campers! The story of Butlin's*, London, 1986

Richards, Thomas, *The commodity culture of Victorian England: advertising and spectacle, 1851–1914*, Stanford CA, 1990, repr. London and New York 1991

Roberts, Elizabeth, *A woman's place: an oral history of working-class women, 1890–1940*, Oxford, 1984

Robinson, David N., *The book of the Lincolnshire seaside*, Buckingham, 1981

Rothstein, Theodore, *From Chartism to labourism*, London, 1929

Schivelbusch, Wolfgang, *The railway journey: trains and travel in the nineteenth century*, Oxford, 1980

Shields, Rob, *Places on the margin: alternative geographies of modernity*, London, 1991

Simmons, J., *Leicester past and present* I, *Ancient borough to 1860*, London, 1974

Smith, Michael A., Parker, Stanley, and Smith, Cyril S. (eds), *Leisure and society in Britain*, London, 1974

Stacey, Margaret, *Tradition and change: a study of Banbury*, Oxford, 1960

Storch, Robert (ed.), *Popular culture and custom in nineteenth-century England*, Beckenham, 1982

Taylor, Harvey, *A claim on the countryside: a history of the British outdoor movement*, Keele, 1997

Tebbutt, Melanie, *Women's talk? A social history of 'gossip' in working-class neighbourhoods, 1880–1960*, Aldershot, 1995

Thompson, F. M. L., *The rise of respectable society: a social history of Britain, 1830–1900*, London, 1988

Urry, John, *The tourist gaze: leisure and travel in contemporary societies*, London, 1990

Urry, John, *Consuming places*, London, 1995

Vamplew, Wray, *Pay up and play the game*, Cambridge, 1988

Walton, John K., *The Blackpool landlady*, Manchester, 1979

Walton, John K., *The English seaside resort: a social history, 1750–1914*, Leicester, 1983

Walton, John K., *The British seaside: holidays and resorts in the twentieth century*, Manchester, 2000

Walton, J. K. and Walvin, J. (eds), *Leisure in Britain, 1780–1939*, London, 1983

Walvin, James, *Beside the seaside*, London, 1978

Walvin, James, *Leisure and society, 1830–1950*, London, 1978

Ward, Colin, and Hardy, Dennis, *Arcadia for all*, London, 1984

Ward, Colin, and Hardy, Dennis, *Goodnight, Campers*, London, 1986

Waters, Chris, *British socialists and the politics of popular culture*, Manchester, 1990

Whitaker, Wilfred B., *Victorian and Edwardian shop workers*, Newton Abbot, 1973

Williams, Allan M., and Shaw, Gareth, *Tourism and economic development: European experiences*, 3rd edn, Chichester, 1998

Williams, Allan M., and Shaw, Gareth, *Critical issues in tourism: a geographical perspective*, 2nd edn, Oxford, 2002

Williams, Francis, *Journey into adventure*, London, 1960

Wilson, Charles, *Benidorm: the truth*, Benidorm, 1999

Wohl, A. S., *Endangered lives*, London, 1983

Yeo, Eileen and Stephen, *Popular culture and class conflict, 1590–1914*, Brighton, 1981

Secondary sources: articles and chapters in edited collections

Barton, Susan, 'The Mechanics' Institutes, pioneers of leisure and excursion travel', *Leicestershire Archaeological and Historical Society, Transactions* LXVII, 1993, pp. 47–58

Beckerson, John, 'Marketing British tourism: government approaches to the stimulation of a service sector', in Hartmut Berghoff, Barbara Korte, Ralf Schneider and Christopher Harvie (eds), *The making of modern tourism: the cultural history of the British experience, 1600–2000*, Basingstoke, 2002, pp. 133–57

Bevir, Mark, 'Labour Churches and ethical socialism', *History Today* 47:3, 1997, pp. 50–5

Bote Gomez, V., and Sinclair, M. Thea, 'Tourism demand and supply in Spain', in M. Barke, J. Towner, and M. Newton (eds), *Tourism in Spain: critical issues*, London, 1995, pp. 65–88

Burke, Peter, 'Viewpoint: the invention of leisure in early modern Europe', *Past and Present* 146, February 1995, pp. 136–50

Cohen, Patricia Cline, 'Women at large: travel in antebellum America', *History Today* 44:12, December 1994

Croll, Andy, 'Coal without dole', *History Today* 49:2, 1999, pp. 14–16

Daunton, M. J., 'Payment and participation: welfare and state formation in Britain, 1900–1951', *Past and Present* 150, February 1996, pp. 169–216

Harrison, J. C., 'Chartism in Leicester', in Asa Briggs (ed.), *Chartist studies*, London, 1959

Horwood, Catherine, 'Housewives' choice: women as consumers between the wars', *History Today* 47:3, 1997, pp. 23–8

Jones, Stephen G., 'The Lancashire wakes: holiday savings and holiday pay in the textile districts', *Eccles and District Local History Society*, 1983, pp. 27–39

Kusamitsu, Toshio, 'Great Exhibitions before 1851', *History Workshop Journal* 9, 1980, pp. 70–89

Marchant, R., 'Early excursion trains', *Railway Magazine*, 100:638, 1954, pp. 426–9

Morris, R. J., 'Leeds and the Crystal Palace', *Victorian Studies* 13, 1970, pp. 283–300

Pi-Sunyer, O., 'Tourism in Catalonia', in M. Barke, J. Towner and M. T. Newton (eds), *Tourism in Spain: critical issues*, London, 1995, pp. 231–64

Reid, D., 'The decline of St Monday, 1766–1876', *Past and Present* 71, 1976, pp. 76–101

Reid, D., 'The "iron roads" and "the happiness of the working classes": the early development of the railway excursion', *Journal of Transport History*, 3rd ser., 17:1, 1996, pp. 57–73

Sheail, John D., 'The impact of recreation on the coast: the Lindsey County Council (Sandhills) Act, 1932', *Landscape Planning* 4, 1977, pp. 53–77

Sherwood, Leslie, 'A second home in Charnwood Forest', *Newsletter of the Living History Unit* (Leicester) 20, 1998

Short, Audrey, 'Workers under glass', *Victorian Studies*, December 1966, pp. 193–202

Steers, J. A., 'Coastal preservation and planning', *Geography Journal* 104, 1944, pp. 7–27

Valenzuela, Manuel, 'Spain from the phenomenon of mass tourism to the search for a more diversified model', in Allan M. Williams and Gareth Shaw (eds), *Tourism and economic development: European experiences*, 3rd edn, Chichester, 1998

Walker, Andrew, 'Pleasurable homes? Victorian model miners' wives and the family wage in a nineteenth-century South Yorkshire colliery district', *Women's History Review* 6:3, 1997, pp. 317–36

Walton, John K., 'The Blackpool landlady revisited', *Manchester Region History Review*, 1994, pp. 23–31

Walton, J. K., 'The demand for working-class seaside holidays in Victorian England', *Economic History Review* 34, 1981, pp. 249–65

Waters, Chris, 'Social reformers, socialists and the opposition to the commercialisation of leisure in late Victorian England', in Wray Vamplew (ed.), *The economic history of leisure: papers presented at the eighth International Economic History Congress*, Budapest, 1982

Wright, Sue, 'Sun, sand and self-expression: mass tourism as an individual experience', in Hartmut Berghoff, Barbara Korte, Ralf Schneider and Christopher Harvie (eds), *The making of modern tourism: the cultural history of the British experience, 1600–2000*, Basingstoke, 2002, pp. 182–202

Unpublished theses and papers

Dunn, Alan, 'Changes in holiday accommodation in the English Riviera since the Second World War', M.A. dissertation, University of Leicester, 1986

Jones, Stephen G., 'The British labour movement and working-class leisure, 1918–1939', Ph.D. thesis, University of Manchester, 1983

Kusamitsu, Toshio, 'British industrialisation and design, 1830–1851', Ph.D. thesis, University of Sheffield, 1982

Martin, G. C., 'Working-class holidaymaking down to 1947', M.A. dissertation, University of Leicester, 1968

Smith, Morris Brooke, 'The growth and development of popular entertainment and pastimes in the Lancashire cotton towns, 1830–1870', M.Litt. dissertation, University of Lancaster, 1970

Wren, Phillip, 'Holiday shanties in Britain: a history and analysis', dissertation, Hull School of Architecture, November 1981

Index

Lightning Source UK Ltd.
Milton Keynes UK
UKOW06f1703200416

272651UK00003B/191/P